Vienna

Mark Honan
Neal Bedford

LONELY PLANET PUBLICATIONS
Melbourne • Oakland • London • Paris

W9-BRI-262

Vienna
3rd edition – April 2001
First published – March 1995

Published by
Lonely Planet Publications Pty Ltd ABN 36 005 607 983
90 Maribyrnong St, Footscray, Victoria 3011, Australia

Lonely Planet Offices
Australia Locked Bag 1, Footscray, Victoria 3011
USA 150 Linden St, Oakland, CA 94607
UK 10a Spring Place, London NW5 3BH
France 1 rue du Dahomey, 75011 Paris

Photographs
All of the images in this guide are available for licensing from
Lonely Planet Images.
email: lpi@lonelyplanet.com.au

Front cover photograph
View of Stephansdom from hotel window, Innere Stadt, Vienna
(Tim Thompson, Stone)

ISBN 1 86450 195 2

text & maps © Lonely Planet 2001
photos © photographers as indicated 2001

Printed by SNP Offset Sdn Bhd
Printed in Malaysia

Contents – Text

Contents – Maps

THINGS TO SEE & DO

EXCURSIONS

COLOUR MAPS   **BACK PAGES**

The Authors

Mark Honan

After a university degree in philosophy opened up a glittering career as an office clerk, Mark decided that there was more to life than form-filling and data-entry. He set off on a two-year trip round the world, armed with a backpack and a vague intent to sell travel stories and pictures upon his return to England. Astonishingly, this barely formed plan succeeded and Mark became the travel correspondent to a London-based magazine. Since 1991 he has written Lonely Planet guidebooks to Vienna, Austria and Switzerland, updated *Solomon Islands* and contributed to guides to Europe, Central America, Mexico and India, as well as to *Lonely Planet Unpacked*, a book of travel horror stories. He is currently cowriting the 1st edition of *Northern India*. Although more than happy not to be a clerk anymore, he finds, curiously, that life as a travel writer still entails a good deal of form-filling and data-entry.

Neal Bedford

Born in Papakura, New Zealand, Neal gave up an exciting career in accounting to experience the mundane life of a traveller. With the urge to move, travel led him through a number of countries and jobs, including au pair in Vienna, lifeguard in the USA, fruit picker in Israel and lettuce washer at rock concerts. Deciding to give his life some direction, he well and truly got his foot stuck in the door by landing the lucrative job of packing books in Lonely Planet's London office. One thing led to another and he managed to cross over to the mystic world of authoring. Neal currently resides in Dublin, but the need to move will probably soon kick in and force him to try his luck somewhere else. He has worked on *Spain*, *Britain*, *England* and *Eastern Caribbean* for Lonely Planet.

FROM THE AUTHORS

Mark Honan

Thanks to everyone who responded to my numerous inquiries – help was requested and received from folk as diverse as a university professor and a passing traffic warden. Among the many are Barbara at ANTO in London and Melanie at Austrian Airlines. Special thanks are due to Irmgard and Sandra for finding me a settled base in Vienna during my research. I'm also indebted to the readers of the last edition who wrote in with useful suggestions. The Bratislava section borrows from Neil Wilson's text that appears in Lonely Planet's *Eastern Europe* 8th edition.

Neal Bedford

From day one Vienna has been a special place for me and held a special place in my heart. Its gorgeous architecture and rich history have captivated me, but the best part has been the people I have met and made lasting friendships with. In no order of importance I would like to thank (and you should know who you are!): Christina for always being there and keeping me sane, Lukas for putting me up and sharing a drink or two (or a doppler if the need arises!), the Ried-am-Riederberg clan (centre of the world!) – The Kurazas, my second family; and Brigit and Wolfgang, Tom 'Mad Dog' Venning and Gorg (Heurigen crawls for mountain climbers), Tina, Astrid, John, Nik, Szusza, Tom P, Hexi, Vivi and Flo, Karin and Helmut, Peter, Slajan, Gigi, Werner, Brigitte, Trixi, Amir and Joachim. If I left anyone out, my apologies. Thanks for all the nights solving the problems of the world over a Krügel or five. Thanks also to Mark Honan for his imput and thoughts. And lastly, thanks to Sturm – the drink of the gods and the hangover from hell.

This Book

Mark Honan wrote the first two editions of this book; for this 3rd edition, his coauthor was Neal Bedford.

From the Publisher

This edition of *Vienna* was produced in Lonely Planet's Melbourne office. Janine Eberle coordinated the editing, and was assisted by Anne Mulvaney, Melanie Dankel and Chris Wyness. Mark Griffiths coordinated mapping, which was produced by Tony Frankhauser with the gracious assistance of Birgit Jordan and Gus Poo y Balbontin. Sally Morgan took care of design, and final checks were done by Kieran Grogan. Illustrations are by Sarah Jolly, Mick Weldon and Matt King. Quentin Frayne produced the Language chapter, Margie Jung designed the cover, and photographs were provided by Lonely Planet Images (LPI). Grateful acknowledgment is made to Wiener Linien GmbH&CoKG for permission to reproduce the Vienna U-bahn map.

Thanks

Many thanks to the following travellers who used the last edition and wrote to us with helpful hints, useful advice and interesting anecdotes:

Kostas Alexopoulos, George Birsic, Lisette Black, Dennis Blazey, Romelle Castle, Thomas P Coohill, Christine Criag Seppi, Teresa Fanning, Lawrence Gowen, Gail Irving, Helmut Kallmann, Peter Keenan, Irene Kontje, Sonny Lee, Cof Linsbauer, Lloyd McCune, H Milton Peek, Marcus Praschinger, Thomas Roush, Saad Saeed, Ivan A Schulman, Ahren Sims, Danidlle Snellen, Johanna Strand, Dr C Tiligada, Michael Vielhaber, Per Wickenberg, Noel Yuseco.

Foreword

ABOUT LONELY PLANET GUIDEBOOKS

The story begins with a classic travel adventure: Tony and Maureen Wheeler's 1972 journey across Europe and Asia to Australia. Useful information about the overland trail did not exist at that time, so Tony and Maureen published the first Lonely Planet guidebook to meet a growing need.

From a kitchen table, then from a tiny office in Melbourne (Australia), Lonely Planet has become the largest independent travel publisher in the world, an international company with offices in Melbourne, Oakland (USA), London (UK) and Paris (France).

Today Lonely Planet guidebooks cover the globe. There is an ever-growing list of books and there's information in a variety of forms and media. Some things haven't changed. The main aim is still to help make it possible for adventurous travellers to get out there – to explore and better understand the world.

At Lonely Planet we believe travellers can make a positive contribution to the countries they visit – if they respect their host communities and spend their money wisely. Since 1986 a percentage of the income from each book has been donated to aid projects and human rights campaigns.

Updates Lonely Planet thoroughly updates each guidebook as often as possible. This usually means there are around two years between editions, although for more unusual or more stable destinations the gap can be longer. Check the imprint page (following the colour map at the beginning of the book) for publication dates.

Between editions up-to-date information is available in two free newsletters – the paper *Planet Talk* and email *Comet* (to subscribe, contact any Lonely Planet office) – and on our Web site at www.lonelyplanet.com. The *Upgrades* section of the Web site covers a number of important and volatile destinations and is regularly updated by Lonely Planet authors. *Scoop* covers news and current affairs relevant to travellers. And, lastly, the *Thorn Tree* bulletin board and *Postcards* section of the site carry unverified, but fascinating, reports from travellers.

Correspondence The process of creating new editions begins with the letters, postcards and emails received from travellers. This correspondence often includes suggestions, criticisms and comments about the current editions. Interesting excerpts are immediately passed on via newsletters and the Web site, and everything goes to our authors to be verified when they're researching on the road. We're keen to get more feedback from organisations or individuals who represent communities visited by travellers.

Lonely Planet gathers information for everyone who's curious about the planet – and especially for those who explore it first-hand. Through guidebooks, phrasebooks, activity guides, maps, literature, newsletters, image library, TV series and Web site we act as an information exchange for a worldwide community of travellers.

Research Authors aim to gather sufficient practical information to enable travellers to make informed choices and to make the mechanics of a journey run smoothly. They also research historical and cultural background to help enrich the travel experience and allow travellers to understand and respond appropriately to cultural and environmental issues.

Authors don't stay in every hotel because that would mean spending a couple of months in each medium-sized city and, no, they don't eat at every restaurant because that would mean stretching belts beyond capacity. They do visit hotels and restaurants to check standards and prices, but feedback based on readers' direct experiences can be very helpful.

Many of our authors work undercover, others aren't so secretive. None of them accept freebies in exchange for positive write-ups. And none of our guidebooks contain any advertising.

Production Authors submit their raw manuscripts and maps to offices in Australia, USA, UK or France. Editors and cartographers – all experienced travellers themselves – then begin the process of assembling the pieces. When the book finally hits the shops, some things are already out of date, we start getting feedback from readers and the process begins again …

WARNING & REQUEST

Things change – prices go up, schedules change, good places go bad and bad places go bankrupt – nothing stays the same. So, if you find things better or worse, recently opened or long since closed, please tell us and help make the next edition even more accurate and useful. We genuinely value all the feedback we receive. A well travelled team reads and acknowledges every letter, postcard and email and ensures that every morsel of information finds its way to the appropriate authors, editors and cartographers for verification.

Everyone who writes to us will find their name in the next edition of the appropriate guidebook. They will also receive the latest issue of *Planet Talk*, our quarterly printed newsletter, or *Comet*, our monthly email newsletter. Subscriptions to both newsletters are free. The very best contributions will be rewarded with a free guidebook.

Excerpts from your correspondence may appear in new editions of Lonely Planet guidebooks, the Lonely Planet Web site, *Planet Talk* or *Comet*, so please let us know if you *don't* want your letter published or your name acknowledged.

Send all correspondence to the Lonely Planet office closest to you:

Australia: Locked Bag 1, Footscray, Victoria 3011
USA: 150 Linden St, Oakland, CA 94607
UK: 10A Spring Place, London NW5 3BH
France: 1 rue du Dahomey, 75011 Paris

Or email us at: talk2us@lonelyplanet.com.au

For news, views and updates see our Web site: www.lonelyplanet.com

HOW TO USE A LONELY PLANET GUIDEBOOK

The best way to use a Lonely Planet guidebook is any way you choose. At Lonely Planet we believe the most memorable travel experiences are often those that are unexpected, and the finest discoveries are those you make yourself. Guidebooks are not intended to be used as if they provide a detailed set of infallible instructions!

Contents All Lonely Planet guidebooks follow roughly the same format. The Facts about the Destination chapters or sections give background information ranging from history to weather. Facts for the Visitor gives practical information on issues like visas and health. Getting There & Away gives a brief starting point for researching travel to and from the destination. Getting Around gives an overview of the transport options when you arrive.

The peculiar demands of each destination determine how subsequent chapters are broken up, but some things remain constant. We always start with background, then proceed to sights, places to stay, places to eat, entertainment, getting there and away, and getting around information – in that order.

Heading Hierarchy Lonely Planet headings are used in a strict hierarchical structure that can be visualised as a set of Russian dolls. Each heading (and its following text) is encompassed by any preceding heading that is higher on the hierarchical ladder.

Entry Points We do not assume guidebooks will be read from beginning to end, but that people will dip into them. The traditional entry points are the list of contents and the index. In addition, however, some books have a complete list of maps and an index map illustrating map coverage.

There may also be a colour map that shows highlights. These highlights are dealt with in greater detail in the Facts for the Visitor chapter, along with planning questions and suggested itineraries. Each chapter covering a geographical region usually begins with a locator map and another list of highlights. Once you find something of interest in a list of highlights, turn to the index.

Maps Maps play a crucial role in Lonely Planet guidebooks and include a huge amount of information. A legend is printed on the back page. We seek to have complete consistency between maps and text, and to have every important place in the text captured on a map. Map key numbers usually start in the top left corner.

Although inclusion in a guidebook usually implies a recommendation we cannot list every good place. Exclusion does not necessarily imply criticism. In fact there are a number of reasons why we might exclude a place – sometimes it is simply inappropriate to encourage an influx of travellers.

Introduction

'The streets of Vienna are paved with culture, those of other cities with asphalt.' So remarked the Austrian writer Karl Kraus (1874–1936). Perhaps that's an exaggeration, but you can see his point. Vienna (Wien) provokes countless images: elaborate imperial palaces, coffee houses crammed with rich cakes and baroque mirrors, angelic choirboys, Art Nouveau masterpieces, and white stallions strutting in measured sequence in the Spanish Riding School.

Then there's the music of Mozart, Beethoven, Haydn, Schubert, Strauss, Brahms, Mahler, Schönberg and many others. Their heritage has an almost physical presence, and adds as much to a view of the city as its many visible traits. The mighty Danube River may slice through 2840km of Europe, from the Black Forest to the Black Sea, but it owes its fame largely to Vienna; thanks to the Strauss waltz, it will be forever 'blue' in the hearts and minds of many.

Today's city is the glorious legacy of the all-conquering Habsburg dynasty, which controlled much of Europe for over 600 years. The attractions for culture seekers are obvious. Monumental architectural gems line the city centre, world-class museums stand bursting with historical and artistic treasures, and internationally established orchestras conjure aural dreams in lavish concert halls. Visitors who want to sidestep the highbrow stuff can do that too, with a hike in the Vienna Woods, some water sports on the river, or an evening in one of Vienna's renowned wine taverns.

There was a time, after the humiliating occupation by the victorious Allies of WWII, when Vienna had an aura of being unable to live up to its own reputation. The hugely impressive building facades seemed just that – facades with no function. Vienna was seen as a haunt for genteel old ladies, whiling away their autumn years sipping coffee in a *Konditorei*.

Yet from the rubble of WWII the Viennese have built a city with enviable economic clout, which has now recovered its old panache and verve. Its architectural gems never stopped shining, its musical prowess never ceased impressing, yet added to the tradition and culture is a new vitality. Modern high-rise developments along the Danube are a manifestation of the city's forward-looking approach. The old ladies may still be in Vienna, endlessly sipping their coffee, but it has become a city in which young people can feel at home again. Visitors of any age can find plenty to enjoy in Vienna.

Facts about Vienna

HISTORY

Evidence of Palaeolithic inhabitation of the Danube Valley is to be found in the 25,000-year-old statuette, the *Venus of Willendorf.* When the Romans arrived on the scene there were already Celtic settlements in the Danube Valley, the result of migrations east from Gaul some 500 years earlier. The Romans established Carnuntum (now Petronell) as a provincial capital of Pannonia in AD 9. Around the same time a military camp, Vindobona, was built about 40km to the west. This effectively marked the northern border of the Roman Empire and served to discourage advances by Germanic tribes north of the Danube. The camp was right in the middle of Vienna's Innere Stadt (the 1st district in the centre of town), within a square bordered by Graben, Tiefer Graben, Ruprechtskirche and Rotenturmstrasse. A civil town sprang up outside the camp, which flourished in the 3rd and 4th centuries. At this time a visiting Roman emperor, Probus, introduced vineyards to the hills of the Wienerwald (Vienna Woods).

In the 5th century the Roman Empire collapsed and the Romans were beaten back by invading tribes. The importance of the Danube Valley as an east-west crossing meant that there were successive waves of tribes and armies trying to wrest control of the region. Before and after the Romans withdrew came the Teutons, Slavs, Huns, Goths, Franks, Bavarians, Avars and the Magyars. In the 7th century the Bavarians controlled territory between the Eastern Alps and the Wienerwald, with the Slavs attempting to encroach on the region from the south-east.

Charlemagne, the king of the Franks, brushed aside all those in his path and in 803 established a territory in the Danube Valley west of Vienna, known as the Ostmark (eastern march). The Ostmark was overrun by Magyars upon his death in 814, but was re-established by Otto I, the Great, in 955. Otto was subsequently crowned the Holy Roman Emperor of the German princes by Pope John XII. In 996 the Ostmark was first referred to as Ostarrichi, a clear forerunner of the modern German Österreich (Austria), meaning eastern empire. The first documentation of a settlement on the site of the old Vindobona military camp appears with a reference to 'Wenia' in the annals of the archbishopric of Salzburg in 881.

The Babenbergs

Leopold von Babenberg, a descendant of a noble Bavarian family, became the *margrave* (German noble above count) of the Ostmark in 976. The Babenbergs proceeded to gradually extend their sphere of influence: in the 11th century most of modern-day Lower Austria (including Vienna) was in their hands; a century later (1192) Styria and much of Upper Austria was safely garnered. This was a period of trade and prosperity for the region. In 1156 the Holy Roman Emperor, Friedrich Barbarossa, elevated the territory to that of a duchy. The same year, the Babenbergs, under Duke Heinrich II, established their permanent residence in Vienna.

Already an important staging point for armies on their way to and from the Crusades, Vienna was first documented as a city *(civitas)* in 1137. The city continued to flourish, welcoming artisans, merchants and minstrels. In 1147 Stephansdom (St Stephen's Cathedral), then a Romanesque church, was consecrated and a city wall was built. A city charter was granted to Vienna by the duke in 1221.

In 1246 Duke Friedrich II died in a battle with the Hungarians over the mutual border. He left no heirs, which allowed the Bohemian king, Ottokar II, to move in and take control. Ottokar held sway over a huge area (all the way from the Sudeten to the Adriatic Sea) and refused to swear allegiance to the new Holy Roman Emperor, Rudolf of Habsburg. His pride was costly –

Ottokar died in a battle against his powerful adversary at Marchfeld in 1278. Rudolf granted his two sons the fiefdoms of Austria and Styria in 1282. Thus began the rule of one of the most powerful dynasties in history – the Habsburgs were to retain the reins of power right up to the 20th century.

The Habsburg Dynasty

The Habsburgs gradually extended their dominion: Carinthia (Kärnten) and Carniola were annexed in 1335, followed by Tirol in 1363. Rudolf IV (who ruled from 1358 to 1365) went as far as forging some documents (the *Privilegium maius*) to elevate his status to that of an archduke. He also laid the foundation stone of Stephansdom and founded the University of Vienna. These acts helped to placate the wealthy Viennese families, who privileges had been reduced in the previous century.

In 1453 Friedrich III managed to genuinely acquire the status that was faked by Rudolf IV and was elected Holy Roman Emperor. Furthermore, he persuaded the pope to raise Vienna to a bishopric in 1469. Friedrich's ambition knew few bounds – his motto was *Austria Est Imperator Orbi Universo* (AEIOU), which expressed the view that the whole world was Austria's empire. To try to prove this he waged war against King Matthias Corvinus of Hungary, who managed to occupy Vienna from 1485 to 1490. Friedrich's tomb rests inside the Stephansdom.

Friedrich III instigated the famous and extremely successful Habsburg policy of acquiring new territories through politically motivated marriages – Burgundy, the Netherlands and Spain (and its overseas lands) were all gained in this manner. Meanwhile, a genetic side effect emerged, albeit discreetly played down in official portraits: the hooked Habsburg nose, thick lips and distended lower jaw became a family trait.

The Habsburg empire was soon too vast to be ruled by one person. In 1521 the Austrian territories were passed on to Ferdinand by his elder brother Charles. Ferdinand later inherited Hungary and Bohemia through his own marriage. Insurrection in Vienna prompted Ferdinand to decree a new city charter under which self-rule was abolished, and Vienna came directly under the control of the sovereign.

The Turkish Threat

Ferdinand became preoccupied with protecting his territories from the incursions of the Turks, who were rampant under the leadership of Suleiman the Magnificent. The Turks overran the Balkans and killed Lewis II in their conquest of Hungary. In 1529 they commenced a siege against Vienna. It lasted for 18 days and was curtailed partly by the early onset of winter. The inner city had not been breached, though the outer districts lay in ruins. Although they withdrew, the Turks remained a powerful force, and it was this ongoing threat that prompted Ferdinand to move his court to Vienna in 1533, the first Habsburg to permanently reside in the city. This move increased the city's prestige.

In 1556 Charles abdicated as emperor and his brother, now Ferdinand I, was crowned in his place. Charles' remaining territory was inherited by his own son, Philip, thereby finalising the split in the Habsburg line. In 1571 the emperor granted religious freedom, upon which the vast majority of Austrians turned to Protestantism. In 1576 the new emperor, Rudolf II, embraced the Counter-Reformation and much of the country reverted to Catholicism – not always without coercion. The problem of religious intolerance was the cause of the Thirty Years' War, which started in 1618 and had a devastating effect on the whole of Central Europe. In 1645 a Protestant Swedish army marched within sight of Vienna but did not attack. The Peace of Westphalia treaty ended the conflict in 1648 and caused Austria to lose territory to France.

For much of the rest of the 17th century, Austria was preoccupied with halting the advance of the Turks into Europe. In the meantime, in 1679, Vienna suffered a severe epidemic of the bubonic plague and between 75,000 and 150,000 Viennese died. The city had barely recovered when the Turks struck again, with a siege in 1683. The Viennese were close to capitulation

The Turks & Vienna

The Ottoman Empire viewed Vienna as 'the city of the golden apple', though it wasn't the *Apfelstrudel* they were after in their two great sieges. The first, in 1529, was undertaken by Suleiman the Magnificent, but the 18-day endeavour was not sufficient to break the resolve of the city. The Turkish sultan subsequently died at the siege of Szigetvár, but his death was kept secret for several days in an attempt to preserve the morale of the army. The subterfuge worked for a while. Messengers were led into the presence of the embalmed body, which was placed in a seated position on the throne, and they then unknowingly relayed their news to the corpse. The lack of the slightest acknowledgment of the sultan towards his minions was interpreted as regal impassiveness.

At the head of the Turkish siege of 1683 was the general Kara Mustapha. Amid the 25,000 tents of the Ottoman army that surrounded Vienna he installed his 1500 concubines. These were guarded by 700 black eunuchs. Their luxurious quarters contained gushing fountains and regal baths, all set up in haste but with great opulence.

Again, it was all to no avail – perhaps the concubines proved too much of a distraction. Whatever the reason, Mustapha failed to put garrisons on the Kahlenberg and was surprised by a quick attack from Charles of Lorraine heading a German army and supported by a Polish army led by King Sobieski. Mustapha was pursued from the battlefield and defeated once again, at Gran. At Belgrade he was met by the emissary of the sultan. The price of failure was death, and Mustapha meekly accepted his fate. When the Austrian imperial army conquered Belgrade in 1718 the grand vizier's head was dug up and brought back to Vienna in triumph, where it is preserved in the Historisches Museum der Stadt Wien (but is no longer exhibited).

---

when they were rescued by a Christian force of German and Polish soldiers. Combined forces subsequently swept the Turks to the south-eastern edge of Europe. The removal of the Turkish threat saw a frenzy of baroque building in Vienna – Johann Bernhard Fischer von Erlach and Johann Lukas von Hildebrandt began to change the face of the city. Under the musical emperor, Leopold I, Vienna also became a magnet for musicians and composers.

The Years of Reform

The death of Charles II, the last of the Spanish line of the Habsburgs, saw Austria get involved in the War of the Spanish Succession (1701–14). At its conclusion Charles VI, the Austrian emperor, was left with only subsidiary Spanish possessions (such as the Low Countries and Italy). Charles then turned to the problem of ensuring his daughter, Maria Theresa, would succeed him as he had no male heirs. To this end he drew up the *Pragmatic Sanction*, cosigned by the main European powers. Maria Theresa duly ascended to the Habsburg

throne in 1740. However, to ensure she stayed there it was first necessary to win the War of the Austrian Succession (1740–48). The Seven Years' War (1756–63) was also fought to retain Habsburg lands (though Prussia won Silesia in this conflict).

Maria Theresa's rule lasted 40 years, and is generally acknowledged as a golden era in which Austria developed as a modern state. Centralised control was established along with a civil service. The army and economy were reformed and a public education system was introduced. Vienna's reputation as a centre for music grew apace. Her son, Joseph II, who ruled from 1780 to 1790 (though was also jointly in charge from 1765), was even more of a zealous reformer. He issued an edict of tolerance for all faiths, secularised religious properties and abolished serfdom. Yet Joseph moved too fast for the staid Viennese and was ultimately forced to rescind some of his measures.

The Crumbling Empire

The rise of Napoleon proved to be a major threat to the Habsburg empire. He inflicted defeats on Austria in 1803, 1805 and 1809, and in the latter two years also occupied Vienna. Franz II, who had taken the Austrian crown in 1804, was forced by Napoleon in 1806 to give up the German crown and the title of Holy Roman Emperor. The cost of the war caused state bankruptcy and a currency collapse in 1811, from which the Viennese economy took years to recover.

European conflict dragged on until the Congress of Vienna, in which Austria and its capital regained some measure of pride. The proceedings were dominated by the Austrian foreign minister, Klemens von Metternich. Austria was left with control of the German Confederation until forced to relinquish it in the Austro-Prussian War in 1866.

On the home front, all was not well in post-Congress Vienna. Although the arts and culture, as pursued by the middle classes, flourished (the so-called Biedermeier period), the general populace had a harder time. Metternich had established a police state and removed civil rights. Coupled with poor wages and housing, this led to revolution in March 1848. The war minister was hanged from a lamppost, Metternich was ousted and Emperor Ferdinand I abdicated. The subsequent liberal interlude was brief, and the army helped reimpose an absolute monarchy. The new emperor, Franz Josef I, was just 18 years old.

Technical advances helped to improve the economic situation and in 1857 Franz Josef ordered the commencement of the massive Ringstrasse developments around the Innere Stadt. The city council *(Gemeinderat)* was re-established in 1861 but only 1% of Viennese – all privileged landowners – were eligible to vote.

Franz Josef became the head of the dual Austro-Hungarian monarchy, created in 1867 by the *Ausgleich* (compromise), Austria's response to defeat by Prussia the previous year. A common defence, foreign and economic policy ensued but unity was not complete, as two separate parliaments remained. Another period of prosperity began, which particularly benefited Vienna. The city hosted the World Fair in 1873. Its infrastructure was improved (trams electrified, electricity stations and gasworks built) and fledgling health and social policies were instigated. Universal male suffrage was introduced in Austro-Hungarian lands in 1906.

Peace in Europe had been maintained by a complex series of alliances (Austria-Hungary was linked to the German empire and Italy under the Triple Alliance). The situation changed in 1914 when Franz Josef's nephew was assassinated in Sarajevo on 28 June. A month later Austria-Hungary declared war on Serbia and WWI began.

The Republic

In 1916 Franz Josef died and his successor, Charles I, abdicated at the conclusion of the war in 1918. The Republic of Austria was created on 12 November 1918. Under the peace treaty signed by the powers on 10 September 1919, the new republic's planned union with Germany was prohibited, and it was forced to recognise the independent states of Czechoslovakia, Poland, Hungary and Yugoslavia. Previously those countries, along with Transylvania (now in Romania), had been largely under the control of the Habsburgs. The loss of so much land caused severe economic difficulties – the new states declined to supply vital raw materials to their old ruler and Vienna's population was soon on the verge of famine. But by the mid-1920s the federal government had succeeded in stabilising the currency and establishing new trading relations.

In 1919 the franchise was extended to women; now all Viennese adults could vote for the city government by secret ballot. The socialists (Social Democrats) gained an absolute majority and retained it in all free elections up until 1996. They embarked on an impressive series of social policies and municipal programs, particularly covering communal housing and health. The Karl-Marx-Hof, designed by Karl Ehn and originally containing 1325 apartments, is the best example of the municipal buildings created in this so-called 'Red Vienna' period. (It stretches for 1km along Heiligenstädter Strasse, north of Franz Josefs Bahnhof.)

The rest of the country, however, was firmly under the sway of the conservative federal government, causing great tensions between city and state. On 15 July 1927, in a very dubious judgement, right-wing extremists were acquitted of an assassination charge. Demonstrators gathered outside the Palace of Justice in Vienna (the seat of the Supreme Court) and set fire to the building. The police responded by opening fire on the crowd, killing 86 people (including five of their own number). The rift between Vienna's Social Democrats and the federal government grew.

The Rise of Fascism

Political and social tensions, coupled with a worldwide economic crisis, gave federal chancellor Engelbert Dollfuss an opportunity in 1933 to establish an authoritarian regime. In February 1934 civil war erupted, with the right wing proving victorious. Vienna's city council was dissolved and all progressive policies instantly stopped. In July the National Socialists (Nazis) assassinated Dollfuss. His successor, Schuschnigg, was unable to stand up to increasing threats from Germany. In 1938 he capitulated and included National Socialists in his government.

On 11 March 1938 German troops marched into Austria and encountered little resistance. Hitler, who had departed Vienna many years before as a failed and disgruntled artist, returned to the city in triumph, and held a huge rally at Heldenplatz. Austria was incorporated into the German Reich under the *Anschluss* on 13 March; a national referendum held in April found most Viennese in favour.

The arrival of the Nazis was to have a devastating affect on Vienna's Jews in particular, though many non-Jewish liberals and intellectuals also fled the city. After May 1938, Germany's Nuremberg racial laws were also applicable in Austria. Jews were stripped of many of their civil rights; they were excluded from some professions and universities and were required to wear the yellow Star of David. Vienna's Jewish community was rocked by racial violence on the night of 9 November 1938, when their shops were looted and all but one of their temples burnt down (for more on this,

see the Jewish Museum in the Things to See & Do chapter). Many Jews managed to flee the country, but about 60,000 Austrian Jews were sent to the concentration camps. All but 2000 perished.

Austria was part of Germany's war machine during WWII from 1939 to 1945. Allied bombing was particularly heavy in Vienna in the last two years of the war and most major public buildings were damaged or destroyed, plus about 86,000 homes. The city was liberated on 11 April 1945 by Russian troops advancing from Hungary.

Post-WWII

Austria was declared independent again on 27 April 1945 and a provisional federal government established under Karl Renner. The country was restored to its 1937 frontiers and was occupied by the victorious Allies – the USA, the Soviet Union, Britain and France. The whole country was divided into four zones, one for each occupying power. Vienna, within the Soviet zone, was itself divided into four zones. Fortunately there was free movement between each zone, and thus Vienna escaped the east-west division suffered by Berlin. Control of the central zone alternated between the four powers on a monthly basis.

Delays caused by frosting relations between the superpowers ensured that the Allied occupation dragged on for 10 years. It was a tough time for the Viennese – the rebuilding of national monuments was slow and expensive and the black market dominated the flow of goods. On 15 May 1955 the Austrian State Treaty was ratified, with Austria proclaiming its permanent neutrality. The Allied forces withdrew, and in December 1955 Austria joined the United Nations. As the capital of a neutral country on the edge of the Warsaw Pact, Vienna attracted spies and diplomats in the Cold War years. Kennedy and Khrushchev met here in 1961, and Carter and Brezhnev in 1979. Various international organisations located themselves in the city.

Austria's international image suffered following the election in 1986 of President Kurt Waldheim who, it was revealed, had served in a German *Wehrmacht* unit implicated in WWII war crimes. A belated recognition of Austria's less-than-spotless WWII record came with Chancellor Franz Vranitzky's admission in 1993 that Austrians were 'willing servants of Nazism'.

The EU Years

In the postwar years Austria worked hard to overcome economic difficulties. It established a free trade treaty with the European Union (EU, then known as the EEC) in 1972, and application for full membership eventually followed. Austrians endorsed their country's entry into the EU in the June 1994 referendum, with a resounding 66.4% voting in favour. Austria officially joined the EU on 1 January 1995, though since then the people have been rather more ambivalent about the advantages of EU membership.

Austria suffered international criticism in February 2000, when the far-right Freedom Party (FPÖ) formed a new federal coalition government with the Austrian People's Party (ÖVP) under the leadership of Chancellor Schlüssel. The new administration, though democratically elected, was condemned before it even had the opportunity to put a foot wrong. The EU immediately imposed sanctions against Austria by freezing all high-level diplomatic contacts.

Many Austrians were angered that ÖVP did a deal with the FPÖ, especially as this excluded the highest-polling party, the SPÖ (with 33% of the vote, compared to 26.9% each for the ÖVP and the FPÖ). Public demonstrations against the FPÖ were held in several Austrian cities – in Vienna these continued throughout 2000 (see Minoritenplatz Vicinity in the Things to See & Do chapter). However, many Austrians, irrespective of their views towards the FPÖ, were also upset at the EU's pre-emptive move, believing that Austria would not have been targeted had it been a more important player in European affairs. In the event, sanctions proved not only futile but counterproductive, and they were withdrawn in September 2000. However, the government remains the subject of close international monitoring.

GEOGRAPHY

Vienna (elevation 156m) occupies an area of 414 sq km in the Danube Valley, the most fertile land for cultivation in Austria. Vines and fruits are grown along the river, with vineyards extending as far as the suburbs of Vienna. More than 700 hectares are under cultivation in the Vienna region, and nearly 90% of the wine produced is white. The largest wine-growing area is Stammersdorf in the north.

The Danube formerly flowed through northern Vienna in a series of offshoots and backwaters, all of which were susceptible to flooding. The flow was regulated from 1870 to 1875 by the digging of a straight channel, which forms the present course of the river. This was supplemented 100 years later by the building of the New Danube channel, a further provision against flooding. The long, thin island that was created between the two channels is now a recreation area. The Old Danube was formerly the main course of the river; it is now an enclosed, curving stretch of water, and the site of beaches and boating activities.

CLIMATE

Austria comes within the central European climatic zone, though the eastern part of the country (where Vienna is situated) has a Continental Pannonian climate, characterised by a mean temperature in July above 19°C and annual rainfall usually under 800mm.

Maximum average temperatures in Vienna are: January 11°C, April 15°C, July 25°C and October 14°C. Minimum average temperatures are lower by about 10°C (summer) to 4°C (winter). The differences in

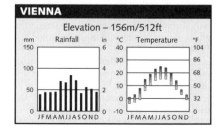

VIENNA
Elevation – 156m/512ft
Rainfall / Temperature

temperature between day and night and summer and winter are greater than in the west of the country. July and August can be very hot, and a hotel with air-conditioning would be an asset at this time. Winter is surprisingly cold, especially in January, and you would need to bring plenty of warm clothing. Damp maritime winds sometimes sweep in from the west. Average rainfall is 710mm per year, with most falling between May and August.

ECOLOGY & ENVIRONMENT

Austrians are well informed about environmental issues and the country has signed up to various international agreements intended to reduce pollution and preserve natural resources. Austria actually exceeds EU environmental dictates in many regards. It spends 3% of its GDP (Gross Domestic Product) on environmental measures.

Recycling is well established in Vienna – about 290kg of waste is recycled annually per inhabitant. Residents diligently divide tin cans, paper and plastic from the rest of their refuse for recycling purposes. This isn't only dictated by conscience – they are compelled to do so by law. In addition, hazardous materials such as aerosols must be put aside to be collected twice a year by the municipal authorities.

Glass containers (especially beer bottles) often have a return value, and some supermarkets have an automatic bottle-returning area *(Flaschen Rücknahme)*. It's all very efficient: you put your bottle into the recess and the machine works out what type it is and the appropriate return value. Once you've deposited all your bottles you press the button and the machine gives you a credit note against the rest of your shopping.

Vienna's widespread use of environmentally friendly trams has helped to keep the city's air of a reasonable quality, and the Wienerwald (Vienna Woods) also helps by acting as an efficient 'air filter'. Data on air quality is shown on display panels in various public locations.

The Spittelau incinerator in the 9th district has one of the lowest emission levels of any incinerator worldwide. This plant re-processes waste matter, burning 260,000 tonnes of waste annually to supply heating for more than 40,000 homes in Vienna.

Vienna's airport is likely to need a new runway by 2010 – an issue bound to inspire much environmental debate.

FLORA & FAUNA

Protected green zones comprising woods, meadows and parks occupy 52% of land in the city of Vienna. Trees include beech, oak, pine and spruce in the Wienerwald, and the famous horse chestnut trees that line avenues in the Prater and elsewhere. Vienna's public parks and gardens are attended to by 1500 gardeners who coax some two million blossoms into life every year.

The Danube River contains 60 fish species native to Austria, including perch, salmon, eels and catfish. The Danube between Vienna and the Slovakian border is a protected area, the Donau-Auen National Park (see the Excursions chapter). Close to Vienna, on the shores of the Neusiedler See, is a protected bird sanctuary (see the Excursions chapter), where there are many rare species. Herons, kingfishers, bitterns, warblers and many others can be seen, and storks nest on the rooftops of nearby towns.

Lainzer Tiergarten is home to wild sheep and boars, and all species of deer that are native to Central Europe. On the domestic front, there are over 46,000 dogs living in the city. The Viennese love their dogs and are unwilling to curtail their canines' habit of excreting in the street. Former mayor Helmut Zilk tried to address this problem by flying in consultants from Paris to demonstrate fancy faeces hoovering machines. Unfortunately, dog owners were unimpressed and have declined to touch their doggies' do-dos with barge poles or anything else. Numerous pigeons provide further waste-disposal problems.

GOVERNMENT & POLITICS

As well as being the capital city of Austria, Vienna is (and has been since 1922) one of nine federal provinces *(Bundesländer)*. Every Austrian federal province has its own head of government *(Landeshauptmann)* and provincial assembly *(Landtag)*. Each provincial assembly has a fair degree of autonomy in deciding local issues and also elects representatives to the Federal Council *(Bundesrat)*, the upper house of the national legislative body. The lower house, the National Council *(Nationalrat)*, is elected every four years by all adults over the age of 18. (In 2000 Carinthia province cut the voting age for local and district elections to 16; there's strong support for a similar initiative in Vienna.) The Austrian head of state is the president; Thomas Klestil was elected to a second six-year term in 1998.

Vienna's provincial assembly is elected every five years. The election in October 1996 ushered in the first postwar coalition. The Social Democrats (SPÖ), formerly with an absolute majority, won 43 seats out of 100, and had to do a deal with the right-wing Austrian People's Party (ÖVP; 15 seats). The opposition includes the far-right Freedom Party (FPÖ; 29 seats) and the Green Party (seven seats).

The FPÖ has seen a huge surge in popularity since 1986 under the leadership of Jörg Haider, who has expressed admiration for several of Adolf Hitler's policies. The FPÖ targeted foreigners and asylum-seekers during the 1996 election, campaigning for zero immigration – this campaign proved to be surprisingly popular in supposedly liberal Vienna. The same themes will be central to its policies for the next election. Haider, the governor of Carinthia province, resigned as head of the FPÖ in early 2000, following the international outcry generated by the FPÖ becoming part of the federal coalition government. However, he remains the party's most influential figure.

Vienna's provincial assembly also functions as the city council *(Gemeinderat)*. Likewise, the offices of provincial governor and mayor are united in the same person. The City Hall *(Rathaus)* is the seat of these offices. Vienna's current incumbent is Michael Häupl of the SPÖ.

ECONOMY

Austria has one of the strongest economies in the EU. Citizens enjoy good welfare services and health care, and a benign pensions and housing policy. In 2000, inflation is expected to be under 2% and national unemployment under 5%. Vienna's registered jobless number around 60,000 people.

Vienna is a base for precision engineering, metal products and the manufacture of electrical and electronic goods. Banking and insurance are also important, as the city's strong trading links with Eastern Europe. The port of Vienna is the largest facility for container transloading in inland Europe, and has increased in importance with the opening of the Main canal connecting the Rhine and the Danube.

Tourism is one of Vienna's biggest earners, and guest workers from Eastern Europe and elsewhere are the backbone of this industry. About 25% of visitors hail from Germany. The easier accessibility of nearby Prague and Budapest, although providing competition to Vienna, has actually helped pull more visitors into the region.

The city coalition government is gradually loosening the old socialist administration's centralised grip on the Viennese economy. It still has fingers in various commercial pies, such as holdings in restaurants and cinemas, but there is an ongoing privatisation program. The city owns around 220,000 residential apartments.

POPULATION & PEOPLE

Vienna has a population of 1,606,000, approximately one-fifth of the population of Austria as a whole. The population density in the city is 388 people per sq km. Native Austrians are mostly of Germanic origin, though Vienna itself has more ethnic diversity. The industrial expansion of the late 19th century brought European migrants into the capital, particularly from the Czech-speaking parts of the then empire.

Around 264,000 foreigners currently live in Vienna, mostly hailing from Yugoslavia (84,000) and Turkey (46,000), plus about 17,000 people apiece from Bosnia, Croatia and Poland. Fears of being overrun by immigrants gained momentum in the early 1990s (thanks in part to a cynical anti-foreigner campaign by the Freedom Party), prompting the federal government to tighten up immigration controls considerably.

National service is compulsory for Austrian males from the age of 18 (six months plus two months at a later time), though they may opt out of the military in favour of civil-service duties.

EDUCATION

Compulsory education lasts to age 15, with many students continuing their education in academic or vocational colleges. Vienna has five universities and three fine arts colleges, attended by a total of 140,000 students. University fees are due to be introduced for the first time in September 2001.

SCIENCE & PHILOSOPHY

The Vienna Circle was a group of philosophers centred on Vienna University in the 1920s and 30s. The term 'logical positivism' was created to describe their philosophy. They owed an initial debt to the work of the Austrian philosopher and scientist Ernst Mach (whose name lives on as a measure of the speed of a body in relation to the speed of sound). The group formulated the verifiability principle as a yardstick for judging whether things are meaningful. Mathematical propositions (eg, $2 + 2 = 4$) are meaningful in that they are tautological and cannot be contradicted. Science is meaningful in that its formulations are answerable and empirically verifiable. However, metaphysical questions (eg, is there a God?) are meaningless because they cannot be verified. The Vienna Circle emigrated with the arrival of the Nazis in 1938. The movement remained influential, though it lost some of its appeal when philosophers couldn't agree whether the verifiability principle itself was tautological or subject to empirical verification.

Sir Karl Popper (1902–94) was loosely connected with the Vienna Circle, but mainly in a critical capacity. He was born in Vienna and lived and worked there until the gathering storm clouds of Nazism compelled him to leave Austria. He had an impact on the way the nature of scientific inquiry was understood, with his views that

the hallmark of science is falsifiability rather than verifiability. He pointed out that general scientific laws could never be logically proved to always apply, they could only be disproved if and when contrary data became manifest. (This would make them meaningless according to the verifiability principle of the logical positivists.) Scientific laws are therefore accepted until they are seen to require revision (as in the way that Newtonian physics was refined by Einstein), thus leading to the advancement of scientific endeavour. Popper was also known for his work in the field of social and political philosophy.

Ludwig Wittgenstein (1889–1951) made a significant impact with his philosophical writings, not least on the Vienna Circle. He was born in Vienna and died in Cambridge, England, where he spent the latter part of his career as a research fellow at the university. Much of his output was concerned with the scope and limitations of language. His *Tractatus* was an adamant treatise ordered as a series of logical statements. He ended up in the paradoxical situation of having to use language to say what he admitted could only be shown using analysis external to language. Nevertheless, Wittgenstein was so convinced that this work had achieved all that it was possible for such a text to do, that it effectively heralded an end to philosophical inquiry. He therefore retired from the scene and retreated to the obscurity of a teaching post in rural Austria.

Wittgenstein returned to Cambridge in 1929 and proceeded to all but contradict the thrust of his earlier work. His new theories were less rigid and attempted to illuminate the inventiveness of language. Wittgenstein has been hailed as one of the most influential 20th-century philosophers. His talents extended to designing a house for his sister – the Wittgenstein Haus (☎ 713 31 64) 03, Parkgasse 18 – which can be visited.

Sigmund Freud (1856–1939), the founder of psychoanalysis, had a love-hate relationship with Vienna, the city where he lived and worked for most of his life. He too fled from the Nazis in 1938. Freud believed that the repression of infantile sexuality was the cause of neurosis in adult life. Central to his

Sigmund Freud

Sigmund Freud was born in Freiberg, Moravia, on 6 May 1856. Three years later his father, a Jewish wool merchant, relocated the family to the Leopoldstadt quarter in Vienna. Freud was educated in Vienna and graduated as a Doctor of Medicine in 1881 (his degree took three years longer to complete than was usual, as he spent much of his time engaged in neurological research that wasn't part of the curriculum). In 1886 he set up his first office as a neurologist at 01, Rathausstrasse 7, and later that year married Martha Bernays, who went on to bear him six children. In 1891 he moved his practice to 09, Berggasse 19. He first came up with the term 'psychoanalysis' in 1896.

The Origin of the Freudian Slip

MATT KING

Although many academics and physicians were hostile towards his published works, Freud was able to gather around him a core of pupils and followers, who would meet in his waiting room on Wednesday evenings. Among their number was the Swiss psychologist Carl Jung, who later severed his links with the group (in 1914) because of personal differences with Freud. In 1923 Freud was diagnosed as having cancer of the palate, an affliction that caused him great pain and forced him to undergo surgery over 30 times. The illness prompted him to mostly withdraw from public life; his daughter, Anna (a child psychiatrist), often appeared in his stead at meetings and conventions.

The arrival of the Nazis in 1938 instigated a mass evacuation by many of Vienna's Jews. Freud was allowed to emigrate to London on 4 June, accompanied by Anna. The rest of his children also managed to escape, but other family members weren't so fortunate – four of his elderly sisters were detained in the city, and finally killed in a concentration camp in 1941. Freud breathed his last in London on 23 September 1939.

treatments was getting the patient to recognise unconscious conflicts. Early on he employed hypnosis to uncover these conflicts, which he later abandoned in favour of free association and the study of symbolism in dreams. *The Interpretation of Dreams* (1900) was his first major work.

In *Beyond the Pleasure Principle* (1920) Freud contended that the two dominant principles of the mind were the pleasure-pain complex and the repression-compulsion complex, the latter being the instinctive drive of an organism to return to its previous state. His last psychoanalytical work was *The Ego and the Id* (1923), a new theory in which the tensions between the id (basic urges), the ego (the conscious personality) and the superego (idealised ingrained precepts) were explored. Inferiority complexes and guilt feelings were the frequent result of such tensions. Although Freud's views have

always been attacked, his legacy to the 20th century remains enormous. A mental landscape of Oedipus complexes, phallic objects and Freudian slips are only a few of the manifestations. Generations of patients supine on couches is another.

ARTS
Sculpture & Design

Sculpture and design have evolved and altered over the years, usually mirroring changes in architectural styles. The Verdun Altar in Klosterneuburg abbey dates from the Romanesque period. Fine examples of baroque sculpture are the Donner Fountain by George Raphael Donner in Neuer Markt, and Balthasar Permoser's statue of Prince Eugene in the Unteres Belvedere. Baroque even extended to funeral caskets, as created by Balthasar Moll for Maria Theresa and Francis I. Neoclassical sculpture is typified in the equestrian statue of Emperor Joseph II in Josefsplatz by the Hofburg.

The Biedermeier period was strongly represented in furniture, examples of which can be seen in the Museum für angewandte Kunst (Museum of Applied Art). After Biedermeier, the technique of bending wood in furniture became popular, particularly in the backs of chairs. The bentwood chair became known as the Viennese chair.

In 1903 the Wiener Werkstätte (Vienna Workshops) were founded. They created a range of quality, if expensive, household products, as well as garments and jewellery. Aesthetic considerations were given precedence over practicality, resulting in some highly distinctive styles, such as Josef Hoffmann's silver tea service (displayed in the Museum für angewandte Kunst). Another key figure involved in the Wiener Werkstätte was Kolo Moser.

Architecture

Excavations of Roman ruins can be seen within Vienna's 1st district at Michaelerplatz, Am Hof 9 and Hoher Markt. Romanesque architecture barely survives in modern Vienna, though some churches (eg, Stephansdom and Michaelerkirche) are built around earlier Romanesque churches.

The Gothic style didn't really take hold in Austria until the accession of the Habsburgs. The most impressive Gothic structure in Austria is Vienna's Stephansdom. It displays a typical characteristic of the Gothic style in Austria with its three naves of equal height, a feature also to be found in the Minorite churches.

While Renaissance architecture had little penetration in Vienna, baroque proved to be a high point for Austria in terms of both architecture and painting. Building fervour was fuelled by the removal of the Turkish threat in 1683. Learning from the Italian model, Johann Bernhard Fischer von Erlach (1656–1723) developed a national style called Austrian baroque. This mirrored the exuberant ornamentation of Italian baroque but gave it a specifically Austrian treatment. Dynamic combinations of colour are coupled with irregular or undulating outlines.

Examples of Fischer von Erlach's work in Vienna include the Nationalbibliothek (national library) and Karlskirche. Another prominent baroque architect was Johann Lukas von Hildebrandt (1668–1745), responsible for the palaces of Belvedere and Schwarzenberg, and the Peterskirche.

Rococo, the extreme version of baroque, was a great favourite with Maria Theresa. She chose this fussy style for most of the rooms of Schloss Schönbrunn when she commissioned Nicolas Pacassi to renovate it in 1744. Austrian rococo is sometimes referred to as late-baroque Theresien style.

Rococo was succeeded by neoclassicism, a less showy style of which Vienna's Technical University is an example. The period between the Congress of Vienna (1814–15) and the revolutions of 1848 was called the Vormärz (pre-March), or Biedermeier when applied to art.

In the second half of the 19th century, historicism took hold – this is seen principally in the Ringstrasse developments instigated by Franz Josef I. A great diversity of retrograde styles can be seen here, such as French Gothic (Votivkirche), Flemish Gothic (Rathaus), Grecian (Parlament), French Renaissance (Staatsoper) and Florentine Renaissance (Museum für angewandte Kunst).

The backlash came at the end of the 19th century with the emergence of Art Nouveau (Jugendstil), an art and architecture style that spread through much of Europe. In Vienna the movement flowered with the founding of the Secession movement in 1897. Otto Wagner – designer of the Postsparkasse (Post Office Savings Bank) and the Kirche am Steinhof – was one of the leading architects in the field (see the boxed text 'Otto Wagner' in the Things to See & Do chapter). It was Wagner who led the movement towards a more modern, functional style as the 20th century unfolded.

Adolf Loos (1870–1933) was perhaps an even more important figure in the move towards a new functionalism. He was a bitter critic of the Ringstrasse buildings, yet he was also quickly disillusioned with the ornamentation in Secessionist buildings.

Architectural Styles

Romanesque This style dates from the 10th to 13th centuries. Romanesque churches are characterised by thick walls, closely spaced columns and heavy, rounded arches. Little of this style remains in Vienna today.

Gothic The Gothic style was popular from the 13th to 16th centuries. This new aesthetic was made possible by engineering advances, permitting thinner walls and (in churches) taller, more delicate columns and great expanses of stained glass. Distinctive features included pointed arches and ribbed ceiling vaults, external 'flying buttresses' to support the thinner walls, and elaborate carved doorway columns.

Renaissance The 16th century saw a new enthusiasm for classical forms and an obsession with grace and symmetry. In Austria, Italian architects were imported to create Renaissance buildings, and they usually incorporated Italian and local features.

Stephansdom's Gothic spire

Baroque This resplendent, triumphal style is closely associated with the rebuilding (and reimposition of Catholicism) in the region after the Thirty Years' War. Emotional sculpture and painting, marble columns, and rich, gilded finishing create the extravagant and awe-inspiring interiors.

Rococo This is essentially late, over-the-top Baroque. Florid in the extreme, elaborate and 'lightweight', it was popular with architects in the late 18th century.

Historicism The revival of old styles of architecture became popular after the 1848 revolution. Neoclassical, neorenaissance and neogothic styles all came to the fore and are evident in most of the building on Vienna's Ringstrasse. The neoclassical style used grand colonnades and pediments, and often huge, simple, symmetrical buildings.

Jugendstil Wagner Apartments

Modern At the end of the 19th century the sensuous and decorative style called Art Nouveau ('new art'; called Jugendstil or Sezessionstil in Austria) took hold, its main practitioners in Vienna being the Secession architects. The more sinuous and decorative features of this style became subservient to functional considerations, both in design and building materials.

The dominance of the Social Democrats in the city government of the new Republic gave rise to a number of municipal building projects, not least the massive Karl-Marx-Hof apartment complex. Postwar architecture was mostly utilitarian.

Since the late 1980s a handful of multicoloured, haphazard-looking structures have appeared in Vienna; these are buildings which have been given a unique design treatment by maverick artist, Friedensreich Hundertwasser (see the boxed text 'Peace

Empire & a Hundred Waters' in the Things to See & Do chapter.

Austria's premier postmodern architect is Hans Hollein, who created Haas Haus opposite Stephansdom.

Literature

The outstanding Viennese work of the Middle Ages was the *Nibelungenlied* (The Song of the Nibelungs), written around 1200 by an unknown hand. This epic poem told a tale of passion, faithfulness and revenge in the Burgundian Court at Worms. Its themes were adapted by Richard Wagner in his *The Ring of the Nibelungen* operatic series.

The first great figure in the modern era was the playwright Franz Grillparzer (1791–1872), who anticipated Freudian themes in his plays which are still performed at the Burgtheater. Other influential playwrights who still regularly get an airing are Johann Nestroy, known for his satirical farces, and Ferdinand Raimaund *(The Misanthrope)*.

Adalbert Stifter (1805–68) is credited as being the seminal influence in the development of an Austrian prose style. Austria's literary tradition really took off around the turn of the century, the same time as the Vienna Secessionists and Sigmund Freud were creating their own waves. Influential writers who emerged at this time included Arthur Schnitzler, Hugo von Hofmannsthal, Karl Kraus and the poet Georg Trakl. Kraus' apocalyptic drama *Die letzten Tage der Menschheit* (The Last Days of Mankind) employed a combination of reports, interviews and press extracts to tell its tale – a very innovative style for its time. Kraus had previously founded *Die Fackel* (The Torch), a critical literary periodical. Peter Altenberg was a poet who depicted the bohemian lifestyle of Vienna, and he currently resides at Café Central in the form of a plaster dummy (see the Places to Eat chapter).

Robert Musil was one of the most important 20th-century writers, but he only achieved international recognition after his death. He was born in Klagenfurt in 1880 and died in poverty in Geneva in 1942, with his major literary achievement, *Der Mann ohne Eigenschaften* (The Man Without Qualities), still unfinished, albeit stretching to several volumes. It reveals a fascinating portrait of the collapsing Austro-Hungarian monarchy. Another major figure in the 20th century was Heimito von Doderer (1896–1966). He grew up in Vienna and first achieved recognition with his novel *The Strudlhof Staircase*. His magnum opus was *Die Dämonen* (The Demons), an epic fictional depiction of the end of the monarchy and the first years of the Austrian Republic, with specific reference to Vienna. *The Demons* and *The Man Without Qualities* have both been translated into English.

Thomas Bernhard (1931–89) was born in Holland but grew up and lived in Austria. He was obsessed with negative themes such as disintegration and death, but in later works like *Cutting Timber* he turned to controversial attacks against social conventions and institutions. His novels are seamless (no chapters or paragraphs, few full stops) and seemingly repetitive, but surprisingly readable once you get into them. He also wrote plays and short stories. Bernhard was influenced by Ludwig Wittgenstein's writings, and even wrote an autobiographical novel about his friendship with the philosopher's nephew. Both *Cutting Timber* and *Wittgenstein's Nephew* are published in English translations.

The best-known contemporary writer is Peter Handke (born 1942). His output encompasses innovative and introspective prose works and stylistic plays. The provocative novelist Elfriede Jelinek dispenses with direct speech and indulges in strange flights of fancy, but she is worth persevering with. Translations of her novels *The Piano Teacher*, *Lust* and *Women as Lovers* have been published in English. Another prominent contemporary author is Friederike Mayröcker, once described as 'the avantgarde's bird of paradise' by a critic.

Film

Austrian endeavours in the film industry go mostly unnoticed outside the German-speaking world. There are a few exceptions. Austrian-born film directors who have made an impact internationally include Fritz Lang *(Metropolis*, 1926), Fred Zinnemann *(High Noon*, 1952) and Billy Wilder *(Some Like it Hot*, 1959). Well-known actors are Klaus Maria Brandauer (who starred in *Mephisto* in 1980), Romy Schneider and Hedy Lamarr; and of course there's former Mr Universe, Arnold Schwarzenegger, whose bulk fills the screen in a range of Hollywood blockbusters, particularly action epics such as *The Terminator* series.

Theatre

Vienna's tradition in the theatre was – and still is – bolstered by the quality of operas and operettas produced in the golden age of music. Greek dramas, avant-garde, mime, comedy, farce and other genres are also regularly performed in Vienna's generous range of federal, municipal and private theatres. The Burgtheater is the premier performance venue in the German-speaking world. The Akademietheater, under the same management, is a more intimate venue that generally stages contemporary plays. The Theater in der Josefstadt is known for the modern style of acting evolved by Max Reinhardt. The Theater an der Wien favours musicals. There are also a couple of English-language theatres – see the Entertainment chapter for details.

Painting

Examples of Gothic church art in Austria are best seen in the Middle Ages collection in the Orangery in the Unteres Belvedere. Early Renaissance art is represented in Austria by the Danube School, which combined landscapes and religious motifs; exponents included Rueland Frueauf the Younger, Wolf Huber, Max Reichlich and Lukas Cranach.

Baroque artists who were responsible for many church frescoes include Johann Michael Rottmayr and Daniel Gran. A prominent canvas painter was Franz Anton Maulbertsch, who combined mastery of colour and light with intensity of expression. The leading Biedermeier painters were Georg Ferdinand Waldmüller (1793–1865) and Friedrich Gauermann (1807–62), who captured the age in portraits, land-

scapes and period scenes. Some of Waldmüller's evocative, if idealised, peasant scenes can now be found in the Historisches Museum der Stadt Wien and in the Oberes Belvedere. Rudolf von Alt was an exponent of watercolour.

Hans Makart (1840–84) was a prominent painter of the historicism period, and Anton Romako (1832–89) anticipated the age of expressionism.

The leading painter of the Art Nouveau age, and one of the founders of the Viennese Secession movement, was Gustav Klimt (1862–1918). Trained in the traditional mould, he soon developed a colourful and distinctive style, full of sensuous female figures, flowing patterns and symbolism.

Viennese Actionism

Viennese Actionism spanned from 1957 to 1968 and was one of the most extreme of all modern art movements. It was linked to the Vienna Group and had its roots in abstract expressionism. Actionism sought access to the unconscious through the frenzy of an extreme and very direct art: the actionists quickly moved from pouring paint over the canvas and slashing it with knives, to using bodies (live people, dead animals) as 'brushes', and using blood, excrement, eggs, mud and whatever came to hand as 'paint'. The traditional canvas was soon dispensed with altogether. The artist's body instead became the canvas, the site of art became a deliberated event (the scripted action, staged both privately and publicly) and even merged with reality.

It was a short step from self-painting to inflicting wounds upon the body, and engaging in physical and psychological endurance tests. For 10 years the actionists scandalised the press and public, incited violence and panic – and got plenty of publicity. Often poetic, humorous and aggressive, the actions became increasingly politicised, addressing the sexual and social repression that pervaded the Austrian state. *Art in Revolution* (1968), the last action to be realised in Vienna, resulted in six months' hard labour all round.

Dr Ed Baxter

Egon Schiele (1890–1918) and Oskar Kokoschka (1886–1980) were important exponents of Viennese expressionism. For more on Schiele's life and work, see Oberes Belvedere (Things to See & Do chapter) and Tulln (Excursions chapter).

The works of most of these 19th- and 20th-century artists are best viewed in the Oberes Belvedere and the Museumsquartier.

The Wienergruppe (Vienna Group) was formed in the 1950s by HC Artmann. Its members incorporated surrealism and Dadaism in their sound compositions, textual montages and actionist happenings (see the boxed text). Public outrage and police intervention were a regular accompaniment to their meetings. The group's activities came to an end in 1964 when Konrad Bayer, its most influential member, committed suicide.

SOCIETY & CONDUCT

It is customary to greet people you come across with the salutation *Grüss Gott* or *Servus* and to say *Auf Wiedersehen* when departing. This applies to shop assistants, cafe servers and the like. Not greeting someone will be taken as a personal affront (and will give the rebuffed party sufficient excuse to demonstrate that the reputation for rude service in Vienna is not wholly unjustified!).

When being introduced to someone it is usual to shake hands, likewise when you leave. This applies even in younger, informal company. At a meal, Austrians dining together normally raise their glasses and say *Prost* before taking their first sip of wine; look people in the eye while you're doing it – some may consider you insincere otherwise. Similarly, there will be a signal before you should start to eat, such as the exchange of a *Guten Appetite*.

Some older Viennese still cling to the language and etiquette of the old empire, known as *Kaiserdeutsch* or *Schönbrunndeutsch*. This can be seen as pompous or charming depending upon your point of view. It may manifest itself at introductions, with men addressing women as *Gnädige Frau* ('gracious lady') and formally adding *Küss die Hand* ('I kiss your hand'), perhaps backing this up by actually performing the act or clicking the heels. People often address each other using full formal titles.

You'll see conservative behaviour exhibited in various other ways too, such as in the rigid respect for the 'don't walk' red figure on traffic lights; even if there's no traffic anywhere in sight, people will obediently wait for the lights to change (in theory you could be fined around €8 if the police spot you jaywalking). The Viennese tend to dress up when going to the opera or theatre, and they'd probably appreciate it if you made a similar effort. Men would be advised to wear a jacket and tie when dining in top-class restaurants.

RELIGION

Religion plays an important part in the lives of many Austrians. If you venture out into the countryside you'll see small roadside shrines decorated with fresh flowers. Freedom of religion is guaranteed under the constitution. Even the religious rights of children are protected: up to age 10 a child's religious affiliation is in parental hands, yet from age 10 to 12 children must be consulted about their preferred religion, and from age 12 to 14 a change of religion cannot be imposed upon any child. Upon reaching 14 children have full independence to choose their own faith.

The 1991 census revealed that in Vienna there were 890,000 Roman Catholics, 80,000 Protestants and 160,000 following other religions; 400,000 people were non-religious or undeclared.

The tourist office has the *Grüss Gott* brochure listing religious services for different denominations and in various languages. In English, there's a Roman Catholic service at the Votivkirche, 09, Rooseveltplatz, at 11 am on Sunday and an interdenominational service at the Reformierte Stadtkirche, 01, Dorotheergasse 16, at 11.30 am on Sunday.

LANGUAGE

The Viennese speak a dialect of German. It's fairly close to standard High German, albeit with some unique words and expressions. See the Language chapter at the back of this book for vocabulary and pronunciation tips.

Above all else, Vienna is known for music. Its reputation grew out of the classical era of the late 1700s and early 1800s, but as early as the 12th century Vienna was known for its troubadours (called *Minnesänger*) and strolling musicians.

In the late 13th century Albrecht I, then head of the Habsburgs, gathered musicians together to perform for him. This led to the birth of the Royal Music Ensemble, which was officially formed by the decree of Maximilian I in 1498, and paved the way for music and musicians to prosper under the Habsburg empire.

The Habsburgs' willingness to patronise music drew composers from all over Europe to Austria and especially Vienna in the 18th and 19th centuries. The Habsburgs were at the height of their power, and their love of music helped elevate it to one of the favourite pastimes of the aristocracy. The three greatest classical composers – Mozart, Haydn and Beethoven – were all drawn to Vienna, and their innovative and inspirational work saw the beginning of a golden era. This short period, from the date Mozart moved to Vienna in 1781 to the year Schubert died in 1828, yielded some of the most memorable music ever produced.

Classical music continued to flourish in Vienna with the coming of the waltz, first penned by Johann Strauss the Elder and then, more famously, by his son. Composers such as Brahms, Mahler and Bruckner flocked to the city to gain inspiration and mix with similar minds.

It is a sign of the importance of music to this city that after both world wars, when resources were so low that people were starving, money was still put aside to keep up performances at the Staatsoper. Today, you can't avoid music in Vienna, as you wander the streets passing by buskers playing the classics or singing opera and people dressed as Mozart peddling tickets to concerts.

Christoph Willibald von Gluck

Although he fell outside the heyday of Viennese classical music, Gluck (1714–87) is worthy of mention, for he played an important part in paving the way for the next generation of composers.

Gluck settled in Vienna in 1751, and after being noticed by Empress Maria Theresa, he became *Kapellmeister* (choir master) to the imperial court. His talent lay in opera, and with such a title he was free to compose his 'reformed' operas – compositions with an emphasis on the dramatic rather than wailing vocalists. The style of his compositions such as *Orfeo* (1762) and *Alceste* (1767) influenced both Mozart and Schubert, and brought about the start of the German romantic era.

Wolfgang Amadeus Mozart

Only 35 when he died, Mozart (1756–91) left some 626 pieces, including 24 operas, 49 symphonies, over 40 concertos, 26 string quartets,

Title page: Statue of Johann Strauss (photograph by Man? Gottschalk)

seven string quintets, and numerous sonatas for piano or violin. Praise for his music came from many quarters – Haydn believed him to be the 'greatest composer' he knew of; Schubert effused on the 'magic of Mozart's music that lights the darkness of our lives'.

MICK WELDON

Wolfgang Amadeus Mozart

Mozart took opera to new heights by achieving a fusion of Germanic and Italianate styles (the librettos were first in Italian and later, innovatively, in German). Pundits consider Mozart's greatest Italian operas to be *The Marriage of Figaro* (1786), *Don Giovanni* (1787) and *Così fan Tutte* (1790). *The Magic Flute* (1791) was a direct precursor of the German opera of the 19th century.

Growing up in Salzburg, Mozart's career started early. His musician father, Leopold, taught him how to play the harpsichord at age three, and two years later gave him a small violin. The five-year-old Mozart asked a quartet of musicians if he could join in their playing; the musicians laughingly agreed, but were amazed when the prodigy proceeded to play his part perfectly. One went so far as to call it witchcraft.

Mozart senior was quick to exploit his son's astounding talent. Along with Wolfgang's sister, Maria Anna (four years older, and also exceptionally gifted), they toured Europe giving recitals and receiving plaudits wherever they went. At age six Wolfgang performed in front of Empress Maria Theresa at Schönbrunn – enthusiastically jumping up into her lap when she marvelled at his performance. At age eight he had already toured London, Paris, Rome, Geneva, Frankfurt and the Hague; four of his sonatas were published before he turned nine.

In 1770, still only 14 years old, Mozart was appointed director of the archbishop of Salzburg's orchestra. The work did not challenge his talents and after petitioning the archbishop to be released he departed for Paris in 1777. He succeeded Gluck as court composer (at less than half the former's salary!) in 1787.

In 1781 Mozart was summoned to Vienna by the archbishop to help with the celebrations of the accession of Joseph II. Although he left the archbishop's employ soon after, he remained in Vienna and it was here that Mozart was to enjoy his most productive years, his music ranging over light-hearted, joyous themes, dramatic emotions and melancholic gloom.

Although always productive musically, Mozart was a compulsive gambler and he lost large sums at billiards, ninepins and cards. He was also something of a ladies' man – at age 24 he proclaimed, 'If I had married everyone I jested with, I would have well over 200 wives'. On 4 August 1782 he married Constanze Weber in the Stephansdom. she bore him six children, but only two survived to be adults.

Mozart was buried on a rainy December day after a meagrely attended, frugal ceremony. His body was wrapped in a sack and doused with lime (an imperial decree to prevent epidemics) before being buried in a ditch in the cemetery of St Mark's.

The film *Amadeus* (1985), by Milos Forman (from Peter Shaffer's play), portrayed Mozart as infuriating, enthusiastic, volatile, emotionally immature and effortlessly gifted. This may be close to the truth, although Mozart once announced that nobody had worked harder than himself at studying musical composition.

Josef Haydn

Although not as famous (or flamboyant) as Mozart or Beethoven, Haydn (1732–1809) is generally considered one of the three greatest classical composers. He was prolific and his life's work includes 108 symphonies, 68 string quartets, 47 piano sonatas and about 20 operas.

Haydn had an extraordinary upbringing. Born in Rohrau, Lower Austria, to humble parents, he left home (virtually never to return) at the age of six, when his musical talent was recognised. He moved to Hainburg to live with a cousin, who was choirmaster. At eight he was invited to be a chorister at the Stephansdom in Vienna, where he stayed for nine years. When his voice broke at 17 he was unceremoniously expelled from the cathedral choir.

Uneducated in musical theory, Haydn studied musical works intensely, most notably those of Bach, so he could compose his own music. After a decade as a freelance musician, he became assistant musical director for the Esterházys, one of the Austrian empire's richest and most influential families. Although the head of the Esterházy family was to change several times, Haydn remained in the family's service until his death 38 years later.

During this period Haydn developed a close friendship with Mozart, teaching him how to write quartets. Mozart dedicated a set of six to his 'beloved friend'.

After the death of Prince Miklós in 1790, most of the court musicians were dismissed by his heir, who did not share his father's love of music. Haydn retained his salary but no duties were required of him. He was persuaded to visit England to write and perform six symphonies. Feted by the aristocracy and royals (King George III invited him to remain), Haydn remained in England for 18 months, and returned there for a shorter period in 1794. He wrote 12 symphonies (including the Symphony No 102 in B-flat Major – one of his greatest works) during his two trips to England.

Back in Vienna, Haydn wrote several significant pieces including the oratorios *The Creation* (1798) and *The Seasons* (1801), and six masses for his new patron, Miklós II, which are among the 18th century's finest.

Haydn's private life was not as successful as his professional life. In 1760 he married Maria Anna Keller, which he described as the biggest mistake of his life. Maria had no love of music – her dislike apparently extended to lining pastry pans with Haydn's manuscripts – and the couple quarrelled frequently. However, Haydn found love with his long-term mistress, Italian soprano Luigia Polzelli.

Just before Haydn died, Vienna was besieged by Napoleon's forces and the elderly composer refused to move to the safety of the inner city. As a mark of respect Napoleon had a guard of honour placed outside his house.

Ludwig van Beethoven

Beethoven (1770–1827), like many other composers of the era, was born into music. His grandfather was Kapellmeister of the choir of the archbishop-elector of Cologne and his father, Johann, was also a singer in the choir. However, unlike Mozart, he was no child prodigy. In spite of his father's urgings, it was not until he was in his teens that Beethoven began to show signs of genius.

After four years with the Bonn opera, Beethoven was sent to Vienna to study with Mozart in 1787; however, his visit was cut short when his mother died two months later. Mozart was very impressed with the young Beethoven, especially his ability to improvise, and predicted he would make a great name for himself.

Beethoven's reputation in Bonn grew. The money he earned from teaching helped support his family, after his father had squandered much of the family fortune on alcohol. Haydn visited Bonn at this time and, after seeing some of Beethoven's manuscripts, agreed to take him as a student.

Beethoven came to Vienna for the second time in late 1792. He was 21 years of age and already a superb piano virtuoso, but he still had much to learn as a composer. Soon after arriving, Beethoven began taking lessons in secret from Johann Georg Albrechtsberger, Stephansdom's organist, who was very learned in musical technique. Later he also studied vocal composition with Antonio Salieri, the imperial Kapellmeister.

Money again became an issue for Beethoven, but patrons such as Prince Lichnowsky (a supporter of Mozart) helped him. Later, when he threatened to leave Vienna after a quarrel with some musicians, several nobles offered him an annuity of 4000 florins. To receive this grand sum all Beethoven had to do was remain in Vienna and write music, which he did until his death.

Beethoven's career had three distinct periods. The first, which largely comprised chamber music, was from his adolescence to his 32nd year. In the second period, when he began

MICK WELDON

Ludwig van Beethoven

to improvise, Beethoven's hearing began to fail him, and he briefly contemplated suicide (what worse fate than deafness could there be for a musician?). As total deafness approached, Beethoven withdrew from the public performances that helped make him so popular. He produced fewer pieces (among them the Symphony No 9 in D Minor, one of his greatest and most influential works), but many consider his final 10 years to have been his best period. He was also greatly inspired by the Viennese countryside (eg, in the Pastoral Symphony of 1808).

Beethoven never married, but appears (from letters) to have contemplated it at least three times. He died from cirrhosis of the liver aged 57, and more than 20,000 people attended his funeral. He lived in over 60 abodes, which can be found all over the city.

Franz Schubert

The last in the great line of composers from the Vienna Classical School is Schubert (1797–1828), who was misunderstood during his lifetime and his work largely overlooked and unappreciated until after his death.

He was born and bred in Vienna, at Nussdorfer Strasse 54, which is now a museum. His musical ability and output is quite staggering – nine symphonies, 11 overtures, seven masses, over 80 smaller choral works, over 30 chamber music works, 450 piano works and over 600 Lieder (over 960 works in total). All this before he died at the age of just 31 – Beethoven's age when he had just completed his first symphony. Beethoven was so impressed with some of Schubert's work that he proclaimed, 'this Schubert certainly has the divine spark in him'.

The 12th child of a schoolteacher father, Schubert began his short but prolific career at the age of 11 when he was enrolled in the *Konvikt*, a boarding school which served as the school for the Vienna Boys' Choir. When his voice broke at the age of 16, he was booted out of the choir and liable for conscription. Schubert sidestepped the army by joining his father as a teacher, and it was at this time that he began to compose. His first symphony and mass were composed during his first year of teaching, and at 17 he switched to a romantic theme and laid the foundations for the German Lied, for which he is so well known.

At only 18, Schubert had one of the most creative years of his life, and quit teaching soon after to devote himself to his true talent. His second burst of creativity occurred in the final year of his life, 1828. His last symphony, in C major, and his Mass in E-flat, were among the pieces composed. It was also the year of the only public performance of his work, a piano trio in E-flat, seven months before his death.

Probably Schubert's most famous piece, his 'Unfinished' Symphony, was written in 1822 when he was only 25. Like almost all of his works, it was performed only after his death, in 1865.

Schubert, like Beethoven, never married. He was considered a bit of a recluse, and only mixed with a few close friends. Unlike the other great composers of the era, he lived most of his life hand-to-mouth, unable to make a living from his music and surviving from the occasional musical tour and the generosity of friends and supporters.

He died only 18 months after his hero Beethoven, and his final wish, to be buried next to him, was carried out. Both now reside in the Central Cemetery of Vienna.

The Strausses & the Waltz

The waltz originated in Vienna at the beginning of the 19th century and went down a storm at the Congress of Vienna (1814–15). The early masters of the genre were Johann Strauss the Elder (1804–49), who was also the composer of the *Radetzky March*, and Josef Lanner (1801–43). Both toured Europe, bringing the waltz to the masses and paving the way for Stauss' son to stamp it into the chronicles of music history.

Johann Strauss the Younger (1825–99) composed over 400 waltzes. He became a musician against the wishes of Strauss senior (who had experienced years of struggle), and set up a rival orchestra to his father's. He composed Vienna's unofficial anthem, *The Blue Danube* (1867), and *Tales from the Vienna Woods*. This joyful, if lightweight, style became so popular that more 'serious' composers began to feel somewhat disenfranchised.

The *Blue Danube* waltz had its first public performance in Paris, and its fame soon spread far and wide. The shrewd young Strauss soon saw the advantages of touring, which helped create the popularity of the waltz.

Strauss also proved also to be a master of the equally fashionable operetta style, especially with his eternally popular *Die Fledermaus* (1874) and *The Gipsy Baron* (1885).

Anton Bruckner

In the late 19th century, Vienna was still attracting musicians and composers from elsewhere in Europe. Bruckner (1824–96) arrived from Upper Austria and settled in Vienna with his appointment as organist to the court in 1868. A very religious man, he is known for lengthy, dramatically intense symphonies (nine in all) and church music.

Bruckner died in Vienna but his body rests in Upper Austria, in the monastery of St Florian where he was originally appointed organist and choirmaster.

Johannes Brahms

At the age of 29, Brahms (1833–97) made a late move to Vienna from his birthplace, Hamburg, and stayed for 35 years. He briefly spent time as artistic director of the Gesellschaft der Musikfreunde but gave it up to pursue a life devoted to composing. As a composer he started late, and completed his first symphony in 1876 at the age of 42.

Brahms enjoyed Vienna's village atmosphere, saying it had a positive effect on his work which was in the classical-romantic tradition. He was held in great public esteem during his life and many of his works were performed by the Vienna Philharmonic. He died in 1897 of cancer of the liver and his funeral was almost as well attended as Beethoven's.

Gustav Mahler

Another famous German to make his mark in Vienna was Mahler (1860–1911). Mahler is known mainly for his nine symphonies, and was director of the Vienna State Opera from 1897 to 1907.

His father enrolled Mahler in the Vienna Conservatorium at the age of 15, and in his three years there he became friends with the likes of Hugo Wolf and Anton Bruckner. Afterwards he embarked on the fruitful career of Kapellmeister for a number of cities around Europe, until his reputation gained him the position of deputy director, then director of the Vienna Opera. It was under Mahler's guidance that the Vienna Opera came into full bloom, with singers beginning to act as well as sing, and stage design playing a part in the performance.

Mahler died at the age of 51 and is buried in Grinzing Cemetery.

Hugo Wolf

Wolf (1860–1903) is probably quite unknown to the average music listener, but he rivalled Schubert in his facility at Lieder composition. Born in what is now Slovenia, it wasn't until he was 15 that he moved to Vienna to begin his music training.

Wolf composed many Lieder in his short life, and had times of intense creativity. His first came in 1888, when he penned no less than

SARAH JOLLY

53 Lieder, and the second towards the end of 1889 and into 1890, when more than 50 Lieder found life on paper.

Tragically, Wolf went insane and died at the age of 43 in a Vienna asylum.

The Second Vienna School

Vienna's musical eminence continued in the 20th century with the innovative work of Arnold Schönberg (1874–1951), who founded the Second Vienna School of Music (dubbed the 'New School') and developed theories on the 12-tone technique. Some of his earlier works (eg, Pieces for the Piano op. 11, composed in 1909) go completely beyond the bounds of tonality and sound more like an orchestra warming up than anything else.

The most influential of his pupils were Viennese-born Alban Berg (1885–1935) and Anton Webern (1883–1945), who both explored the 12-tone technique. Their compositions were not well received by the general public. At the first public performance of Berg's composition *Altenberg-Lieder*, conducted by Schönberg, the concert had to be cut short due to the audience's outraged reaction to the unconventional instrumental effects.

Vienna Philharmonic Orchestra

The Vienna Philharmonic is one of the best-known orchestras in the world, and plays to packed houses wherever it tours. Like the Vienna Boys' Choir, the Philharmonic is a Vienna institution.

Started as an experiment in March 1842, it grew in popularity in Vienna but did not venture on its first foreign tour until 1898, under

SARAH JOLLY

the baton of Gustav Mahler. Its first tour outside Europe took place in 1922, with a trip to South America.

The Philharmonic has the privilege of choosing its conductors, whose ranks have included the likes of Mahler, Richard Strauss and Felix von Weingartner. Conductors stick around for years (19 in the case of Weingartner) or for a few concerts, depending on the whim of the orchestra members and management.

The instruments used by the Philharmonic generally follow pre-19th-century design and more accurately reflect the music Mozart and Beethoven wrote. Most of its members have been born and bred in Vienna, making it a truly Viennese affair.

Music Today

The *Heurigen* (wine taverns) in Vienna have a musical tradition all their own – *Schrammelmusik* – with the songs often expressing very maudlin themes. It is usually played by musicians wielding a combination of violin, accordion, guitar and clarinet and has a small but loyal following in Vienna.

In the field of rock and pop Vienna has made little impact (unless you count the briefly emergent Falco), though the city does have several jazz clubs, and was home to Joe Zawinul of Weather Report. The local rock scene is alive and kicking, with many acts drawing large crowds. Particularly popular is Ostbahn Kurti (or Kurt Ostbahn, depending on how he feels at the time), who sings in a thick Viennese dialect which is often hard to understand. The mainstream Austrian pop of Wolfgang Ambros, Georg Danzer and Reinhard Fendrich also draws large crowds.

Vienna is making small waves on the DJ and clubbing scene worldwide, and attracts well-known international acts. Local DJs Kruder & Dorfmeister and the Sofa Surfers have both enjoyed international success and are slowly putting Vienna on the map of modern music.

Facts for the Visitor

WHEN TO GO

Visitors descend on Vienna year-round. When to go depends on what you want to do or see. In July and August, for example, you won't be able to see the Lipizzaner stallions or the Vienna Boys' Choir, but you will be able to enjoy the Vienna Summer of Music. See the Public Holidays & Special Events section later in this chapter for seasonal events to aim for.

It's not only singers and horses that disappear in July and August – many Viennese also go on holiday at this time. These months can be oppressively hot, yet summer remains the most popular time for tourists to visit. June is dire for budget accommodation, but from July to September things are much easier with the opening of student residences. In winter you'll find things less crowded and the hotel prices lower (except over Christmas and Easter), though it can get too cold for comfort around the New Year. Weatherwise, spring and autumn are probably the most comfortable seasons for sightseeing. September is a busy month for tourism.

ORIENTATION

Vienna stands imperiously in the Danube Valley, with the rolling hills of the Wienerwald (Vienna Woods) undulating beyond the suburbs in the north and west. The Danube River divides the city into two unequal halves. The old city centre and nearly all the tourist sights are south of the river. The Danube Canal (Donaukanal) branches off from the main river and winds a sinewy course south, forming one of the borders of the historic centre, the 1st district (known as the Innere Stadt). The rest of the old centre is encircled by the Ringstrasse, or Ring, a series of broad roads sporting sturdy public buildings and sites of touristic interest. Beyond the Ring is a larger traffic artery, the Gürtel (literally meaning 'belt'), which is fed by the flow of vehicles from the outlying motorways.

Stephansdom (St Stephen's Cathedral), with its distinctive slender spire, is in the heart of the Innere Stadt and is the city's principal landmark. The majority of hotels, pensions, restaurants and bars are in the Innere Stadt, and west of the centre between the Gürtel and the Ringstrasse. Farther west is an important tourist sight, Schloss Schönbrunn.

The long, thin Danube Island (Donauinsel) is a recreation area which is flanked by the Danube and the New Danube (Neue Donau). A loop of water to the east is the Old Danube (Alte Donau), known for its beaches and water sports. Enclosed by the Old Danube are Donaupark and the UNO business district. North and east of the Old Danube are relatively poor residential districts, of no real interest to tourists.

Addresses

Vienna is divided into 23 districts *(Bezirke)*, fanning out from the 1st district, the Innere Stadt. Take care when reading addresses. The number of a building within a street *follows* the street name. Any number *before* the street name denotes the district. This system has been used throughout this book. If you know the postcode of somewhere you can always work out approximately where it is, as the middle two digits of the four-number code correspond to the district, eg, a postcode of 1010 means the place is in district one, and 1230 refers to district 23.

> ### Fax Numbers in this Book
>
> In this book some fax numbers are presented as extensions (eg, fax -30) of the phone numbers that they follow. To send a fax dial the main phone number and add the fax extension.
>
> Throughout Vienna you'll also see telephone numbers presented with extensions. For an explanation of this system see the boxed text 'Telephone Numbers Explained' in the Post & Communications section later in this chapter.

Generally speaking, the higher the district number the farther it is from the centre. Another thing to note is that the same street number may cover several adjoining premises, so if you find that what is supposed to be a pizza restaurant at Wienstrasse 4 is really a rubber fetish shop, check a few doors either side before you resign yourself to a radical change of diet.

MAPS

For most purposes, the free map of Vienna provided by the tourist office will be sufficient. It shows bus, tram and U-Bahn routes and major city-wide sights on a general map and a central blow-up. (Some of its key items aren't explained – for that you'll have to buy *Vienna From A to Z*; see the introduction to the Things to See & Do chapter). For a street index, you'll need to buy a map. The most authoritative series of maps on Vienna and Austria are produced by Freytag & Berndt. It has maps to different scales; at 1:20,000 you can get either a fold-up map or a more extensive, book-style *Städteatlas*.

RESPONSIBLE TOURISM

As a visitor, you have a responsibility to the local people and to the environment. For guidelines on how to avoid offending the people you meet, read Society & Conduct in the Facts about Vienna chapter. When it comes to the environment, the key rules are to preserve natural resources and avoid degrading your surroundings. One way you can do this is to follow the local habit of recycling. For more on this, see Ecology & Environment, also in the Facts about Vienna chapter. Traffic congestion on the roads is a major problem, and visitors will do themselves and residents a favour if they forgo driving and use public transport.

TOURIST OFFICES
Local Tourist Offices

The main tourist office (Map 7) is at 01, Am Albertinaplatz, and has extensive free literature including an excellent city map. *Ten good reasons for Vienna*, clearly aimed at the young with its overly hip style, contains lots of useful information for everyone, as

does the biannual *Vienna Scene*. There are also free lists of museums, events, hotels and restaurants, as well as a room-finding service (€2.95 commission per reservation). The office is open 9 am to 7 pm daily.

Advance requests for brochures, telephone inquiries and anything out of the ordinary are better dealt with at the head office of the Vienna Tourist Board (Map 4; ☎ 211 14, fax 216 84 92, **e** wtv@info.wien.at) at Obere Augartenstrasse 40, A-1025, Wien. Opening hours are 8 am to 4 pm Monday to Friday; but the office is not set up to handle visits in person from the public. Check the Web site at www.info.wien.at.

Lower Austria (Niederösterreich) surrounds Vienna and includes areas like the wine-growing Wachau and the Wienerwald (see the Excursions chapter). There is a Lower Austria Information Centre (Map 7) at 01, Kärntner Strasse 38, but it's only part of the Intropa travel agency and its main intent is to sell you packages. For detailed information you'll need to contact the region's local tourist offices. Alternatively, try the Niederösterreich Information head office (☎ 536 10-6200, fax -6060, **e** noe .tourist-info@ping.at), with a Web site at www.noe.co.at.

The Österreich Werbung, or Austria Information Office (Map 6; ☎ 587 20 00, fax 588 66 48, **e** oeinfo@oewwien.via.at), 04, Margaretenstrasse 1, is open 9.30 am to 5 pm Monday to Friday (to 6 pm on Thursday), and has information about the whole country. The Web site is at www.austria-tourism.at.

Information and room reservations (usually €2.95 commission) are also available in offices open daily at various entry points to the city:

Airport – Arrivals hall, 8.30 am to 9 pm
Train stations – Westbahnhof (Map 5), 7 am to 10 pm; and Südbahnhof (Map 6), 6.30 am to 10 pm (to 9 pm from 1 November to 30 April)
From the west by road – A1 autobahn exit Wien-Auhof (Map 2), 8 am to 10 pm (April to October) and 10 am to 6 pm (November to March)
From the south by road – A2 exit Zentrum (Map 2), Triester Strasse, 9 am to 7 pm (Easter to June, and October) and 8 am to 10 pm (July to September); closed in winter

From the north by road – At Floridsdorfer Brücke (bridge; Map 2) on Donauinsel (Danube Island), 10 am to 6 pm; closed October to April

Tourist Offices Abroad

The Austrian National Tourist Office (ANTO) has branches in about 20 countries. Elsewhere, its functions may be taken care of by the Austrian Trade Commission, or the commercial counsellor at the Austrian embassy. Make contact by telephone, letter or email in the first instance – some offices are not geared to receive personal callers.

Australia (☎ 02-9299 3621, fax 9299 3808, ⓔ oewsyd@world.net) 1st floor, 36 Carrington St, Sydney, NSW 2000

Canada (☎ 416-967 3381, fax 967 4101, ⓔ anto.tor@sympatico.ca) 2 Bloor St East, Suite 3330, Toronto, Ont M4W 1A8

Czech Republic Österreich Werbung (☎ 2-222 11 282, fax 222 10 256, ⓔ oewprag@dovolena-v-rakousku.cz) Krakovská 7, CR-12543 Prague 1

Germany Österreich Information (☎ 089-666 70 100, fax 666 70 200, ⓔ info@oewmuc.de) Postfach 701580, D-81315, Munich

Hungary Osztrák Nemzeti Idegenforgalmi Képviselet (☎ 1-391 43 11, fax 391 43 20, ⓔ info@oewbud.hu) PF 1022, H-1387, Budapest 62

Italy Austria Turismo (☎ 02-439 90 185, fax 439 90 176, ⓔ informazioni@austria-turismo.it) Casella Postale No 1255, I-20121, Milan

Japan (☎ 03-358 209 31, fax 381 463 79, ⓔ antoyo@magical.egg.or.jp) Akasaka-Dori Post Office, Tokyo 107-0052

South Africa (☎ 11-442 7235, fax 788 2367, ⓔ oewjnb@cis.co.za) Cradock Heights, 2nd floor, 21 Cradock Ave, Rosebank, 2196 Johannesburg

Switzerland Österreich Werbung (☎ 01-451 15 51, fax 451 11 80, ⓔ info@oewzrh.ch) Postfach, CH-8036, Zürich

UK (☎ 020-7629 0461, fax 7499 6038, ⓔ info@anto.co.uk) PO Box 2363, London W1A 2QB

USA
New York: (☎ 212-944 6880, fax 730 4568, ⓔ info@oewnyc.com) PO Box 1142, New York, NY 10108-1142
Los Angeles: (☎ 310-477 2038, fax 477 5141, ⓔ info@oewlax.com) 11601 Wilshire Blvd, Suite 2480, Los Angeles, CA 90025

There are also tourist offices in Amsterdam, Brussels, Copenhagen, Paris, Russia and Stockholm; the complete list is at www.austria-tourism.at. New Zealanders can use the Austrian consulate in Wellington (see the Embassies & Consulates section).

Other Information Offices

The city information office in the Rathaus (City Hall; Map 7) is open 8 am to 6 pm Monday to Friday. Phone inquiries (☎ 525 50) will also be answered from 8 am to 4 pm on Saturday and Sunday, as well as during office hours. It provides information on social, cultural and practical matters, geared as much to residents as to tourists. There are two touch-screen computer terminals with useful information.

Jugendinfo (Youth Info; Map 7; ☎ 17 79, ⓔ jugendinfowien@wienXtra.at), at 01, Babenbergerstrasse 1, sells tickets for a variety of events at reduced rates for those aged between 14 and 26. Staff can tell you about events around town, and places where you can log onto the Internet. It's open noon to 7 pm Monday to Saturday.

TRAVEL AGENCIES

Ökista is a specialist in student and budget fares. The head office (☎ 401 48, fax -2290, ⓔ info@oekista.at), 09, Garnisongasse 7, is the location for telephone sales and Vienna accommodation bookings. Opening hours are 9 am to 5.30 pm Monday to Friday. For face-to-face ticket sales, or to get an International Student Identity Card (ISIC; €5.10 fee, proof of status required), visit one of the branch offices:

09, Türkenstrasse 6–8 (Map 3; ☎ 401 48-7000), open 9 am to 6.30 pm weekdays
04, Karlsgasse 3 (Map 7; ☎ 505 01 28), open 9 am to 5.30 pm weekdays
Altes AKH-Campus, 09, Alserstrasse 4/Hof 1 (Map 3; ☎ 902 07), open 9 am to 6.30 pm weekdays, 9 am to 5 pm Saturday
DZ-Im Libro, Donaustadtstrasse 1/2 (☎ 202 48 08), same opening hours as Altes AKH-Campus

Österreichisches Verkehrsbüro (Map 7; ☎ 588 00, fax 586 85 33, ⓔ info@verkehrs buero.at), 01, Friedrichstrasse 7 (and elsewhere), is a major national agency. Čedok (Map 7; ☎ 512 43 72, fax -85), 01, Parkring

FACTS FOR THE VISITOR

10 (entry from Liebenberggasse), is a specialist agency to the Czech Republic, open 9 am to 5 pm weekdays.

DOCUMENTS
Visas

Visas are not required for citizens from the EU, EEA (European Economic Area), USA, Canada, Australia or New Zealand. Most visitors may stay a maximum of three months (six months for Japanese). If you need to stay longer you should simply leave the country and re-enter. British and other EU nationals, plus the Swiss, may stay as long as they like, though if they are taking up residency they should register with the local police within five days of arrival. Any other nationals seeking residency should apply in advance in their home country.

Nationals of most African and Arab nations (South Africa included) require a visa; see the Ministry of Foreign Affairs Web site at www.bmaa.gv.at (it also lists Austrian embassy addresses worldwide). The visa has a validity of up to three months and the procedure varies depending upon the nationality – some nationals may be required to show a return ticket. Visa extensions are not possible – you will need to leave and reapply.

There are no border controls between EU nations signed up to the Schengen Agreement, which currently includes all member states except Britain and Ireland. Once you've entered one of these countries, you don't need a passport to move between them (though you should carry one anyway for identification purposes). Similarly, a visa valid for any of them ought to be valid for them all, but double-check with the relevant embassy.

Other Documents & Cards

Don't forget to arrange travel insurance before you leave home – good-value annual policies are available nowadays. An International Student Identity Card (ISIC) can get the holder decent discounts on admission prices, but in Austria these discounts will usually only apply to those under 25 or 27. Hostelling International (HI) membership is required if you want to stay in youth hostels;

it is cheaper to join in your home country than to pay for the guest stamp in Austria.

See the Getting There & Away chapter for required documentation and useful travel passes for car drivers.

Copies

It's a good idea to photocopy all important document details, leaving one copy with someone at home and keeping the other with you, separate from the originals.

It's also a good idea to store details of your vital travel documents in Lonely Planet's free online Travel Vault, just in case you lose the photocopies or can't be bothered with them. Your password-protected Travel Vault is accessible online anywhere in the world – create it at www.ekno.lonelyplanet.com.

EMBASSIES & CONSULATES
Austrian Embassies Abroad

Austrian embassies abroad include:

Australia (☎ 02-6295 1533, fax 6239 6751) 12 Talbot St, Forrest, Canberra, ACT 2603
Canada (☎ 613-789 1444, fax 789 3431) 445 Wilbrod St, Ottawa, Ontario K1N 6M7
Ireland (☎ 01-269 4577, fax 283 0860) 15 Ailesbury Court Apartments, 93 Ailesbury Rd, Dublin 4
New Zealand (☎ 04-499 6393, fax 499 6392) Austrian Consulate, Level 2, Willbank House, 57 Willis St, Wellington – does not issue visas or passports; contact the Australian office for these services
UK (☎ 020-7235 3731, fax 7344 0292) 18 Belgrave Mews West, London SW1X 8HU
USA (☎ 202-895 6700, fax 895 6750) 3524 International Court NW, Washington, DC 20008

Foreign Embassies in Vienna

For a complete listing, look in the telephone book under *Botschaften* (embassies) or *Konsulate* (consulates). Of the embassies mentioned below, consulate details are the same unless indicated. Double-check visa requirements if you plan to make excursions to neighbouring Hungary, the Czech Republic or Slovakia: currently, Americans, Britons and New Zealanders do not require a visa for these countries, but Australians need one for the Czech Republic and Hungary. According to a reader's report, it takes a week for Australians to get a Czech visa in Vienna, but if you go to the border you can get one on the spot.

Australia (Map 7; ☎ 512 85 80-0) 04, Mattiellistrasse 2–4
Canada (Map 7; ☎ 531 38-3000) 01, Laurenzerberg 2
Czech Republic (☎ 894 31 11) 14, Penzingerstrasse 11–13
France
  Embassy: (☎ 502 75-0) 04, Technikerstrasse 2
  Consulate: (☎ 536 12) 01, Wipplinger Strasse 24–26
Germany (☎ 711 54-0) 03, Metternichgasse 3
Hungary (Map 7; ☎ 533 26 31-0) 01, Bankgasse 4–6
Ireland (☎ 715 42 46-0) 03, Landstrasser Hauptstrasse 2, Hilton Center
Italy
  Embassy: (☎ 712 51 21-0) 03, Rennweg 27
  Consulate: (☎ 713 56 71-0) 03, Ungarngasse 43
Japan (☎ 531 92-0) 01, Hessgasse 6
New Zealand New Zealand embassy (☎ 030-20 62 10) in Berlin, Germany, has responsibility for Austria
  Consulate: (☎ 318 85 05) 19, Springsiedelgasse 28
Slovakia (☎ 318 90 60) 19, Armbrustergasse 24
Slovenia (☎ 586 13 09) 01, Nibelungengasse 13
South Africa (☎ 320 64 93-0) 19, Sandgasse 33
Switzerland (☎ 795 05-0) 03, Prinz Eugen Strasse 7
UK
  Embassy: (Map 6; ☎ 716 13-0) 03, Jaurèsgasse 12
  Consulate: (☎ 716 13-5151) 03, Jaurèsgasse 10
USA
  Embassy: (Map 3; ☎ 313 39-0) 09, Boltzmanngasse 16
  Consulate: (Map 7; ☎ 313 39) 01, Gartenbaupromenade 2–4

CUSTOMS

Duty-free shopping within the EU was abolished in July 1999. If you buy duty-paid alcohol and tobacco in high-street shops in other EU countries, there is theoretically no restriction on how much you can bring into Austria. However, to ensure these goods remain for personal use, guideline limits are 800 cigarettes, 200 cigars, 1kg tobacco, 10L of spirits, 90L of wine, 110L of beer and 20L of other alcoholic beverages.

For duty-free purchases made outside the EU, anybody aged 17 or over may bring into Austria 200 cigarettes or 50 cigars or 250g tobacco, plus 2L of wine and 1L of spirits.

MONEY
Currency

Austria is part of the European Monetary Union (EMU), along with Belgium, Finland, France, Germany, Ireland, Italy, Luxembourg, the Netherlands, Portugal and Spain. By 1 January 2002, euro notes and coins will be legal tender in these countries, and bank accounts will be converted to euros. During the first two months, the existing currencies, like the Austrian schilling (AS, or *ÖS* in German), will remain in circulation. The schilling will cease to be legal tender on 28 February 2002, though you will be able to unload old schillings at banks after that date.

Schilling banknotes come in denominations of AS20, AS50, AS100, AS500, AS1000 and AS5000, and schilling coins are to the value of 500, 100, 50, 25, 10, five and one schillings. There are 100 groschen in each schilling. The euro is divided into 100 cents. There are coins for one, two, five, 10, 20 and 50 cents, and €1 and €2. There are notes to the value of €5, €10, €20, €50, €100, €200 and €500. There is no limit on the value of schillings or euros that can be imported or exported.

Exchange Rates

The following are approximate exchange rates for Austrian schillings and euros when this book went to press:

country	unit		schilling		euro
Australia	A$1	=	AS8.43	=	€0.61
Canada	C$1	=	AS10.13	=	€0.73
Czech Republic	100K	=	AS39.60	=	€2.88
France	10FF	=	AS20.96	=	€1.52
Germany	DM1	=	AS7.03	=	€0.51
Hungary	Ft100	=	AS5.19	=	€0.38
Italy	L1000	=	AS7.11	=	€0.52
Japan	¥100	=	AS14.08	=	€1.02
New Zealand	NZ$1	=	AS6.57	=	€0.48
Switzerland	Sfr1	=	AS9.12	=	€0.66
UK	UK£1	=	AS22.42	=	€1.63
USA	US$1	=	AS15.64	=	€1.14

euro currency converter AS10 = €0.73

Euro Note

This book was researched when the schilling still reigned supreme, with the embryonic euro merely a bit-part player in paperless transactions.

Though euro notes and coins were not yet in circulation, dual pricing (in schillings and euros) was already the norm. By law, prices had to show the exact conversion to the euro to two decimal places, and with the euro being fixed at an unwieldy rate of €1 to 13.7603 Austrian schillings (AS), strange prices such as €1.03, €26.34 and €193.87 were appearing all over the place.

In this book we list prices in euros. We've assumed there will be some rationalisation of these weird euro prices once the schilling has been consigned to the piggy bank of history. Accordingly, euro prices quoted have been rounded up to the nearest five or 10 cents.

If you're using this book while the schilling is still in circulation, you might find yourself having to convert back and forth between schillings and euros. Currency converters, sold cheaply, will allow you to do this easily. Without one, to make a quick, approximate calculation of schillings to euros, divide by 10 and take off one third, eg, AS150 is 15 – 5 = €10. For an approximate euro conversion back to schillings, add 50% and times by 10; hence €20 is 20 + 10 x 10 = AS300. However, these approximates do undervalue the schilling slightly, so when shopping in schillings you'll be spending a little more than you think you are.

Here's a more exact table of schilling rates in euros:

AS5	= €0.37		AS100 =	€7.27
AS10	= €0.73		AS125 =	€9.09
AS15	= €1.09		AS150 =	€10.90
AS20	= €1.46		AS175 =	€12.72
AS25	= €1.82		AS200 =	€14.54
AS30	= €2.18		AS250 =	€18.17
AS40	= €2.91		AS300 =	€21.81
AS50	= €3.64		AS400 =	€29.07
AS60	= €4.36		AS500 =	€36.34
AS70	= €5.09		AS1000 =	€72.68
AS80	= €5.82		AS1500 =	€109.01
AS90	= €6.54		AS2000 =	€145.35

Exchanging Money

Exchange rates can vary a little between banks. It pays to shop around, not only for exchange rates but also for commission charges. Changing cash usually attracts lower commission rates, but always check first.

The American Express office (Map 7; ☎ 515 40, fax 515 67-3), 01, Kärntner Strasse 21–23, is open 9 am to 5.30 pm Monday to Friday and 9 am to noon Saturday. It has a travel section and financial services, and will hold mail (not parcels) free of charge for up to one month for customers who have American Express cards. There is no commission on cashing AmEx travellers cheques. Commission on the cheques of

other institutions is €3.65 (up to US$100) or €5.85 (over US$100). The commission for exchanging cash is €0.75 for tiny amounts, and €1.10 for up to US$200. The exchange rates aren't great, but you may come out ahead given the relatively low commissions.

The post office charges €2.20 minimum for cash but doesn't change cheques. Train stations charge about €2.95 for cash and €4.70 minimum for cheques. Banks typically charge €7.30 or more. Avoid changing a lot of low-value cheques because commission costs will be higher. Look especially carefully at the commission rates charged by exchange booths (Wechselstuben) – we've seen scandalous rates of 10% plus a charge per cheque! Moneychangers at the airport tend to charge high commissions though the exchange rates are standard.

Most banks are open 9 am to 3 pm Monday to Friday (until 5.30 pm on Thursday), with smaller branches closing from 12.30 to 1.30 pm. Train stations have extended hours for exchange at ticket counters or at exchange offices. Exchange offices are open 7 am to 10 pm daily in Westbahnhof, and 6.30 am to 10 pm daily (to 9 pm from 1 November to 31 March) in Südbahnhof. Branch post offices can exchange money until up to 5 pm on weekdays, and on Saturday morning. Some post offices have longer hours for exchange.

Travellers Cheques & ATMs American Express and Thomas Cook are the best-known travellers cheques. An alternative (or additional) way to manage your money is to rely on getting cash advances with a Visa card, EuroCard or MasterCard. ATM Bankomat machines for this are numerous, including at all the main train stations, the airport and 200 branches of Bank Austria. They are accessible 24 hours a day, and there's no commission to pay at the Austrian end. You can avoid the daily charge by feeding money into your credit card account at the beginning of your trip (though the credit card company will still make a transaction charge of around 1.5% to 2.5%), and you'll get a better rate of exchange than with cash or travellers cheque exchanges. A couple of readers have reported problems with getting cash advances using Australian-issued cards, so check with your bank before leaving home. Using a debit card or cash card in ATMs to draw money directly out of your home bank account will probably attract lower charges – ask your bank for advice.

Credit Cards Visa, EuroCard and MasterCard are accepted a little more widely than American Express and Diners Club, although a surprising number of shops and restaurants refuse to accept any credit cards at all. Plush shops and restaurants will accept cards, though, and the same applies for hotels. Train tickets can be bought by credit card in main stations.

International Transfers To get money sent internationally, transferring funds bank to bank is not always straightforward if you don't have a bank account in the receiving country. It's quicker and easier to have money wired via Western Union's Money Transfer system – receiving offices are in Westbahnhof, Südbahnhof and elsewhere. Or there's the MoneyGram service used by American Express (for AmEx cardholders only), Thomas Cook and some post offices; minimum commission is about US$20/UK£12.

Security
Using a moneybelt or something similar to carry your money is a wise precaution. Consider also hiding a small amount of emergency cash (eg, US$50) away from the rest of your banknotes.

Costs
Vienna is averagely expensive for a European city – cheaper than Paris, Zürich or Rome, similar to Munich, more expensive than Prague or Budapest. Britons and Americans will probably find things pretty cheap, given the relentless slide of the euro against sterling and the dollar.

Budget travellers will be able to survive on about €33 (US$28) per day – €12 for a hostel bed, €12 for cheap meals or self-catering, €1.65 for transport (based on a weekly travel pass for €11.30) and €7.35 for admissions and incidentals. However, this is a very stringent estimate – you could spend double per day and still feel you're economising. Purchasing 'luxuries' like a beer in a bar (€2.85), a cup of coffee in a coffee house (€2.20), a foreign newspaper (€2.55) or souvenirs can add up to a sizable sum very quickly.

To stay in a room with a private bathroom, and have a moderate lunch, a decent dinner, some money to spend on evening entertainment and not be too concerned about how expensive a cup of coffee is, a daily allowance of above €120 (US$100) would be needed.

Note that children pay lower prices; students and senior citizens often do, too.

FACTS FOR THE VISITOR

Tipping & Bargaining

Restaurant bills include a service charge, though it is customary to tip in restaurants and cafes. Round up small bills and add about 10% to larger ones – in all but the most formal places you simply say the total amount you want the server to take when you hand over the money. Taxi fares do not include an element for tips and the driver will expect around 10% extra. Tour guides, cloakroom attendants, hairdressers, hotel porters and cleaning staff are also usually tipped.

Bargain hard in flea markets. Otherwise, prices are fixed, but it can't hurt to ask for 'a discount for cash' if you're making several purchases. In theory, hotel prices are not negotiable; in practice, you can often haggle for a better rate in the low season or if you're staying more than a few days.

Taxes & Refunds

Value-added tax (*Mehrwertsteuer*, or MWST) is set at 20% for most goods. Prices are displayed inclusive of all taxes, even (usually) service charges in hotels and restaurants.

All non-EU tourists are entitled to a refund of the MWST on purchases over €72.68 (AS1000). To claim the tax, a tax-refund cheque must be filled out by the shop at the time of purchase (show your passport), and you then get it stamped by border officials when you leave the EU. (If you're leaving Austria for another EU country, you can't get this customs stamp in Austria, you have to get it from customs staff where you finally quit the EU.) Vienna airport has a counter for payment of instant refunds, as do those at Salzburg, Innsbruck, Linz and Graz. Counters are also at Westbahnhof and Südbahnhof, and at major border crossings. The refund is best claimed upon departing the EU, as otherwise you'll have to track down an international refund office or make a claim by post.

Before making a purchase, ensure the shop has the required paperwork; some places display a 'Tax Free for Tourists' sticker. Also confirm the value of the refund; it's usually advertised as 13%, which is the refund of the 20% standard rate of VAT after various commissions have been taken. But some items are subject to a lower rate of VAT – for paintings and sculpture it's only 10%.

POST & COMMUNICATIONS
Post

The main post office (Map 7) is at 01, Fleischmarkt 19. It's open 24 hours a day for collecting and sending mail, changing money and using the telephone. Only a few services (like using a Privatsparbuch) are not round the clock. There are also post offices open extended hours daily at Südbahnhof (8 am to 10 pm), Franz Josefs Bahnhof (6 or 7 am to 10 pm) and Westbahnhof (6 am to 11 pm). Post offices usually have photocopiers but they're expensive (€0.25) – instead, try branches of Metzer (eg, in Westbahnhof, where copies are €0.10).

Branch post offices are open 8 am to noon and 2 to 6 pm weekdays (some stay open lunchtimes nowadays), and 8 to 10 am Saturday. They generally have a counter for changing money, but this closes at 5 pm on weekdays.

Sending Mail Stamps are available in tobacconist *(Tabak)* shops as well as post offices. Sending ordinary mail (up to 50g) within Austria costs €0.51. Letters (up to 20g) cost €0.51 nonpriority/priority to Europe and €1.05/1.10 elsewhere. The normal weight limit for letter post *(Briefsendung)* is 2kg, which would cost €10.20/18.20 to Europe and €10.20/32.75 to elsewhere. Printed matter (books, brochures etc) can be sent at a reduced rate, and up to a 5kg limit. Airmail takes about four days to the UK, seven days to the USA and about 10 days to Australasia. By surface mail *(Erdwegpakete)* you can send packages up to 20kg.

Receiving Mail Poste restante is *Postlagernde Briefe* in German. Mail can be sent care of any post office and is held for a month; a passport must be shown on collection. Ask people who are sending you letters to write your surname in capitals and underline it. The full address for the main post office is: Hauptpostlagernde, Fleischmarkt 19, A-1010, Wien.

Note that like other Continentals, the Viennese 'cross' the number seven with a horizontal line and begin the number one with a rising diagonal stroke connecting to the top of the vertical downstroke, which looks rather like a lopsided, uncrossed seven. The net result of this is that unless you (or whoever writes to you) gets into the habit of crossing sevens when addressing envelopes, letters to No 77 will probably be delivered to confused residents of No 11, and eventually returned to sender or dispatched with due diligence to the recycling bin.

Telephone

The telephone code for Vienna is 01, or 1 if calling from abroad.

Telekom Austria has two zones for national calls – Regional-Zone (up to 50km) and Österreich-Zone (over 50km), which is about 300% more expensive. Cheap rates for national calls are from 6 pm to 8 am, and at weekends; rates drop greatly during these times. The minimum tariff in phone boxes is €0.15. You can easily beat Telekom's rates at various cut-price telephone call centres dotted around the city.

Post offices invariably have telephones outside. Be wary of using telephones in hotels, as they are two or three times more expensive than using normal call boxes. You can save money and avoid messing around with change by buying a phonecard (Telefon-Wertkarte); they come in various denominations, some of which give you extra calls for your money.

If you make a call and get the rising three-bleep anthem it means you've dialled an invalid number. Check the phone book or call ☎ 11811 for directory assistance.

There's a wide range of local and international phonecards. Lonely Planet's eKno global communication service provides low-cost international calls – for local calls you're usually better off with a local phonecard. eKno also offers free messaging services, email, travel information and an on-line travel vault, where you can securely store all your important documents. You can join online at www.ekno.lonelyplanet.com, where you will find the local-access numbers

for 24-hour customer service. Once you have joined, always check the eKno Web site for the latest access numbers for each country and updates on new features. To join and use eKno from Austria, call ☎ 0800-291 018.

International Calls For directory assistance for international telephone numbers, dial ☎ 11811 for Germany or ☎ 11812 for everywhere else. To direct-dial abroad, first call the overseas access code (00), then the appropriate country code, then the relevant area code (minus the initial '0' if there is one), and finally the subscriber number. To call Austria from abroad, the country code is ☎ 43.

Per minute at normal/cheap rates, telephone calls from Austria cost about €0.55/0.45 to the UK, €0.60/0.55 to the

Telephone Numbers Explained

In Vienna, telephone numbers don't always have the same number of digits: the reason for this is that some telephone numbers have an individual line, others a party line, and sometimes numbers are listed with an extension that you can dial direct (without a pause after the main number).

This is relevant for reading phone numbers listed in the telephone book: if, for example, you see the number '123 45 67...-0', the '0' signifies the number has extensions. Dialling the '0' will get through to that subscriber's main telephone reception. If you know the specific extension of somebody you want to speak to, dial that instead of the '0' and you'll get straight through to that person.

Fax numbers are often a telephone extension of the main number, and it's fairly common to see them listed only by their extension, perhaps following the letters 'DW' (an abbreviation for *Durchwahl*, indicating 'extension'). In this book, any telephone extensions are separated from the main number by a hyphen, and fax extensions are shown only by a hyphen and the extension number (ie, you'd have to dial the main number first to reach it). We show the fax number in full if it's different to the main telephone number.

USA, €0.85/0.80 to Australia or South Africa, and €1.05/0.95 to New Zealand.

To reverse the charges (ie, call collect), you have to call a freephone number to place the call. Some of the numbers are listed below (ask directory assistance for others):

Australia:	☎ 0800-200 202
Canada:	☎ 0800-200 224
Ireland:	☎ 0800-200 213
New Zealand:	☎ 0800-200 222
South Africa:	☎ 0800-200 230
UK:	☎ 0800-200 209
USA (AT&T)	☎ 0800-200 288
USA (MCI)	☎ 0800-200 235
USA (Sprint):	☎ 0800-200 236

Fax
Luxury hotels offer fax services but it's cheaper to use the post office. To send a fax from the post office costs €1.35 for five pages plus the cost of the telephone time; receiving faxes costs just the €1.35. Some hotels *may* let you receive the odd fax free of charge.

Email & Internet Access
Vienna has dozens of places offering public access to online services. Happily, some are free, like Haus Wien Energie (Map 5; ☎ 581 05 00), 06, Mariahilfer Strasse 63, open 9 am to 6 pm (to 8 pm Thursday, to 3 pm Friday; closed weekends) and Amadeus branches (see Books & CD ROMs in the Shopping chapter). There's also free Internet access at some bars and clubs, and people aged under 19 can log on free at the youth centre *(Jugendzentrum)* in most Viennese districts. Details of all these venues, in addition to the conventional Internet cafes, are listed in the excellent *internet jugendinfo* booklet. It's updated several times a year and is available free from the Jugendinfo office (see earlier under Other Information Offices).

If you're not prepared to queue, stick to outlets that charge. Café Stein (Map 7; ☎ 319 72 411), 09, Währinger Strasse 6, charges €4.75 for 30 minutes (10 am to 11 pm daily). There's also the Nationalbibliothek in the Hofburg (€3.65 for 30 minutes;

see under Libraries later in this chapter). Most hostels have Internet access.

INTERNET RESOURCES
The World Wide Web is a rich resource for travellers. You can research your trip, hunt down bargain air fares, book hotels, check on weather conditions or chat with locals and other travellers about the best places to visit (or avoid!).

There's no better place to start your Web explorations than the Lonely Planet Web site (www.lonelyplanet.com). Here you'll find succinct summaries on travelling to most places on earth, postcards from other travellers and the Thorn Tree bulletin board, where you can ask questions before you go or dispense advice when you get back. You can also find travel news and updates to many of our most popular guidebooks, and the subWWWay section links you to the most useful travel resources elsewhere on the Web.

The Vienna Tourist Board's site (www.info.wien.at) and the ANTO's site (www.austria-tourism.at) are both good for tourist information and background data. The government site, www.wien.gv.at, has some great features, including maps and an address-searching facility. A US-based press and information service is at www.austria.org; you'll find current news and good links for a range of topics. The online version of *Austria Today* (www.austriatoday.at) has a directory of business services.

More specific Web sites are listed later in this book, eg, travel-related sites are mentioned in the Getting There & Away chapter.

BOOKS
A great deal has been written about Vienna. See the Shopping chapter for information or bookshops in the city; these will have a good selection (especially the British Bookshop). Note that imported titles will cost more in euros than the cover price would imply.

Lonely Planet
Austria covers the whole country, and gives more detail on the places mentioned under the Excursions chapter in this book. Vienna

is also covered in the *Western Europe, Central Europe* and *Europe* guidebooks, and each has a companion phrasebook.

Guidebooks

Check Vienna's bookshops, particularly the British Bookshop, for locally produced guides in English. These include *Living in Vienna*, a practical guide put together by the American Women's Association in Vienna. The tongue-in-cheek *Xenophobe's guide to the Austrians* contains some amusing and revealing insights into Austrian people and society.

Falter's Best of Vienna (€3.30) is a locally available seasonal magazine giving over 250 current and useful recommendations for eating, drinking, shopping and entertainment. Some categories are typically quirky and playful; past highlights include best wall to lean against, best worker's Beisl with a parrot, best U-Bahn clock and best wild boar farm in the city. The same publisher releases various other guides, including one dedicated to eating, *Wien, wie es isst*. Falter's guidebooks are in German only, which is a pity for monolinguists, as Falter is known for its witty wordplay.

History & Politics

You can probably guess the topic of *Austria, Empire and Republic* by Barbara Jelavich. *A History of the Habsburg Empire 1526–1918* is a large tome by Robert A Kann. Steven Beller's *Vienna and the Jews* (Cambridge University Press) is concerned specifically with the years from 1867 to 1938. For an up-to-date perspective, see *Guilty Victim* by Hella Pick, which analyses Austria from the Holocaust to Haider (published 2000).

A number of other books deal with Vienna's history from the slant of its musical heritage. *Mozart and the Enlightenment* by Nicholas Till is a scholarly work placing Mozart in his historical context, with detailed analysis of his operatic works. *Mozart and Vienna*, by HC Robbins Landon, focuses on the Vienna years, and successfully evokes the city of the time by quoting extensively from a contemporary work, *Sketch of Vienna* by Johann Pezzl.

General

The title *Mozart – his Character, his Work*, by Alfred Einstein, is self-explanatory, as is *Gustav Mahler – Memories and Letters* by Alma Mahler. *Freud's Women* by Lisa Appignanesi & John Forrester is a large volume that offers an insight into the psychoanalyst. There's also *The Life and Work of Sigmund Freud* by Ernest Jones.

The Third Man is Graham Greene's famous Viennese spy story. John Irving's *Setting Free the Bears* is a fine tale about a plan to release the animals from the zoo at Schönbrunn. The zoo plot takes place in 1967, yet the book is also very evocative of life in Austria and Vienna before, during and after WWII. Vienna zoo also puts in an appearance in *Invisible Architecture*, a collection of three stories by Steven Kelly. The architecture in question is more to do with the make-up of the Viennese soul than the buildings in the city. *An Equal Music* by Vikram Seth is partially set in Vienna's Music Academy.

Mozart & the Wolf Gang, by Anthony Burgess, is a learned but enjoyable celestial fantasy in which the great composers discourse on music and Mozart. *The Strange Case of Mademoiselle P*, by Brian O'Doherty, is about an attempted medical cure in Maria Theresa's Vienna. It's based on a real incident and provides an insight into the petty power struggles in the imperial court, but it does rather peter out at the end.

See Literature in the Facts about Vienna chapter for fiction by Austrian authors.

NEWSPAPERS & MAGAZINES

English-language newspapers are widely available in Vienna, usually late in the afternoon of the day they're published. Prices are between €2.20 and €3.65. The first to hit the stands are the *Financial Times* and the *International Herald Tribune*. *USA Today*, *Time*, *Newsweek*, the *Economist* and most British newspapers are easy to find. The News & Books shop in Westbahnhof stocks many newspapers and magazines from around the world; it's open 6 am to 11 pm daily (to 10 pm on Sunday and public holidays). A smaller branch in Südbahnhof closes one hour earlier.

Of the several German-language daily newspapers available, the magazine-size *Neue Kronen Zeitung* (€0.70) has the largest circulation; the tabloid-size *Die Presse* adopts a more serious approach. *Austria Today* is a weekly national newspaper in English (€1.85), with current news and listings of cultural events.

Austrian newspapers are often dispensed from bags attached to pavement posts, and rely on the honesty of readers to pay for the copies they take. Foreign-language titles are only available from newsstands or pavement sellers.

RADIO & TV

Home-grown commercial TV and radio is a recent phenomenon in Austria, and the state-run network still dominates.

State-run national radio channels are Ö1 (87.8 and 92 FM), giving a highbrow diet of music, literature and science, and Ö3 (99.9 FM), offering pop music and topical information. There's also a network of local stations, such as Radio Wien (89.9 and 95.3 FM). FM4 (103.8 FM) is a music and chat station broadcasting in English and German. Most of the English segments are between 6 am and 2 pm, including news on the hour, discussions and reports on cultural events.

The two state-run national TV channels are ÖRF1 and ÖRF2. However, many homes (and hotels) have satellite or cable and can pick up a whole host of TV channels from Germany and elsewhere, plus MTV, Eurosport, CNN (the 24-hour news network) and NBC (featuring American chat shows in the evening). ATV, Austria's first domestic cable/satellite station, started up in 2000. The local newspapers and events magazines give full program listings of all channels.

PHOTOGRAPHY & VIDEO

Vienna provides a great number of photo opportunities. Don't use a camera flash at the opera, theatre or similar event; it's very distracting for the performers, whether they be humans or stallions. Film is widely available and fairly reasonably priced, though developing costs are high. Note that slide film *(Diafilm)* usually excludes processing *(Entwicklung)* and mounting *(Rahmung)*, but you may get a voucher for free or cheap processing valid only at the store where you purchased the film.

The Niedermeyer chain store is one of the cheapest places to buy film, especially if you buy multipacks: a three-pack of 36-exposure Kodak 100 film costs €8 and a twin-pack of Ektachrome 200 slide film is €8.75. Niedermeyer also has its own brand of film which is much cheaper. The chain has over 50 branches in Vienna, including a huge branch at 09, Alserbachstrasse 28–30 (Map 3; ☎ 406 06 02), two on Mariahilfer Strasse (Nos 51 and 102), one at 01, Graben 11, and another one opposite Franz Josefs Bahnhof. All its stores sell cameras and other electronic gadgets. Hartlauer is another competitively priced chain of stores, selling everything from camera gear to spectacles. Cosmos has fewer outlets, but is also cheap.

Photo processing (9cm by 13cm) at Niedermeyer costs €3.65 plus €0.21 per picture for the two-day service (express service is a shocking €0.58 per print). These prices may be high, but they're typical for Austria. The cheapest place we've found for film developing is the larger branches of Libro bookshops, where developing is €2.20 and the per photo price is €0.14.

Videos purchased in Austria will be recorded using the PAL image system (also used in Britain and Australia), which is incompatible with the NTSC system in use in North America and Japan.

TIME

Austrians use the 24-hour clock for anything written down, instead of dividing the day into am and pm. Austrian time is GMT/UTC plus one hour. If it's noon in Vienna it is 6 am in New York and Toronto, 3 am in San Francisco, 9 pm in Sydney and 11 pm in Auckland. Clocks go forward one hour on the last Saturday night in March and back again on the last Saturday night in October.

Note that in German *halb* is used to indicate the half-hour before the hour, hence *halb acht* means 7.30, not 8.30.

Sunset on the Alte Burg at the Hofburg ...

... and over Vienna

The illuminated Burgtheatre

Some of the 250,000-odd tiles that make up the roof of Stephansdom

The imposing Karlskirche, designed by Johann Bernhard Fischer von Erlach

The gardens of Schloss Belvedere

Oberes Belvedere, royalty's dining room

ELECTRICITY
The current used is 220V, 50Hz AC. Sockets are the round two-pin type, which are standard throughout most of Continental Europe. North American appliances will need a transformer if they don't have built-in voltage adjustment.

WEIGHTS & MEASURES
The metric system is used. Like other Continental Europeans, Austrians indicate decimals with commas and thousands with points. You will sometimes see meat and cheese priced per *dag*, which is an abbreviation referring to 10g (to ask for this quantity say *'deca'*).

LAUNDRY
Look out for *Wäscherei* for self-service *(Selbstbedienung)* or service washes. Many youth hostels have cheaper laundry facilities, and most good hotels have a laundry service, albeit expensive.

Schnell & Sauber Waschcenter (Map 5), 07, Urban Loritz Platz, Westbahnstrasse, is open 24 hours daily, and has instructions in English. It costs €4.40 to wash a 6kg load, plus €0.40 for powder, €0.75 to spin and from €0.75 to dry. Another branch is at 09, Nussdorfer Strasse 80 (Map 3), open 6 am to 11 pm daily.

Another place is Miele Selbstbedienung (Map 3; ☎ 405 02 55), 08, Josefstädter Strasse 59, but it's more expensive and only open from 7 am to 6.30 pm weekdays. Dry-cleaning is available here.

TOILETS
Toilets are found in restaurants, museums and galleries, and these are unattended and free to use. If toilets are attended a small charge is made (eg, at train station toilets), or cubicles may be coin-operated (about €0.40). There are many public toilets to be found, eg, at Graben and Hoher Markt. *Damen* is for women and *Herren* is for men.

LEFT LUGGAGE
The most convenient places to store bags are the train stations – see Vienna's Train Stations in the Getting There & Away chapter.

HEALTH
No immunisations are required for entry into Austria, unless you're coming from an infected area. However, everyone should keep up-to-date with diptheria, tetanus and polio vaccinations.

Vienna is a healthy place and if you're healthy when you arrive, there's no reason why you should experience any particular health problems. Even streetside snack stands have adequate sanitary standards. Tap water is high quality and perfectly drinkable (except in the rare instance when you'll come across a sign announcing *Kein Trinkwasser*).

Ticks might be a problem in forested areas in east Austria. A very small proportion of ticks carry encephalitis (a cerebral inflammation that can cause death), so if you plan to spend a lot of time in the woods get an encephalitis immunisation before you leave.

If you wear glasses, it's wise to carry a spare pair or a copy of your prescription.

EU and EEA nationals can get free emergency medical treatment, although payment may have to be made for medication, private consultations and non-urgent treatment. Inquire before leaving home about the documentation required. British citizens normally need to show an E111 form (available from post offices) to take advantage of reciprocal health agreements in Europe, so it's worth getting one if you're travelling through the Continent. However, in Austria you only need to show a British passport, though if you're staying a long time in Vienna it would facilitate matters if you get a certificate from the health insurance office, the Gebietskrankenkasse (☎ 601 22-0), 10, Wienerbergstrasse 15–19. This office can also tell you the countries that have reciprocal agreements with Austria (the USA, Canada, Australia and New Zealand don't).

A straightforward, non-urgent appointment with a doctor costs anything from €20 to €70. Make sure your travel insurance includes medical cover.

WOMEN TRAVELLERS
In Vienna, women enjoy equal status and opportunity with men. Although men still predominate in influential and high-ranking

positions, the situation is changing, helped by a recent mayoral campaign to address this inequality. Women make up around one-third of the 100-strong Vienna city council, and a (female) councillor has responsibility for women's issues. In a recent breakthrough, women were allowed to join the formerly all-male Vienna Philharmonic Orchestra – it currently includes a female harpist in its line-up.

Overall, Vienna is a very safe city and women travellers should experience no special problems. Attacks and verbal harassment are less common than in many countries. However, normal caution should be exercised in unfamiliar situations (which occur quite often when travelling).

Organisations

There is an emergency, 24-hour hotline for women to report rape and sexual violence; call the Frauennotruf on ☎ 71 719. The Frauentelefon (☎ 408 70 66) is a non-urgent helpline for women to discuss work, family and social problems; it operates 8 am to noon Monday and Wednesday, and 1 to 5 pm Thursday.

GAY & LESBIAN TRAVELLERS

Vienna is reasonably tolerant towards gays and lesbians, more so than the rest of Austria, and the situation is improving all the time. Gay bashing is virtually unknown here (unlike in ostensibly more gay-tolerant cities like Amsterdam or Berlin). Recently, two of the three federal statutes concerning homosexuality were repealed – these had banned gay meetings and the promotion of homosexuality. The third statute relates to the age of consent: between men this is 18, in contrast to 14 for heterosexuals. The Austrian government is resisting any change on this inequality, despite pressure from the European parliament. There is no set age of consent for lesbian sex, apparently because the legislators decided there was no discernible difference between mutual washing of bodily parts and intimate sexual contact. While lesbians welcome the lack of legislation, they see this as a typical (male) denial of female sexuality.

At gay venues in Vienna (see Gay & Lesbian Venues in the Entertainment chapter) you can pick up the Gay City Map, showing gay-friendly hotels, shops, bars, cafes and clubs, and the free monthly *Bussi* magazine.

Look out for the Regenbogenparade (Rainbow Parade) on the last Saturday in June. Around 100,000 gays and lesbians parade along the Ringstrasse, in an event that has only been fully established since 1996. Vienna's other big gay occasion is the Life Ball, an Aids fundraising event held in the Rathaus in July. Tickets are pretty steep, selling for around €72.70. For more information about the Parade on the Web check www.pride.at, and for the Life Ball see www.lifeball.at.

Organisations

Probably the best organisation to contact is Rosa Lila Villa (Map 5), 06, Linke Wienzeile 102; big letters outside proclaim it's a 'Lesben & Schwulenhaus' (lesbian & gay house). There's telephone counselling, a small library with books in English, and advice and information on what's on offer in the city. Opening hours are 5 to 8 pm Monday to Friday. The lesbian centre (☎ 586 81 50, @ lesbenberatung@villa.at) is on the ground floor, and the gay men's centre (☎ 585 43 43, @ schwulenberatung@villa.at) is on the 1st floor. Also on the premises is Café Willendorf, open 6 pm to 2 am daily (with good food till midnight).

The Homosexualle Initiative Wien (HOSI; Map 4), 02, Novaragasse 40, also has telephone counselling (☎ 216 66 04, @ office@hosiwien.at) from 6 to 8 pm on Tuesday and 7 to 9 pm Wednesday and Thursday. It's open to visitors on Tuesday from 5 to 10 pm.

The Frauenzentrum (Map 3; ☎ 408 50 57), 09, Währinger Strasse 59 (entry via Prechtlgasse), is a women's centre which is run mainly by lesbians, but facilities are open to all women

DISABLED TRAVELLERS

Disabled people often get reduced, concessionary admission prices – look for the word *Behinderte*. All stations on the U3 and

U6 lines have lifts or ramps, but only about half the others do. Drivers displaying the international handicapped sticker can ignore time restrictions in short parking zones. The two state-run TV channels have a teletext service, and traffic lights 'bleep' when pedestrians can safely cross.

The tourist office can give advice and information. It has a detailed (albeit out-of-date) booklet in German or English that gives information on hotels and restaurants with disabled access, plus addresses of hospitals, medical equipment shops, parking places, toilets and much more. The tourist office's brochures on museums and hotels indicate disabled access; ramps are fairly common but by no means ubiquitous.

Organisations

There's no national organisation that provides help for the disabled in Austria, but the city of Vienna runs an advice centre for disabled people, the Behindertenberatungsstelle (Map 7; ☎ 531 14-85359), 01, Schottenring 24, open 3 to 6.30 pm Monday and Thursday.

SENIOR TRAVELLERS

Senior citizens are often entitled to reduced admission prices; the qualifying age is usually 60 and above for women and 65 and above for men, though sometimes it's 60 for both. Always carry proof of age. Travel benefits include cheaper flights, rail tickets and discount tickets on Vienna's public transport. Cheaper (and smaller) 'senior' meals are available in some restaurants, but this isn't very common.

Organisations

The Seniorenbeauftragter der Stadt Wien (☎ 4000-8580) can give information on reductions for seniors, plus travel, cultural and leisure-time tips; it's staffed 8 am to 3.30 pm weekdays.

VIENNA FOR CHILDREN

It is sometimes said that the Viennese love dogs more than they love children, but children are fairly well received. There are sometimes special events put on for children – inquire at the tourist office. Children's menus are available in some restaurants. Your hotel should be able to advise you on local babysitting services.

Vienna has museums devoted to teddy bears, dolls and toys, circuses and clowns – all of which children might enjoy; there's even a children's museum, the Kindermuseum ZOOM in the Museumsquartier. Also look out for the puppets in the Marionettentheater at Schönbrunn, and the Niedermair Kindertheater (Map 7; ☎ 408 44 92), 08, Lenaugasse 1a. Schönbrunn zoo has a section where children can stroke the animals. The Volksprater funfair is also ideal for children.

There are lots of enjoyable indoor and outdoor swimming pools in Vienna. City-owned pools offer free entry for children (up to age 15) during the summer school holidays, and perhaps during other school holidays; phone 60112-8044 for the latest information. The Stadt Kinderfreibad (Map 4) is an open-air pool specially for kids aged six to 15 (open 10 am to 6 pm weekdays). Children also travel free on public transport during school holidays. Children under 12 can often stay in their parents' hotel room free of charge.

Teenagers can get good information at Jugendinfo (see Other Information Offices earlier in this chapter).

LIBRARIES

You need to be a resident (and show the appropriate police stamp to this effect) to borrow books from Vienna's libraries, but anybody is welcome to peruse books on the premises.

The Nationalbibliothek in the Hofburg has huge reference and lending sections plus CD ROM, papyrus and sheet-music collections. Upstairs is a room with newspapers such as the *Times* and the *International Herald Tribune*, and magazines and periodicals (many in English) covering all sorts of academic and recreational subjects. The main part of the library is open 9 am to 7 pm Monday to Friday (to 3.45 pm from 1 July to 31 August) and 9 am to 12.45 pm Saturday.

Libraries are dotted around Vienna. The main branch is the Städtische Hauptbücherei

(Map 3; ☎ 4000-84 551), 08, Skodagasse 20, open 10 am to 7.30 pm Monday and Thursday and 2 to 7.30 pm Tuesday and Friday. There's also a library on the 2nd floor (the periodicals room is on the 1st floor) in the main university building (Map 7) on the corner of Dr Karl Lueger Ring and Universitätsstrasse.

The British Council (Map 7; ☎ 533 26 16-81), 01, Schenkenstrasse 4, has a library, including newspapers and magazines in English. It's open 11 am to 5 pm weekdays (to 6 pm Monday and 1 pm Friday).

CULTURAL CENTRES
The Museumsquartier (Map 7; ☎ 523 58 81), 07, Museumsplatz 1, is the former imperial barracks. It is now a cultural centre, and there will be dozens of different organisations based here by the time it fully opens in September 2001. Already there are museums, theatres, exhibitions, galleries, cafes and discussion groups – see the Things to See & Do chapter for more on its museums.

The American Reference Center (Map 3; ☎ 405 30 33), 08, Schmidgasse 14, is linked to the US embassy, and has many publications in English about or from the USA. It's a resource for people undertaking research (ie, not for normal tourists), and you need to make an appointment to visit.

The traditional coffee houses (see the Places to Eat chapter) are the most enjoyable places to go for reading; most carry English-language newspapers.

DANGERS & ANNOYANCES
Overall, Vienna is a very safe city to visit. There is some anti-foreigner feeling, but it rarely erupts into violence and is directed more towards immigrant residents than to tourists. Crime rates are low by international standards, but you should still always be security-conscious. Reception staff will usually look after valuables like cameras or electronic equipment. If you do have something stolen, get a police report as it will be needed to claim on your travel insurance.

There are police stations all over the place: each district has a head office and branches. The Innere Stadt head office (Map 4; ☎ 313 47-0) is at 01, Deutschmeisterplatz 3, and the police are also in the Stephansplatz and Karlsplatz U-Bahn stations. For other districts look in the phone book under *Polizei* and the subheading *Bezirkspolizeikommissariate u Wachzimmer*.

Train stations are a habitual haunt of drunks and down-and-outs who can be annoying and occasionally intimidating. Drug addicts sometimes congregate in the Karlsplatz U-Bahn station near the Secession exit.

EMERGENCIES
Emergency telephone numbers in Vienna include:

Ambulance:	☎ 144
Doctor:	☎ 141
Police:	☎ 133
Fire:	☎ 122

The Europe-wide emergency number for the police, the Euronotruf (☎ 112), also works in Vienna.

Get medical treatment at the general hospital, the Allgemeines Krankenhaus (Map 3 ☎ 404 00, extension -1964 for emergencies) at 09, Währinger Gürtel 18–20. Other hospitals with 24-hour emergency departments include Lorenz Böhler Unfallkrankenhaus (Map 4; ☎ 331 10-0), 20, Donaueschingenstrasse 13; Unfallkrankenhaus Meidling (Map 2; ☎ 601 50-0), 12, Kundratstrasse 37; and Hanusch-Krankenhaus (Map 5; ☎ 910 21-0), 14, Heinrich Collin Strasse 30.

The University Dental Hospital, Universitäts-Zahnklinik (☎ 42 77-0), is at 09, Währinger Strasse 25a. For recorded information on out-of-hours dental treatment, call ☎ 512 20 78.

Chemist shops or drugstores *(Apotheken)* are open normal shop hours, though they operate an out-of-hours service in rotation. Dial ☎ 1550 for recorded information in German.

LOST PROPERTY
For items lost on Vienna public transport, contact the Zentral Fundstelle (☎ 7909-43500) at U3 Station Erdberg, open 6 am to

10 pm daily. After a few days, items here end up at the main lost property office, the Polizeifundamt (Map 3), 09, Wasagasse 22; call ☎ 313 44-9214 within two weeks of the loss, thereafter call ☎ 313 44-9211. Unless you're still in Vienna when the item is found they'll usually forward it to your embassy (in the case of the USA they'll post items home). For items lost on Austrian railways call the office in Südbahnhof (☎ 9300-35656).

LEGAL MATTERS

Austria offers the level of civil and legal rights you would expect of any industrialised Western nation. If you are arrested, the police must inform you of your rights in a language that you understand.

In Austria, legal offences are divided into two categories: criminal *(Gerichtdelikt)* and administrative *(Verwaltungsübertretung)*. If you are suspected of having committed a criminal offence (such as assault or theft) you can be detained for a maximum of 48 hours before you are committed to trial. If you are arrested for a less serious administrative offence (eg, drunk and disorderly, breach of the peace) you will be released within 24 hours. Drink driving is an administrative matter, even if you have an accident, but if someone is hurt in the accident it becomes a criminal offence. Possession of a controlled drug is a criminal offence, although it is common for possession of a small amount of marijuana to attract only a caution.

If you are arrested, you have the right to make one phone call to a 'person in your confidence' within Austria, and another to inform legal counsel. A legal emergency service is available in Vienna out of normal office hours (the police will give you details). If you can't afford legal representation, you can apply to the judge in writing for legal aid.

You can consult a lawyer free of charge at the Rechtsanwaltskammer (☎ 533 27 18-45), 01, Rotenturmstrasse 13. The service is offered Monday to Thursday, but there is a lengthy queuing system involved. There are also special sessions at district courts *(Bezirksgerichte)* where you are able to get free legal advice, eg, (☎ 515 28) at 01, Riemergasse 7.

As a foreigner, your best bet when encountering legal problems is to contact your national consulate in the first instance. If you have a complaint about the conduct of the Viennese police, contact the Vienna Police Headquarters, the Bundespolizeidirektion (Map 7; ☎ 313 10-0), 01, Schottenring 7–9.

BUSINESS HOURS

In the 1990s shopping hours were liberalised – shops may stay open till 7.30 pm on weekdays and 5 pm on Saturday, though many close at 6 pm and noon respectively. Business hours for offices and government departments vary, but are usually 8 am to 3.30, 4 or 5 pm Monday to Friday. Municipal museums are closed on Monday, though the opening hours for other museums and galleries don't follow any set pattern – some are open daily.

PUBLIC HOLIDAYS & SPECIAL EVENTS

Public holidays are 1 January (New Year's Day), 6 January (Epiphany; *Heilige Drei Könige*), Easter Monday *(Ostermontag)*, 1 May (Labour Day), Ascension Day *(Christihimmelfahrt*; 40 days after Easter), Whit Monday *(Pfingstmontag)*, Corpus Christi *(Fronleichnam)*, 15 August (Assumption; *Maria Himmelfahrt*), 26 October (National Day), 1 November (All Saints' Day; *Allerheiligen)*, 8 December (Immaculate Conception; *Mariä Empfängnis*), 25 December (Christmas Day; *Weihnachten*) and 26 December (St Stephen's Day; *Stephanitag)*. Some people also take a holiday on Good Friday.

The national tourist office compiles an annual list of events in Austria, and the Vienna tourist office releases a monthly listing of events in the city. No matter what time of year you visit Vienna, there will always be something special going on. The cycle of musical events is unceasing. Mozart features heavily, as he had his most productive years in Vienna (1781–91), but all varieties of music get a look-in. You may find colourful processions on religious feast days. The following is by no means a complete listing of annual events.

January & February

The Opera Ball at the Staatsoper is one of the most lavish of the 300 or so balls put on in January and February. Men wear black tails and women wear ball gowns (usually white). Get tickets from Opernballbüro (☎ 514 44-2606), 01, Goethegasse 1.

The Imperial Ball, another sumptuous affair, allows you to see in the New Year at the Hofburg; for (very expensive!) tickets apply to Kongresszentrum Hofburg (☎ 587 36 66-23), A-1014 Wien.

Some districts have events for *Fasching* (Shrovetide carnival) in early February.

March & April

Mid-March sees the start of a month-long Spring Festival of classical music in the Konzerthaus. At Easter there's 10 days of classical music in the OsterKlang Festival. Check the Web site at www.osterklang.at.

May & June

The Vienna Marathon is run in May; the Web site is at www.vienna-marathon.com.

The Vienna Festival (from mid-May to mid-June) has a wide-ranging program of the arts, based in various venues. It's considered to be one of the highlights of the year. Contact Wiener Festwochen (☎ 589 22-22, fax -49), Lehárgasse 11, A-1060 Wien, for details after December, and visit the Web site at www.festwochen.or.at.

Over a weekend in late June there's three days of free rock, jazz and folk concerts, plus general outdoor fun, in the Donauinselfest. It's a major party, with about half a million visitors pouring in each day. On 21 June there's Midsummer night celebrations in the Wachau.

July & August

The KlangBogen Festival, from early July to mid-August, ensures that things don't flag during the summer holidays. Musical events take place at various locations around town, with reduced student tickets going on sale at the venue 10 minutes before the performance. Contact KlangBogen (☎ 4000-8410), 01, Stadiongasse 9; the Web site is at www.klangbogen.at.

In the first two weeks of July there's a Jazz Festival at the Staatsoper and elsewhere; check the Web site at www.viennajazz.org.

The free open-air Opera Film Festival on Rathausplatz runs throughout July and August. Films of operas, operettas and concerts are shown on a large screen at dusk. Food stands and bars are erected to take care of bodily needs.

The International Dance Festival goes from mid-July to mid-August.

September & October

September is a month of trade fairs, as well as heralding the start of the new opera season. There's also the Vienna in-line marathon.

Expect much flag-waving on National Day (26 October).

In the second half of October there's the Viennale Film Festival (☎ 713 2000); the Web site is at www.viennale.at.

November & December

Throughout November there's the Wien Modern festival, featuring modern classical and avant-garde music, performed in the Konzerthaus and elsewhere.

Vienna's traditional Christmas market *(Christkindlmarkt)* takes place in front of the City Hall from mid-November to 24 December. Trees are decorated in the Rathaus park, and inside the Rathaus there are free concerts of seasonal music. Other Christmas markets spring up, such as the one on Freyung.

On New Year's Eve various celebrations are arranged in the Innere Stadt, and one of the evening's musical events is relayed onto a giant screen at Stephansplatz.

DOING BUSINESS

Vienna is a major conference location, which hosts hundreds of international conferences annually. Not surprisingly, the city can provide a multitude of facilities and services for the business visitor. If you want to start a business in Austria, there are a lot of bureaucratic hoops to leap through, though various organisations are on hand to make things easier for you. The first useful port of call you could try would most probably be the trade office at the Austrian embassy in your home country.

Business Locales

Vienna International Center (UNO City) in the 22nd district is where international organisations are based, including the UN (the third-most important base after New York and Geneva) and the International Atomic Energy Agency (rather ironic, considering that Austrians rejected nuclear power in a 1978 referendum). UNO City has extraterritorial status so take your passport when visiting. Also here you'll find the Austria Center Vienna (Map 4; ☎ 260 69-0, fax -303), Austria's largest convention hall, with 14 conference rooms and 170 offices and meeting rooms.

The Hofburg (Map 7; ☎ 587 36 66, fax 535 64 26), in the Innere Stadt, also hosts conferences, banquets and exhibitions. Over a third of international conferences are held in Vienna's hotels. The Vienna Tourist Board head office (see the Tourist Offices section earlier) has congress information. The main centre for trade fairs is the Messegelände (☎ 7272-0208) in the Prater.

Business Park Wien Süd is a new business park just beyond the city precincts, near the Shopping City Süd, by the A21 motorway. It's the biggest business park in Austria, and includes offices as well as production, manufacturing and storage buildings.

Business Services

The following organisations could help you set up and run a business in Vienna.

Dun & Bradstreet Information Services (☎ 588 61-0, fax 586 33 59, ⓔ service-at@dnb.com), 01, Opernring 3–5 – marketing information and credit reports

Kreditschutzverband von 1870 (KSV; ☎ 534 84), 01, Zelinkagasse 10 – Austrian association for the protection of creditors; compiles business information databases

Österreichische Wirtschaftswerbungs (☎ 588 58-0, fax 586 86 59, ⓔ austrian.business@telecom.at), 01, Opernring 3 – Austrian Business Agency. (Both this agency and the WWFF can provide copious free information.) Web site: www.aba.gv.at

PriceWaterhouseCoopers (☎ 501 88-0, fax -4), 04, Prinz Eugene Strasse 72 – public accountants and tax advisers

Regus Business Centre (☎ 599 99-0, fax -700), 06, Mariahilfer Strasse 123 and elsewhere – office rental from a few hours upwards; secretarial services, telephone service, catering and conference facilities Web site: www.regus.com

Wiener Wirtschaftsförderungsfonds (WWFF; ☎ 4000-867 90, fax -7073, ⓔ vienna@wwff.gv.at), 08, Ebensdorferstrasse 2 – Vienna Business Agency, a nonprofit organisation selling Vienna as a business location to potential investors Web site: www.wwff.gv.at

Wirtschaftskammer Österreich (☎ 501 05-0), 04, Wiedner Hauptstrasse 63 – Austrian Chamber of Commerce

WORK

Job opportunities in Vienna are as varied as in any other large city. Since January 1993 EU nationals have been able to obtain work in Austria without needing a work permit or residency permit, though as intending residents they need to register with the police within five days of arrival.

Non-EU nationals need both a work permit and a residency permit, and will find it pretty hard to get either. Inquire (in German) about job possibilities via the Arbeitsmarktservice für Wien (☎ 515 25-0, fax -340), Weihburggasse 30, A-1010, Wien. The work permit needs to be applied for by your employer in Austria. Applications for residency permits must be applied for via the Austrian embassy in your home country. In theory, a residency permit might be granted without a prearranged work permit, but you would need sufficient funds, confirmed accommodation in Austria, and perhaps some form of Austrian sponsorship. Non-EU nationals do not require a residency permit if they are undertaking seasonal work for up to six months.

Getting There & Away

AIR

Air travel can be a bargain if you carefully research the best deals. You can buy discounted tickets from budget travel agents but stick to agencies that are bonded or have a protection scheme so your money is safe if they go bust.

Buying direct from the airline often means paying full price, though some airlines do sell discounted tickets via their Web site, and 'no-frills' airlines also sell budget tickets direct to the customer. Always be clear about restrictions and conditions before parting with your money, and remember that most airlines require you to confirm return trips at least 72 hours before departure.

High season varies from airline to airline, but you can expect slightly higher prices from April to October. Youth fares can apply to people up to 30, depending on the airline, though 26 is the usual cut-off age. You may find you have to pay more if

---

Warning

The information in this chapter is particularly vulnerable to change: Prices for international travel are volatile, routes are introduced and cancelled, schedules change, special deals come and go, and rules and visa requirements are amended. Airlines and governments seem to take a perverse pleasure in making price structures and regulations as complicated as possible. You should check directly with the airline or a travel agent to make sure that you understand how a fare (and ticket you may buy) works. In addition, the travel industry is highly competitive and there are many lurks and perks.

The upshot of this is that you should get opinions, quotes and advice from as many airlines and travel agents as possible before you part with your hard-earned cash. The details given in this chapter should be regarded as pointers and are not a substitute for your own careful, up-to-date research.

---

you don't stay a Saturday night or if your trip exceeds one month.

Austrian Airlines is the national carrier and has the most extensive services to Vienna. Lauda Air is another home-grown airline. Their Web sites are www.aua.com and www.laudaair.com.

Departure Tax

There is no departure tax to pay at the airport when leaving Vienna, as all Austrian taxes are already included in the ticket price. These include two taxes levied by the Austrian government totalling around €16. Your ticket price may also include a departure tax and 'passenger service charge' levied by your departure country/airport.

Other Parts of Austria

Domestic services by Austrian Airlines to and from the rest of Austria are run jointly with Tyrolean Airlines. There are several flights a day to Graz, Klagenfurt and Innsbruck and at least one a day to Salzburg and Linz. Check schedules as they vary according to the season.

North America

Council Travel (☎ 800-226-8624) and STA (☎ 800-777-0112) have offices in major cities nationwide. See the Web sites www .ciee.org and www.statravel.com. Ticket Planet (☎ 1-800-799 8888) has a good itinerary search facility on its Web site at www.ticketplanet.com. An APEX return on a daily Austrian Airlines flight from New York can be as low as US$430. From Los Angeles, Delta flies daily (via Paris), as does Swissair (via Zürich). Expect to pay at least US$700 return. Lauda Air (☎ 1-800-588 8399) has four flights a week from Miami; promotional return fares can be as low as US$399. Add around US$60 taxes to all the above fares.

In Canada, Travel CUTS (☎ 800-667-2887) has offices in all major cities and a Web site at www.travelcuts.com. You'll

Air Travel Glossary

Cancellation Penalties If you have to cancel or change a discounted ticket, there are often heavy penalties involved; insurance can sometimes be taken out against these penalties. Some airlines impose penalties on regular tickets as well, particularly against 'no-show' passengers.

Courier Fares Businesses often need to send urgent documents or freight securely and quickly. Courier companies hire people to accompany the package through customs and, in return, offer a discount ticket which is sometimes a phenomenal bargain. However, you may have to surrender all your baggage allowance and take only carry-on luggage.

Full Fares Airlines traditionally offer 1st class (coded F), business class (coded J) and economy class (coded Y) tickets. These days there are so many promotional and discounted fares available that few passengers pay full economy fare.

Lost Tickets If you lose your airline ticket an airline will usually treat it like a travellers cheque and, after inquiries, issue you with another one. Legally, however, an airline is entitled to treat it like cash and if you lose it then it's gone forever. Take good care of your tickets.

Onward Tickets An entry requirement for many countries is that you have a ticket out of the country. If you're unsure of your next move, the easiest solution is to buy the cheapest onward ticket to a neighbouring country or a ticket from a reliable airline which can later be refunded if you do not use it.

Open-Jaw Tickets These are return tickets where you fly out to one place but return from another. If available, this can save you backtracking to your arrival point.

Overbooking Since every flight has some passengers who fail to show up, airlines often book more passengers than they have seats. Usually excess passengers make up for the no-shows, but occasionally somebody gets 'bumped' onto the next available flight. Guess who it is most likely to be? The passengers who check in late.

Promotional Fares These are officially discounted fares, available from travel agencies or direct from the airline.

Reconfirmation If you don't reconfirm your flight at least 72 hours prior to departure, the airline may delete your name from the passenger list. Ring to find out if your airline requires reconfirmation.

Restrictions Discounted tickets often have various restrictions on them – such as needing to be paid for in advance and incurring a penalty to be altered. Others are restrictions on the minimum and maximum period you must be away.

Round-the-World Tickets RTW tickets give you a limited period (usually a year) in which to circumnavigate the globe. You can go anywhere the carrying airlines go, as long as you don't backtrack. The number of stopovers or total number of separate flights is decided before you set off and they usually cost a bit more than a basic return flight.

Transferred Tickets Airline tickets cannot be transferred from one person to another. Travellers sometimes try to sell the return half of their ticket, but officials can ask you to prove that you are the person named on the ticket. On an international flight tickets are compared with passports.

Travel Periods Ticket prices vary with the time of year. There is a low (off-peak) season and a high (peak) season, and often a low-shoulder season and a high-shoulder season as well. Usually the fare depends on your outward flight – if you depart in the high season and return in the low season, you pay the high-season fare.

GETTING THERE & AWAY

Lauda Air Takes Off, Hits Turbulence

Austria's Niki Lauda, three-times Formula One racing world champion, founded Lauda Air in 1979. It initially operated as a charter airline, with Lauda himself, a trained pilot, often taking the controls. In 1985 a long battle to operate scheduled flights began. Lauda Air's struggle to establish itself was made harder by the attitude of the state-owned Austrian Airlines. It halved prices on certain routes, denigrated the fledgling airline in the press and was often uncooperative in air traffic rights negotiations.

Though partial approval was given in 1987 it took another three years of intensive political and public pressure (greatly aided by Lauda's status as a national hero) before Lauda Air finally received a worldwide concession to operate scheduled flights. Ironically, the airline's erstwhile foe Austrian Airlines later purchased a 36% stake in Lauda Air, which flies to Europe, the USA, Asia and Australia in aircraft named after the likes of Johann Strauss, Enzo Ferrari, James Dean and Bob Marley. Lauda Air's innovative style saw it introduce quality in-flight meals (supplied by DO & CO), jeans as part of the staff uniform, and in-flight gambling on the Vienna-Australia route.

Niki Lauda's management became the subject of criticism during 2000. It emerged that the airline was on the verge of bankruptcy, with estimated losses of €73 million. The final blow came in October when an auditing firm denounced the lack of internal financial control in the airline's foreign currency dealings. The report was instrumental in Niki Lauda's decision to resign on 21 November 2000.

Austrian Airlines may yet have the last laugh in its chequered relationship with Lauda Air – it is hoping to take a controlling interest in the airline. In November 2000 it purchased a further 11% in Lauda Air from Lufthansa, bringing its total to 47%.

usually have to change planes in a European gateway city like Paris or Frankfurt, though United Airlines can get you from Toronto to Vienna via Chicago (around C$1025 return, plus taxes; 15 hours total).

Australasia

STA (☎ 131 776) and Flight Centre (☎ 131 600) are major dealers in cheap air fares from Australia and New Zealand, with Web sites at www.statravel.com.au and www.flightcentre.com.au. In New Zealand, call ☎ 09-309 0458 for STA and ☎ 09-309 6171 for Flight Centre.

From Australia, Lauda Air (☎ 1800-642 438) operates the only direct flight to Vienna (via Kuala Lumpur), departing from Melbourne/Sydney on Monday, Wednesday and Saturday; 'red hot special' fares on this route can be as low as A$900/1440 single/return. From New Zealand, you can just get an Auckland–Melbourne return (from NZ$395) and pick up the Lauda flight from there. Or consider buying a round-the-world (RTW) ticket; prices are upwards of NZ$2200.

Europe

There are several daily nonstop flights to all the major European transport hubs from Vienna. STA has offices in London (☎ 020-7361 6161) and other cities in Britain and Europe; check the Web site at www.sta.com. Additionally, many travel agents in Europe have ties with STA Travel where STA-issued tickets can be altered (usually for a US$25 fee). Outlets include: Voyages Wasteels (☎ 01 43 43 46 10), 2 Rue Michel Chasles, Paris and ISYTS (☎ 01-323 37 67), 1st floor, 11 Nikis St, Syntagma Square, Athens. Currently there is no travel agent in Austria linked with STA.

London is one of the world's major centres for discounted air tickets. London–Vienna return usually costs in excess of UK£150, though the no-frills airline buzz (☎ 0870-240 7070) may offer London Stansted–Vienna return for as low as £95. See the Web site at www.buzzaway.com.

Austrian Airlines (☎ 0845-601 0948) has low fares on its early morning weekday flights, flying from London Heathrow. Lauda Air (☎ 0800-767 737) has a daily flight (except Saturday) from Manchester. British Airways sells its own discounted tickets, called World Offers (☎ 0345-222 111). It has four daily flights from Heathrow; its Web site is at www.britishairways.co.uk. Mondial Travel (☎ 01580-714714), The Four Wents, Goudhurst Rd, Cranbrook, Kent, is a specialist in budget flights to Austria and can arrange fly-drive deals and city breaks. Other recommended places with branches throughout the UK are Usit Campus (☎ 0870-240 1010) and Trailfinders (☎ 020-7937 5400). See Organised Tours at the end of this chapter for more outlets.

Airline Offices
Many airline offices in Vienna are on Opernring, opposite the Staatsoper. For a complete listing, look under *Fluggesellschaften* in the Yellow Pages *(Gelbe Seiten)* section of the Wien telephone book. They include:

Aer Lingus (☎ 369 28 85) 19, Scheibengasse 12
Air Canada Inquire at Austrian Airlines (see below)
Air France (☎ 502 22-2400) 01, Kärntner Strasse 49
Alitalia (☎ 505 17 07-0) 01, Kärntner Ring 2
Austrian Airlines (Map 7; ☎ 1789) 01, Kärntner Ring 18
British Airways (BA; Map 7; ☎ 795 67-567) 01, Kärntner Ring 10
Delta Air Lines (☎ 512 66 46-0) 01, Kärntner Ring 17
Iberia (☎ 586 76 36-0) 01, Opernring 11
Japan Airlines (JAL; ☎ 512 75 22) 01, Kärntner Strasse 11
KLM – Royal Dutch Airlines (☎ 589 24-0) 02, Schlachthausgasse 23–29
Lauda Air (Map 7; ☎ 7000-777) 01, Opernring 6
Lufthansa Airlines (☎ 0800-900 800) 06, Mariahilfer Strasse 123 or c/o Austrian Airlines
Malév – Hungarian Airlines (☎ 587 33 18-0) 01, Opernring 3–5
South African Airways (SAA; ☎ 587 15 85-0) 01, Opernring 1/R
Swissair (Map 7; ☎ 960 07) 01, Rotenturmstrasse 5–9

BUS
Other Parts of Austria
The yellow and red Bundesbus services are ideal for getting to the more out-of-the-way

places. Buses are efficient and usually depart from train stations. Fares work out at around €10.50 per 100km, but shorter journeys are proportionately more expensive. Bus timetable information is available on ☎ 711 01 between 7 am and 7 pm. The Bundesbus counters in Busbahnhof Wien Mitte are open 6.15 am to 1 pm and 1.45 to 6 pm daily.

Other Countries
Buses are generally slower, cheaper and less comfortable than trains. Europe's biggest network of international buses is provided by a group of companies operating under the name Eurolines, with a Web site at www.eurolines.com. Addresses for Eurolines include:

Deutsche-Touring (☎ 069-790 30) Am Römerhof 17, Frankfurt
Eurolines France (☎ 08-36 69 52 52) Gare Routière Internationale, 28 Ave du Général de Gaulle, 75020 Paris
Eurolines Italy (☎ Florence: 055-35 71 10) Ciconvallazione Nonentana 574, Lato Stazione Tiburtina, Rome
Eurolines Nederland (☎ 020-560 87 87) Rokin 10, 1012 KR Amsterdam
Eurolines UK (☎ 0870-514 3219) 52 Grosvenor Gardens, London SW1

In Austria, Eurolines (☎ 712 04 53, ℮ info@eurolines.at) has a counter at Busbahnhof Wien Mitte (bus station; Map 7), open noon to 9 pm daily. There are bus connections across Western and Eastern Europe, with reduced prices (of 10% or more, depending on the operator) for people under 26 and over 60. Some Eurolines seats can be reserved by telephone, but with many services heading east you have to pay in person at the counter in advance.

Eurolines buses to Budapest (€26.90/ 37.80 one way/return, 3½ hours) depart from Wien Mitte several times daily, starting at 7 or 8 am. Buses run every two hours or so to Bratislava in Slovakia (€10.20 /18.20 one way/return, 90 minutes), via the airport and Hainburg; but note that it works out cheaper to buy the return leg in Bratislava.

Eurolines buses to/from London (Victoria Coach Station) operate five days a week

GETTING THERE & AWAY

European Rail Passes

These may not work out much more expensive than a straightforward return ticket, and are worth considering if you want to explore a number of destinations en route to Austria. Always study the terms and conditions attached to passes. For information on a range of rail passes, visit the Web sites at www.raileurope.com and www.raileurope.co.uk.

Eurail Pass

This pass can only be bought by residents of non-European countries. Eurail passes are valid for unlimited travel on national railways and some private lines in Austria, Belgium, Denmark, Finland, France (including Monaco), Germany, Greece, Hungary, Ireland, Italy, Luxembourg, the Netherlands, Norway, Portugal, Spain, Sweden and Switzerland (including Liechtenstein). The pass is also valid for free or discounted travel on various international ferries and national lake/river steamers.

A standard **Youthpass** for travellers under 26 is valid for unlimited 2nd-class travel within the given time period, ranging from 15 days (US$388) up to three months (US$1089). The **Youth Flexipass**, also for 2nd class, is valid for freely chosen days within a two-month period: 10 days for US$458 or 15 days for US$599.

The corresponding passes for those aged over 26 are available in 1st class only. The standard Eurail pass costs from US$554 for 15 days up to US$1558 for three months. The Flexipass costs US$654 for 10 days or US$862 for 15 days. Two people travelling together can save around 15% each by buying 'saver' versions of these passes. Eurail passes for children are also available.

Europass is basically a cut-down version of the Eurail pass, covering only France, Germany, Italy, Spain and Switzerland. The youth/adult price is US$296/348 for a minimum five travel days, or US$620/728 for a maximum 15 days. Some countries can be added as 'associate' countries to the scheme. The cost to add any one/two countries is US$52/86 for youths or US$60/100 for adults. Austria and Hungary can be added, and together they count as one country. The Eurail and Europass Aid Office (☎ 5800-335 98) is in Vienna's Westbahnhof station, open 9 am to 4 pm Monday to Saturday.

(daily in summer). The trip costs UK£72/111 one way/return and takes 22 hours. Eurolines UK also has circular explorer routes: a round-trip ticket from London includes stops in Vienna, Budapest and Prague and costs UK£116 (no youth reductions).

Austrobus has buses to Prague (sometimes continuing to Karlsbad in Germany), leaving Vienna from its stop at 01, Rathausplatz 5. Departures are at 7 am Monday to Saturday, and 2 pm Sunday (€23.65, five hours). From Prague, buses leave at 9 am Monday to Thursday and 2 pm Friday to Sunday. Buy tickets from the driver, or in advance from Columbus Reisen (Map 7; ☎ 534 11-123), 01, Dr Karl Lueger Ring 8.

If you want to visit several countries by bus, Eurolines has passes linking 48 cities: a 30-day pass in the high season costs €370 for adults or €296 for youths/seniors. Another option is the UK-based Busabout (☎ 020-

7950 1661), which has buses running along set routes around Europe from April to October. There are consecutive passes (eg, UK£155/139 for adults/students, valid 15 days) or flexipasses (valid up to four months). See the Web site at www.busabout.com.

TRAIN
Other Parts of Austria

Austrian trains are efficient and frequent. The country is well covered by the state network, with only a few private lines operating. Eurail and Inter-Rail passes are valid on the former. Many stations have information centres where the staff speak English. Train information can be obtained on ☎ 05-1717 (local rate). Tickets can be purchased on the train but they may cost €2.20 extra. Unless otherwise specified, 2nd-class fares are quoted in this book. Reserving train seats usually incurs a €2.95 fee.

European Rail Passes

Inter-Rail Pass

Inter-Rail passes are available in Europe to people who have been resident there for at least six months. The standard Inter-Rail pass is for travellers aged under 26, though older people can get the Inter-Rail 26+ version. The pass divides Europe into eight zones (A to H); Austria is in zone C, along with Denmark, Germany and Switzerland. The standard/26+ fare for any one zone is UK£129/179, valid 22 days. To purchase two/three/all zones (valid one month) costs UK£169/195/219, or UK£235/269/309 for the 26+ version.

The all-zone (global) pass would take you everywhere covered by Eurail, plus to the following countries: Bulgaria, Croatia, Czech Republic, Macedonia, Poland, Romania, Slovakia, Slovenia, Turkey and Yugoslavia. As with Eurail, the pass gives discounts or free travel on ferry, ship and steamer routes.

European East Pass

This is sold in North America and Australia and is valid in Austria, Hungary, Poland, the Czech Republic and Slovakia. In the USA, Rail Europe charges US$205 for five days' 1st-class travel within one month; extra rail days (five maximum) cost US$23 each.

National Rail Passes

There is a **Euro-Domino Pass** for each of the countries covered in the Inter-Rail pass. Adults (travelling 1st or 2nd class) and youths under 26 can opt for three to eight days' free travel within one month. The Austrian version costs UK£68 for three days, rising by £6 or £8 per day up to £108 for eight days. They're sold in Europe to European residents. Outside Europe, travellers can buy a similar product under a different name. In the USA, for example, Rail Europe sells an **Austrian Flexipass**, which is valid on Austrian railways for three to eight days over a 15-day period. The price in 2nd class is US$104 for three days, with extra days costing $16 each.

Ordinary single/return tickets (over 100km) are valid for three days/one month, and you can break your journey, but tell the conductor first. Trains are expensive (eg, €12.95 for 100km, €21.80 for 200km), and Austria has withdrawn most of its rail passes. Still available is the VORTEILScard (€93.75, valid one year) which reduces fares by 50% – fine if you stay a while, but of no value for short stays. Two or more people travelling together can get fare reductions on journeys over 100km (1 Plus-Ticket). Alternatively, if you plan on doing a lot of travel outside Vienna you could consider buying a European or national rail pass before you leave home – see the boxed text.

Other Countries

Vienna is the main rail hub in Central Europe, and has excellent rail connections to all important destinations. However, if you don't want to fly and need to take a long rail trip, you might be better off buying a rail pass instead of a standard ticket (see the boxed text). London–Vienna, for example, costs as much as £305 return via the Eurostar service to Paris (14 hours).

Travellers under 26 can pick up Billet International de Jeunesse (BIJ) tickets that cut fares by up to 30%. Various agents issue BIJ tickets in Europe, eg, Voyages Wasteels (☎ 01 43 43 46 10), 2 Rue Michel Chasles, Paris, and elsewhere. Rail Europe (☎ 08705-848 848), 179 Piccadilly, London, sells BIJ tickets, Eurail and Inter-Rail passes; check the Web site at www.raileurope.co.uk.

Express trains can be identified by the symbols EC (EuroCity) or IC (InterCity). The French TGV and the German ICE trains are even faster. Supplements can apply on international and express trains, and it is a good idea (sometimes obligatory) to make seat reservations at peak times and on certain lines.

Europeans over 60 should inquire about the Railplus Card, which is good for fare reductions.

Vienna's Train Stations

Vienna has several train stations and not all destinations are exclusively serviced by one station. Check with train information centres in stations or telephone the 24-hour information line (☎ 05-1717). Remember to ask about reduced fares if you're under 26. Sometimes there are also cheap fares on international return tickets valid less than four days (eg, Budapest return costs €44.65 and includes city transport in Budapest). All the following stations (except Meidling) have lockers (from €2.20), money exchange (including Bankomat ATMs), and places to eat and buy provisions. Train stations are usually closed from around 1 to 4 am.

Westbahnhof Westbahnhof (Map 5) services trains to Western and northern Europe and western Austria. There are services about every hour to Salzburg (€31.25, 3¼ hours); some continue to Munich and terminate in Paris Est (14½ hours total). To Zürich, there are two day trains (€81.55, nine hours) and one night train that departs at 9.15 pm (€80.05, plus charge for fold-down seat/couchette). A direct overnight train departs at 8.05 pm for Bucharest (€90.55, 18 hours). Eight trains a day go to Budapest (€32, 3½ hours). Westbahnhof is also a U-Bahn station for lines U3 and U6, and many trams stop outside.

Südbahnhof The Südbahnhof (Map 6) station services trains to Italy, the Czech Republic, Slovakia, Hungary and Poland. Express trains to Rome (via Venice and Florence) depart at 7.34 am and 7.36 pm (14 hours). Five trains a day go to Bratislava (€12.10/16 one way/return, 1½ hours); four go to Prague (€37.10, five hours), with two continuing to Berlin (10 hours total). Trams D (to the Ring and Franz Josefs Bahnhof) and O (to Wien Mitte and Praterstern) stop outside. The quickest way to transfer to

Westbahnhof is to take tram No 18, or the S-Bahn to Meidling and then the U6.

Franz Josefs Bahnhof Franz Josefs Bahnhof (Map 3) handles regional and local trains, including trains to Tulln, Krems and the Wachau region. From outside, tram D goes to the Ring, and tram No 5 goes to Westbahnhof (via Kaiserstrasse) in one direction and Praterstern (Wien Nord) in the other.

Other Stations Wien Mitte (Map 7) services local trains, and is adjacent to the Landstrasse stop on the U3. Wien Nord (Map 4), at the Praterstern stop on the U1, handles local and regional trains, including the airport service (which also stops at Wien Mitte). Meidling (Map 5) is a stop for most trains going to and from Südbahnhof, and it is linked to the Philadelphiabrücke stop on the U6.

CAR & MOTORCYCLE

By road there are numerous entry points from Germany, the Czech Republic, Slovakia, Hungary, Slovenia, Italy and Switzerland. All main border crossings are open 24 hours a day. To and from Germany and Italy there are no border controls, thanks to the EU Schengen Agreement. Driving into Vienna is straightforward: the A1 from Linz and Salzburg and the A2 from Graz join the Gürtel ring road; the A4 from the airport leads directly to the Ring, and the A22 runs to the city centre along the northern bank of the Danube.

To avoid a long drive, consider a motorail service: many head south from Calais and Paris, and Vienna is linked by a daily motorail to Salzburg, Innsbruck, Feldkirch and Villach.

Paperwork & Preparations

Proof of ownership of a private vehicle should always be carried (Vehicle Registration Document for British-registered cars) when touring Europe. A British (except for the old green version) or other Western European driving licence is valid throughout Europe. If you have any other type of licence you should obtain an International

Driving Permit (IDP). Third-party insurance is a minimum requirement in Europe, and you'll need proof of this in the form of a Green Card. Taking out a European breakdown assistance policy is a good investment, such as AA Five Star Service or RAC European Motoring Assistance.

Every vehicle travelling across an international border should display a nationality plate of its country of registration. A warning triangle, to be used in the event of breakdown, is compulsory almost everywhere (including Austria). Recommended or compulsory accessories are a first-aid kit (compulsory in Austria and several neighbouring countries), a spare bulb kit and a fire extinguisher. Contact a motoring organisation for more information.

Road Rules

Some motoring organisations publish handy guides to European motoring regulations, rules and procedures; the RAC has some of this sort of information on its Web site at www.rac.co.uk. Driving is on the right throughout Continental Europe, and priority is usually given to traffic approaching from the right. Road signs are generally standard throughout Europe. *Umleitung* in German means 'diversion', though in Austria you may see *Ausweiche* instead.

The blood alcohol concentration (BAC) limit when driving in Europe is usually between 0.05% and 0.08%, but in some areas (Gibraltar, Eastern Europe, Scandinavia) it can be *zero* per cent. In Austria it's 0.05%, and the penalty for drink driving is a hefty on-the-spot fine and confiscation of your driving licence.

Crash helmets for motorcyclists and their passengers are compulsory everywhere in Europe. Austria, Belgium, Croatia, France, Germany, Luxembourg, Portugal, Spain, Scandinavia, Yugoslavia and most of Eastern Europe also require motorcyclists to use headlights during the day; in other countries it is recommended.

There are toll charges for some of the Alpine tunnels, and some mountain roads and passes are closed in winter. On mountain roads, postbuses always have priority, otherwise priority lies with uphill traffic. Drive in low gear on steep downhill stretches.

Speed limits for driving on Austrian roads are 50km/h in towns, 130km/h on motorways and 100km/h on other roads. Cars towing a caravan or trailer are limited to 100km/h on motorways. Snow chains are recommended in winter. Seatbelts must be used, if fitted, and children under 12 should have a special seat or restraint. Austrian police have the authority to impose fines for various traffic offences. As a foreigner you may have to pay on the spot (ask for a receipt), and the police have the power to impound goods if you can't pay up.

Fuel

Leaded petrol is no longer available in Austria, but Super Plus petrol has a special additive that allows it to be used with leaded petrol engines. Prices per litre are about €1.05 for Super Plus, compared to €1 for unleaded petrol and €0.90 for diesel. Petrol is cheaper in the Czech Republic, Slovakia, Hungary and Switzerland, so fill up before departing those countries. Prices in Germany and Italy are comparable to those in Austria.

Motorway Tax

Tolls were introduced on Austrian motorways in 1997. The annual fee is €72.70 for cars (below 3.5 tonnes) and €29.10 for motorcycles. But, unlike in neighbouring Switzerland, tourists have the option of buying short-term passes. The weekly disc costs €7.65/4.40 for cars/motorcycles and is actually valid for up to 10 days: from Friday to midnight two Sundays hence. The two-month disc, valid for consecutive calendar months, costs €21.85/10.90 for cars/motorcycles. The tax doesn't cover the toll fee for other roads and tunnels.

BICYCLE

Getting to Vienna by bike is certainly possible. A cycle track, for example, runs all the way along the Danube from Germany's Black Forest to Vienna and on to Bratislava. If you get weary of pedalling or simply want to skip a boring leg, you can put your feet up on the train. On slower trains, bikes

GETTING THERE & AWAY

can usually be taken on board as luggage, subject to a small supplementary fee. Fast trains (IC, EC etc) can sometimes accommodate bikes; otherwise, they need to be sent as registered luggage (costs vary) and may end up on a different train from the one you take. With the exception of Eurostar, British trains are not part of the European luggage registration scheme. Bikes can also be carried by aeroplane, but check with the carrier in advance.

Within Austria, you can take your bike with you on trains by buying a pass. For local and regional trains it costs €2.95/6.55/19.65 for one day/week/month. The daily pass for IC/EC trains is €7.30 within Austria or €10.20 for international journeys. Sending your bike as registered luggage costs €6.55/10.20 national/international.

HITCHING

Hitching is never entirely safe in any country, and we don't recommend it. Travellers who decide to hitch should understand that they are taking a small but potentially serious risk. People who do choose to hitch will be safer if they travel in pairs and let someone know where they are going.

Throughout Europe, hitching is illegal on motorways – stand on the entrance roads, or approach drivers at petrol stations and truck stops. Ferry tickets for vehicles sometimes include a full load of passengers, so hitchers may be able to get free passage this way.

Hitching in Austria is not too bad overall. Trying to hitch rides on trucks is often the best bet: check border customs posts and truck stops. *Autohof* indicates a parking place able to accommodate trucks. It is against the law for minors under 16 to hitch in Burgenland, Upper Austria, Styria and Vorarlberg. Heading west from Vienna, the lay-by across the footbridge from the U4 Unter St Veit stop has been recommended.

A safer way to hitch is to arrange a lift through an organisation that links drivers and hitchers, such as Allostop Provoya or Auto-Partage in France and Mitfahrzentrale in Germany. You could also try scanning university notice boards. In Vienna, Rot-Weiss-Rot Mitfahrzentrale (☎ 408 22 10,

e office@mfz.at) has set charges for hitchers, and drivers get the balance after the agency takes its cut. Lifts across Austria tend to be limited, but there are usually many cars going to Germany. Examples of fares for hitchers are: Salzburg €18.20, Innsbruck €25.45, Klagenfurt €19.65, Vorarlberg €29.10, Brussels €43.65, Cologne €43.65, Frankfurt €36.35 and Munich €25.45. There's no walk-in office but you can telephone 24 hours, seven days a week.

BOAT

Since the early 1990s the Danube has been connected to the Rhine by the River Main tributary and the Main-Danube canal in southern Germany. The MS *River Queen* does 13-day cruises along this route, from Amsterdam to Vienna, between May and September. It departs monthly in each direction. In Britain, bookings can be made through Noble Caledonia (☎ 020-7409 0376); deck prices start at UK£1995. In the USA, you can book through Uniworld (☎ 800-733 7820). Respective Web sites are at www.noble-caledonia.co.uk and www.cruiseuniworld.com.

From Vienna, hydrofoils travel eastwards to Bratislava and Budapest. The trip to Bratislava costs €17.45/26.90 one way/return (1½ hours; once daily Wednesday to Sunday between mid-April and late October). Budapest costs €56.70/79.95 one way/return and takes at least 5½ hours; there's one daily departure from early April to late October, except from late July to early September when there are two daily. Bookings can be made through Mahart Tours (Map 4; ☎ 7292-161) or G Glaser (☎ 726 08 201), both at 02, Handelskai 265; or DDSG Blue Danube (Map 7; ☎ 588 80-0, fax -440), 01, Friedrichstrasse 7, with a Web site at www.ddsg-blue-danube.at.

Hydrofoils are more expensive than the bus or the train, but make a pleasant change. Likewise, the steamers that ply the Danube west of Vienna to Passau (Germany) provide an enjoyable excursion, but are rather slow, especially upstream. Yet they're well worth it if you like lounging on deck and having the scenery come to you rather than the

GETTING THERE & AWAY

Fiacre coachman – driver of a hard bargain

Inside the Naturhistorisches Museum

Cafe society – sipping, watching, relaxing

The Gothic arches of the Rathaus

Schönbrunn Palace – Vienna's Versailles

Neuer Markt was a flour market in medieval times

Tying the knot at the Kunsthistorisches Museum

other way round. The most enjoyable stretch of the river is the Wachau region, and several operators run boats here (see the Danube Valley section in the Excursions chapter for details).

ORGANISED TOURS

Various packages are available – see your travel agent or check the travel pages in Sunday newspapers. Austrian Holidays (☎ 020-7434 7399), the UK tour operator of Austrian Airlines, can do flight-only deals or arrange holidays based around tourist sights, winter sights or the opera. Austria Travel (☎ 01708-222 000), 54 Station Rd, Upminster, RM14 2TT, UK, has competi-

tive air fares, and can construct a tailor-made tour for you.

Young revellers can take bus tours based on hotel or camping accommodation. Some of Contiki's tours include Austria, though you only get one day in Vienna – check www.contiki.com. For people over 50, Saga offers holidays ranging from cheap coach tours to luxury cruises. Saga Holidays in Britain (☎ 0800-300 500), Saga Building, Middelburg Square, Folkestone, Kent CT20 1AZ, has a 'four countries cruise' that kicks off with three nights in Vienna (£899, 10 nights). In the USA, Saga Holidays (☎ 800-343 0273) is at 222 Berkeley St, Boston, MA 02116.

Getting Around

SCHWECHAT AIRPORT

Flughafen Wien Schwechat (☎ 7007; 7007-22233 for flight inquiries), Vienna's airport, is 19km east of the city centre. Schwechat handles over 12 million passengers a year and has all the facilities expected of a major airport, such as tourist information, money-exchange counters (high commission rates), a supermarket (open daily) and car rental counters.

TO/FROM THE AIRPORT

The cheapest way to get to the airport is by S-Bahn on line S7. The fare is €2.80, or €1.40 supplement if you already have a city pass for the day. Trains usually leave at three and 33 minutes past the hour from Wien Nord, calling at Wien Mitte three minutes later. The trip takes about 35 minutes and the first/last train departs at 5.03 am/9.33 pm. From the airport, trains usually depart at 14 and 44 minutes past the hour, with the first/last service at 6.10 am/10.24 pm. (There are earlier trains in both directions on weekdays only.)

Airport buses run from the City Air Terminal (Map 7) at the Hotel Hilton to the airport every 20 or 30 minutes from 4.30 am (5 am in the opposite direction) to 12.30 am (1 am) every day. From 1 April to late October buses also run throughout the night, though less frequently. The 20-minute journey costs €5.10/9.45 one way/return, including three pieces of luggage. Buses also run from Westbahnhof between 5.30 am and 10 pm (to 1.10 am in summer), stopping at Südbahnhof 15 minutes later. The fare is also €5.10/9.45 and departures are every 30 or 60 minutes. For more information on airport bus services, telephone ☎ 930 00-2300.

If taking a taxi is the only option, you're usually quoted around €29 to €33. However, C&K Airport Service (☎ 1731, fax 689 69 69) does the trip for €19.65 fixed fare. Reserve ahead if you can, though in the airport you could approach their drivers holding signs by the passenger exit point and ask them to point out the coordinator.

PUBLIC TRANSPORT

Vienna has a comprehensive and unified public transport network that is one of the most efficient in Europe. Flat-fare tickets are valid for trains, trams, buses, the underground (U-Bahn) and the S-Bahn regional trains. Services are frequent, and you rarely have to wait more than five or 10 minutes. Public transport kicks off around 5 or 6 am. Buses and trams usually finish by midnight (except for night buses), though some S-Bahn and U-Bahn services may continue until 1 am.

Information

Transport routes are shown in the free tourist office map, and there's a transport map at the back of this book. For a more detailed listing, buy a map (€1.50) from a Vienna Line ticket office. These offices are located in many U-Bahn stations. Transport information offices at Karlsplatz, Stephansplatz and Westbahnhof are open 6.30 am to 6.30 pm Monday to Friday and 8.30 am to 4 pm weekends and holidays; those at Floridsdorf, Landstrasse, Philadelphiabrücke, Praterstern, Spittelau and Volkstheater are open 6.30 or 7 am to 6.30 pm Monday to Friday only. For public transport information in German call ☎ 7909-105.

Tickets & Passes

Single-trip tickets cost €1.60 from drivers or the ticket machines on buses and trams. They're only €1.40 each from ticket machines in U-Bahn stations; it's the same rate in multiples of four/five from ticket offices, machines or Tabak shops. You may change lines on the same trip. Single tickets are valid for immediate use; strip tickets have to be validated in the blue boxes (inside buses and trams and beside U-Bahn escalators) before your journey. Some ticket machines don't give change or will only change certain bills – be sure to use the correct money unless you can follow the German instructions.

Daily city passes *(Stunden-Netzkarte)* are the better deal for extensive sightseeing. Costs are €4.40 (valid 24 hours from first use) and €10.90 (valid 72 hours). Validate the ticket before your first journey. An eight-day, multiple-user pass *(8-Tage-Karte)* costs €21.80. The validity depends upon the number of people travelling on the same card: one person gets eight days of travel, two people get four days, and so on. Validate the ticket each day (and for each person) at the beginning of your journey.

Weekly passes, valid from the start of services Monday to 9 am the following Monday, cost €11.30; monthly passes, valid from the first of the month to the second of the following month, cost €40.70. These passes are much better value than the previously mentioned passes, provided the commencement date fits in with your visit. Both are transferable, so you can let someone else travel on your ticket or sell any unexpired days. The yearly pass for €385.20 can start any month; it has a photo ID and is not transferable.

Children aged six to 15 travel for half-price, or for free on Sunday, public holidays and during Vienna school holidays (photo ID necessary); younger children always travel free. Senior citizens (women aged 60, men aged 65) can buy a ticket for €1.90 that is valid for two trips; inquire at transport information offices. Students up to 19 studying in Vienna can get cheap deals.

All passes can be purchased at ticket offices and Tabak shops. Ticket inspections are not very frequent, but if you're caught ticketless you'll pay an on-the-spot fine of €40.70 plus the fare. Some young Viennese are prepared to take the risk, but most people are happy to support their enviable transport network.

Train
S-Bahn S-Bahn trains, designated by a number preceded by an 'S', operate from the main train stations, and are mainly used as a service to the suburbs or satellite towns. Inter-Rail, Eurail and Austrian rail passes are valid on the S-Bahn. Regional trains ('R' services) cover some of the same routes.

U-Bahn The U-Bahn is a quick and efficient way to get around the city, albeit mostly underground and therefore lacking in visual stimulus. There are five lines, U1 to U6 (there is no U5). The U2 line will be extended to Praterstern and beyond over the next few years. Platforms have timetable information and signs showing the different exits and nearby facilities. Station exits are often a fair distance apart, so after disembarking, orientate yourself instead of blindly striking out for the nearest exit. Platforms are often accessible by lift or escalator from street level. Platforms and trains are no-smoking zones.

Bus & Tram
Buses and trams are slower than the U-Bahn, but at least allow you to see the city while you're travelling. Trams are usually numbered but may be lettered instead, and cover the city centre and some suburbs. Buses go everywhere, including inside the Ring (unlike trams). They also cover the suburbs more extensively than trams. Most buses have a number followed by an 'A' or 'B'. Very logically, buses connecting with a tram service often have the same number, eg, 38A connects with 38, and 72A continues from the terminus of 72.

Night Bus
There's a comprehensive 'Nightline' service, marked with an 'N' on the buses and bus stops. They run every 30 minutes from 12.30 or 1 am to about 5 am, and stretch into all suburbs. Most routes hit the Ringstrasse, with Schwedenplatz, Schottentor and the Oper being the most important intersection points. Vienna Line offices can give you a timetable and route map. The fares are not covered by daily passes: pay €1.10 for one ticket or €3.27 for a strip of four.

CAR & MOTORCYCLE
You're probably better off planning to use the excellent public transport system in Vienna. The Viennese can be impatient drivers

GETTING AROUND

and you'll find it difficult or expensive to park in the centre. Take special care if you've never driven in a city with trams before; they always have priority and no matter how much you might swear at them, they're never going to deviate from their tracks just to suit you. Vehicles must wait behind the tram when it stops to pick up or set down passengers. Parking is not permitted on roads with tram tracks from 10 pm to 5 am between 15 December and 31 March (because of snow-clearing). Use of the horn is prohibited near hospitals.

The evening rush hour starts at about 4 pm. Petrol stations are dotted around the city; some are self-service but only a handful are open 24 hours. Tankstelle Brunnbauer (Map 5), 07, Zieglerstrasse 53, is cheaper than most and it's open till 9 pm (8 pm Sunday and holidays).

Parking

There are many underground parking garages. The Staatsoper garage on Kärntner Strasse charges €2.20 per hour, €26.20 for the first 24 hours and €21.85 for subsequent 24-hour periods. It's open 24 hours. The cheapest central garage is the one in front of the Museumsquartier, charging €1.85 per hour and €10.90 for 24 hours, but it's closed from midnight to 6 am (8 am on weekends and holidays). The multistorey car parks at Südbahnhof and Westbahnhof charge €2.15 per hour or €16.90 per day (open 24 hours).

All of the Innere Stadt is a short-term parking zone (Kurzparkzone), meaning that on-street parking is limited to a maximum 1½ hours between 9 am and 7 pm from Monday to Friday. Outside these hours there are no parking restrictions. Vouchers (Parkschein) for parking on these streets, designated as blue zones from their blue markings, must be purchased from Tabak shops and displayed on the windscreen. Vouchers cost €0.45 per 30 minutes.

On some streets, parking or stopping may be prohibited altogether (blue sign circled in red with a red cross – Parking Verboten) or only permitted for 10 minutes (blue sign circled in red with a single diagonal line –

a Halten area). Plaques under the sign will state any exceptions or specific conditions (eg, the 'Halten' sign may also be marked as 'Kurzparkzone', allowing a 1½-hour stop).

Blue zones have gradually crept into all the districts bordering the Innere Stadt, ie, districts 2–9 and 20. The Kurzparkzone restrictions in these districts apply on weekdays from 9 am to 8 pm, and the maximum stop permitted is two hours. Elsewhere, you can still find white zones where there are no time restrictions on parking. The 1½- or two-hour limit can be ignored upon purchase of a €3.65 parking card – inquire at your hotel.

Parking tickets incur a fine of €21.85 if you pay within two weeks. Don't assume you can get away with it if you're due to leave the country, as Austria has reciprocal agreements with some countries for the collection of such debts. And don't risk getting towed, as you'll find it expensive (at least €75) and inconvenient to retrieve your car.

Car Rental

For the lowest rates, organise car rental before departure. Holiday Autos has low rates and offices or representatives in over 20 countries; check their Web site at www .holidayautos.com. In the UK call ☎ 0870 300 400; in the USA call Kemwel Holiday Autos (☎ 800-576 1590). In the UK, a competitor with even lower prices is Autos Abroad (☎ 020-7287 6000); the Web site at www.autosabroad.co.uk. Autos Abroad charges UK£159 (about €260) for one week for its lowest category car including airport surcharge, unlimited mileage and collision damage waiver (CDW).

All the multinational rental companies are present in Austria. You should be able to make advance reservations online. Central reservation numbers in Austria and international Web sites are:

Avis: ☎ 0800-0800 87 57 (toll free),
    Web site: www.avis.com
Budget: ☎ 07242-777 74
    Web site: www.budget.com
Europcar: ☎ 01-740 50-4000
    Web site: www.europcar.com
Hertz: ☎ 01-795 32
    Web site: www.hertz.com

cal walk-in rates are pretty expensive.
u'll be looking at around €50 to €60 per
/ in the lowest category with unlimited
metres, though there may be special of-
s from time to time. Also inquire about
aper weekend deals – they work out at
und €30 to €40 per day. Quoted rates
lude 20% MWST (VAT) and are subject
1% contract tax, plus about €1 to €4
day to cover road tax. All the multi-
ional companies have an airport office,
ugh prices are 10% to 12% higher than
city offices.

Other companies to try include Sixt (Map
, ☎ 01-503 66 16), at Wiedner Gürtel 1a,
arking Südbahnhof, which is linked to Eu-
odollar; or National, known in Austria as
ARAC (Map 7; ☎ 01-866 16-33), at 01,
Schubertring 9. You can make online reservations with Sixt at www.sixt.de. At the
ime of writing, the cheapest walk-in rates
were offered by Europa Service (☎ 0810 00
1027, local rate call), which has an office in
the airport and at the City Air Terminal. Its
prices start at €29 per day or €59 from 4
pm Friday to 9 am Monday.

The minimum age for renting is 19 for
small cars and 25 for prestige models. You
ll need to have held a valid licence for at
st a year. CDW is offered for an add-
al charge of about €22 per day. Be sure
inquire about all terms and conditions
efore commencing a rental, such as if you
can drive it across the border.

A place offering motorbike rental is 2
Rad-Börse (Map 7; ☎ 214 85 95-0, fax -26),
47. It has various Ho

For 24-hour emergency assistance within
Austria dial ☎ 120. Assistance is free for
ÖAMTC members and for members of motoring clubs in other countries that have reciprocal agreements with ÖAMTC. If
you're not entitled to free assistance, call-
out charges are €87.25 during the day or
€98.15 from 10 pm to 6 am. ÖAMTC also
offers travel agency services.

Another national motoring club, the
Auto, Motor und Radfahrerbund Österre-
ichs (ARBÖ; ☎ 891 21-0), 15, Mariahilfer
Strasse 180, offers 24-hour emergency assistance on ☎ 123; call-out charges are
slightly higher than those of ÖAMTC, and
it has fewer international affiliations.

TAXI

Taxis are metered for city journeys. The flag
fall starts at €1.90 (€2 on Sunday, holidays
and from 11 pm to 6 am). The rate is then
about €1.10 per kilometre (€1.20 on Sunday etc), plus €0.15 per 22 seconds of being
stuck in traffic. The rate for trips outside the
city borders is double, in order to pay for the
driver's trip back, though it may be possible
to negotiate a fare. Taxis are easily found at
train stations and top hotels, or just flag them
down in the street. There is a €1.90 surcharge for phoning a taxi; numbers to call are
☎ 31 300, ☎ 40 100, ☎ 60 160 and ☎ 81 400.

BICYCLE

There are 700km of bicycle tracks in and
around Vienna, including along the banks of
the Danube. Pick up the *Tips für Radfahrer*
booklet from the tourist office. It's in German, but it has maps showing bike tours, eg,
circular tours through the Prater and along
the Old and New Danubes. It also lists bike
rental places *(Radverleih)*.

Argus (Map 6; ☎ 505 84 35), 04,
Frankenberggasse 11, is an organisation pro-
moting cycling, and has maps and cycling
information for Austria. It's open 2 to 6 pm
Monday to Thursday and 2 to 8 pm Friday.

The cheapest places to rent bikes are at
the train stations: Westbahnhof, Südbahnhof, Franz Josefs Bahnhof, Wien Nord and
Floridsdorf. You can return them at a different station, subject to a €6.55 fee. Rates
r AS10 = €0.73

Cycling in Vienna

Vienna is a great city for cycling. We asked Pedal Power, Vienna's cycling-tour specialists, for their recommendations on where to go biking in and around Vienna, and this is what they came up with.

The old city is surrounded by a bike path on the Ringstrasse that gives travellers access to all the main sights except Schönbrunn Palace. For those who want to sweat, just head for the Vienna Woods. All trails there are open to biking.

If you want to get away from the normal sights then you can do a cemetery tour (Central Cemetery and St Mark's Cemetery) or a music tour to the places where Beethoven, Johann Strauss, Haydn and Mozart lived, worked and died. Or how about a Heurigen tour (*heurige* = new wine) to Bisamberg where the Viennese go to enjoy a Spritzer, or a ride through the new Donau-Auen National Park on the Danube just south-east of Vienna? Pedal Power has maps and written descriptions for all of these, as well as information on scenic train routes that you can combine with a bike trip.

Want to get out of the city? Take a bike and head north-west or south-east on the Danube Valley Bike Trail. The 335km from Passau (German border) to Vienna is an unforgettable trip, always on the river, winding back and forth, riding through vineyards and villages with cheap accommodation (private rooms) and good wine and food. Heading south-east you can bike all the way to Budapest or turn south in Hainburg and cycle around Lake Neusiedl. Half of the lake is in Austria and half of it is in Hungary. Again, there is a bike path the whole way.

Rick (USA), Laurie (NZ) & Susanne (Austria)

are €13.10 per day, reduced to €8.75 after 3 pm or with that day's train ticket. At Südbahnhof you can return them as late as midnight; in Westbahnhof it's until 10 pm. Bikes can be carried on the S-Bahn and U-Bahn (in a separate carriage on the U6 line) outside rush-hour times, for half the adult fare. Pedal Power (see under Other Tours at the end of this chapter) also rents out bikes and supplies cycling accessories. The city of Vienna has plans to make bicycles available for free rental – inquire at the Rathaus.

WALKING

The sights in the Innere Stadt can easily be seen on foot; indeed, the main arteries of Kärntner Strasse, Graben and Kohlmarkt are pedestrian only. To visit anything else it's best to buy a transport pass. Be careful not to walk in the cycle lanes that dissect many pavements.

A walking tour of the city centre is suggested under Innere Stadt in the Things to See & Do chapter; for walks farther afield, turn to the Hiking section under Activities later in that chapter.

FIACRES

More of a tourist novelty than a mode of transport, a fiacre *(Fiaker)* is a traditional-style open carriage drawn by a pair of horses. They can be found lined up Stephansplatz, Albertinaplatz and Held platz at the Hofburg. Commanding €36 for a 15- to 20-minute trot, these hors must be among Vienna's richest inhabitants Drivers generally speak English and point out places of interest en route. Drivers al quote the same price, but you could try to ain.

euro currency c

Reisebuchladen (Map 7; ☎ 317 33 84, e robinreisen@vienna.at), 09, Kolingasse 6, conducts an alternative to the normal sightseeing tour, concentrating on 'Red Vienna' buildings like the Karl-Marx-Hof and Art Nouveau sights like Otto Wagner's Kirche am Steinhof. The tour is called 'Traum & Wirklichkeit' (Dream & Reality) and costs around €27 per person. The guide is not afraid to reveal uncomplimentary details about Vienna. Schedules depend upon demand and the tour is in German unless there are enough English speakers.

Boat Tours

These operate from early April to late October. DDSG Blue Danube (Map 7; ☎ 588 80-0, fax -440, e info@ddsg-blue-danube .at) has a 95-minute 'Hundertwasser Tour', in a boat that's been given the Hundertwasser design treatment (€9.45). It departs four times a day – get on board at the Danube Canal (Schwedenplatz) or at the Danube River (Reichsbrücke).

don't see as much of the water as you might expect. Donau Schiffahrt Pyringer-Zopper (☎ 715 15 25-20, e dspz@donau schiffahrtwien.at) does almost identical Danube circuits (€8.75 or €13.10). Its departure points are also Schwedenplatz and Reichsbrücke.

Tickets for all tours are available from the departure point.

Other Tours

Pedal Power (Map 4; ☎ 729 72 34, fax 729 72 35, e office@pedalpower.at), 02, Ausstellungsstrasse 3, conducts half-day bicycle tours in and around Vienna from 1 May to 31 October, starting 10 am. Tours cost €23 (€19 for students), or €16 if you have your own bike. You can register online at www.pedalpower.at.

On weekends and holidays from May to October you can take a one-hour tour of Vienna by 'old-time tram'. The departure point is Karlsplatz and the cost is €14.55 (€5.10 for children); for information call ☎ 7909-440 26.

THINGS

centre, called the Innere Stadt (inner city, ie, the 1st district). Many lesser sights that are not covered in this chapter are mentioned in *Vienna from A to Z*, a 110-page booklet available from the tourist office (€3.65) and shops. This outlines over 200 sights, and includes walking-tour suggestions. The tourist office has a useful museums leaflet listing opening times and

Highlights

The prime sights in the centre are Stephansdom, the Hofburg, and the Kunsthistoriches Museum. Farther afield, other main attractions are the palaces of Schönbrunn and Belvedere. In addition to exploring these places, visitors might enjoy:

- A tram ride round the Ringstrasse
- The chaos and clutter of the Naschmarkt flea market
- The sights and sounds of Kärntner Strasse and Graben
- People-watching in a traditional coffee house
- A night on the wine in a *Heurigen*
- The elaborate rides and strange sculptures in the Prater amusement park
- The bizarre waxworks in the Josephinum museum
- The unusual architecture of Friedensreich Hundertwasser
- The fountain and façade of the Parlament
- Art Nouveau creations: the Kirche am Steinhof and the Secession building

Some of these options are covered in the Places to Eat and Entertainment chapters. Overrated attractions include the Lipizzaner stallions in the Spanish Riding School, the 'Bermuda Triangle' drinking area, and touristy waltz shows. Taking a ride around the centre in a fiacre (Fiaker), one of Vienna's horse-drawn carriages, is fun but overpriced.

cle architecture.

The Vienna Card, which is valid for three days, is available from the tourist office, transport offices and hotels. It's worth getting if you plan on doing a lot of sightseeing in a concentrated period. It costs €15.20 and includes a public transport pass (worth €10.90) and gives discounts of 10% to 50% on some admission prices (museums, galleries, theatres etc), as well as shopping discounts.

Innere Stadt

The majestic architecture you see today in the city centre is largely due to the efforts of Emperor Franz Josef I. In 1857 he decided to tear down the redundant military fortifications and exercise grounds that surrounded the Innere Stadt and replace them with grandiose public buildings that would better reflect the power and the wealth of the Habsburg empire. The Ringstrasse, or Ring Boulevard, was laid out between 1858 and 1865, and in the decade that followed most of the impressive edifices that now line this thoroughfare were under construction. Franz Josef had extremely deep pockets to match his elaborate plans; consider this for an architectural shopping list: Staatsoper (built 1861–69), Musikverein (1867–69), Museum für angewandte Kunst (1868–71), Akademie der bildenden Künste (1872–76), Naturhistorisches Museum (1872–81), Rathaus (1872–83), Kunsthistorisches Museum (1872–91), Parlament (1873–83), Universität (1873–84), Burgtheater (1874–88), Justizpalast (1875–81) and the Heldenplatz section of the Neue Burg (1881–1908).

Ironically, WWI intervened and the empire was lost before Franz Josef's grand scheme was fully realised: a further wing the Hofburg was planned, and the palace and the giant museums opposite were to linked by a majestic walkway, rising arches over the Ringstrasse. Nevertheless, what was achieved is still extremely impressive. To fully appreciate the sheer scale of this endeavour, you should take a tour of at least some of the Ringstrasse by foot. The whole ring is about 5km long, but the grandest section, between the university and the opera, is under 2km (see the Ringstrasse section later in this chapter).

Instead of walking, you can pedal along the bike path on either side of the Ringstrasse, take tram No 1 (clockwise) or No 2 (anticlockwise), drive in a clockwise direction, or even hire a *fiaker* (fiacre; horse-drawn carriage).

All the sights in this section can be found on Map 7.

WALKING TOUR

This walk covers about 2.5km within the Innere Stadt, starting at the intersection of the Ringstrasse and Kärntner Strasse.

Kärntner Strasse

Walk north along Kärntner Strasse, passing the **Staatsoper** (State Opera) on your left. This may appear the equal of any other Ringstrasse edifice, but initial public reaction was so poor Eduard van der Nüll, one of the designers, ended up committing suicide. The building was all but destroyed in WWII and reopened only in 1955. The opulent interior is best explored during the interval of a performance (see the Entertainment chapter), though you can also take a guided tour for €4.40 (students €2.20, seniors €3.30); usually at 2 and 3 pm daily except Sunday – see the timetable outside.

Kärntner Strasse soon becomes an elegant pedestrian-only walkway of plush shops, trees, cafe tables and street entertainers. The oldest building here is **Esterházy Palace** at No 41, dating from 1698. It now houses the casino. Detour left down short Donnergasse to look at the **Donnerbrunnen** (1739) in Neuer Markt. The four naked figures (which were too revealing for Maria Theresa's taste) on this fountain represent the four main tributary rivers to the Danube: the Enns, March, Traun and Ybbs. Across the square is the **Kapuzinerkirche** (Church of the Capuchin Friars) and the **Kaisergruft** (see the Hofburg section later in this chapter for details).

Back on Kärntner Strasse, detour again down the second street on the left, Kärntner Durchgang. Here you'll find the **American Bar** designed by Adolf Loos in 1908. Loos was one of the prime exponents of a functional Art Nouveau style, though the facade here is somewhat garish. Next door is a strip club, **Chez Nous**. The dancers who disrobe for a living here forge a tenuous link with the artists of the 1950s who undressed in this same building. The premises was the base for the art club of the Wienergruppe (Vienna Group), performance artists and writers who indulged in all sorts of weird and wonderful activities. Events often involved the removal of clothing and the adoption of apparently obscene poses, both of which were guaranteed to enrage the conservative elite of the time (see Arts in the Facts about Vienna chapter for more information).

Stephansplatz to Michaelerplatz

From Kärntner Strasse, the street opens out into Stock im Eisen Platz. On the left-side corner, flush against the building and surrounded by protective perspex, is a **nail-studded stump**. Nobody quite knows why this 16th-century tree trunk acquired its crude metal jacket, but the commonly touted explanation is that each blacksmith who left the city would bang in a nail for luck. Across the square is Stephansplatz and Vienna's prime landmark, **Stephansdom** (see separate heading later). Facing it is the unashamedly modern **Haas Haus**, built by Hans Hollein and opened in 1990. Many Viennese were rather unhappy about this curving silver structure crowding their beloved cathedral, but tourists seem happy enough to snap the spindly reflections of the Stephansdom spire in its rectangular windows.

Leading north-west from Stock im Eisen Platz is the broad pedestrian thoroughfare of Graben, another plush shopping street. Like Kärntner Strasse and Stephansplatz, it's a fine place to linger, soak up the atmosphere, and absorb the hubbub of voices and appreciate the musicianship of the buskers. Graben is dominated by the knobbly outline of the **Pestsäule** (Plague Column), completed in 1693 to commemorate the 75,000 or more victims of the Black Plague who perished in Vienna some 20 years earlier. Loos was also busy in Graben, creating the Schneidersalon Knize at No 10 and, rather appropriately given his surname, the toilets nearby.

Turn left into Kohlmarkt, so named because charcoal was once sold here. At No 14 is one of the most famous of the Konditorei-style cafes in Vienna, **Demel** (see Coffee Houses in the Places to Eat chapter). Just beyond is Michaelerplatz, with the dome of St Michael's Gate to the **Hofburg** towering above.

Loos Haus on Michaelerplatz (housing the Raiffeisenbank) is a typical example of the clean lines of Loos' work. Its austere appearance raised eyebrows when it was erected in 1910. It had the opposite effect on Franz Josef's eyebrows, causing him to frown in fury every time he saw it. His complaint? The lintel-less windows seemed to him to be 'windows without eyebrows'. The excavations in the middle of the square are of Roman origin. **Michaelerkirche**, on the square, betrays five centuries of architectural styles – 1327 (Romanesque chancel) to 1792 (baroque doorway angels).

Ringstrasse

Pass through St Michael's Gate and the adjacent courtyard to find yourself in Heldenplatz, with the vast curve of the new section of the Hofburg (see separate heading later in this chapter) on your left. Walk past the line of fiacres, noting the Gothic spire of the **Rathaus** rising above the trees to the right. Ahead, on the far side of the Ring, stand the rival identical twins, the **Naturhistorisches Museum** and the **Kunsthistorisches Museum** (the museums and the Rathaus are covered in more detail later in this chapter). These huge buildings are mirror-images of each other, and were the work of Gottfried Semper and Karl von Hasenauer. Between the museums is a large statue of Maria Theresa, surrounded by key figures of her reign. She sits regally, holding her right

hand out, palm upwards, in an early version of the 'gimme five' greeting.

Walk anticlockwise round the north side of the Ring and pause for a relaxing meander around the **Burggarten**. This garden was formerly reserved for the pleasure of the imperial family and high-ranking officials. Statues here include those of Mozart (1896; originally at Albertinaplatz) and of Franz Josef. It also has the **Schmetterlinghaus** (Butterfly House), in an Art Nouveau glasshouse, which is open 10 am to 4 pm daily (5 pm or later in summer); admission is €4.75 (€3.30 concession).

Return to the Ring and continue anticlockwise, passing a vast statue of a seated Goethe, until you reach the Staatsoper. Take a left down Operngasse to get to **Albertinaplatz**. The south-eastern extremity of the Hofburg is on your left, which contains the famous Albertina collection of graphic arts (see separate heading later in this chapter). On the square is a troubling work by Alfred Hrdlicka, created in 1988. This series of pale block-like sculptures commemorates Jews and other victims of war and fascism. The dark, squat shape with the barbed wire is a Jew washing the floor; the greyish block originally came from the Mauthausen concentration camp. The tourist office is opposite.

Turn right along Philharmonikerstrasse, passing between the opera and the **Hotel Sacher** (see the Places to Stay chapter), a famous five-star hotel and purveyor of an equally famous cake, the Sacher Torte. Sacher and Demel had a long-running dispute over who was the true creator of the authentic chocolate torte: Sacher was Metternich's cook, while Demel was pastry cook to the Habsburgs (see the boxed text 'Sacher Torte – More Than Just a Cake' in the Places to Eat chapter). Graham Greene was staying in the Hotel Sacher in 1948 (despite the fact that at the time the hotel was requisitioned solely for the use of British army officers) when he came up with the plot for *The Third Man*.

Another few steps will bring you back to Kärntner Strasse, with the Lower Austria tourist office on your left.

The Story behind the Story of *The Third Man*

'I had paid my last farewell to Harry a week ago, when his coffin was lowered into the frozen February ground, so that it was with incredulity that I saw him pass by, without a sign of recognition, among the host of strangers in the Strand.' Thus wrote Graham Greene on the back of an envelope. There it stayed, for many years, an idea without a context. Then Sir Alexander Korda asked him to write a film about the four-power occupation of postwar Vienna. The film was to be directed by Carol Reed, who had worked with Greene on an earlier film, *The Fallen Idol*.

Greene now had an opening scene and a framework. He still needed a plot. He flew to Vienna in 1948 and roamed the bomb-damaged streets, searching with increasing desperation for inspiration. Nothing came to mind until, with his departure imminent, Greene had lunch with a British intelligence officer. The conversation proved more nourishing than the meal. The officer told him about the underground police who patrolled the huge network of sewers beneath the city. He also waxed on the subject of the black-market trade in penicillin, which the racketeers exploited with no regard for the consequences. Greene put the two ideas together and created his story.

Another chance encounter completed the picture. After filming one night, Carol Reed went drinking in the Heurigen area of Sievering. There he discovered Anton Karas playing a zither and was mesmerised by the hypnotic rhythms the instrument produced. Although Karas could neither read nor write music, Reed flew him to London where he recorded the soundtrack. The bouncing, staggering refrain that became Harry Lime's theme dominated the film, became a chart hit and earned Karas a fortune.

As a final twist of serendipity, the most memorable lines of dialogue came not from the measured pen of Greene, but from the improvising mind of Orson Welles as Harry Lime. They were delivered in front of the camera in the Prater, under the towering stanchions of the Ferris wheel: 'In Italy for 30 years under the Borgias they had warfare, terror, murder, bloodshed – they produced Michelangelo, Leonardo da Vinci and the Renaissance. In Switzerland they had brotherly love, 500 years of democracy and peace, and what did that produce? The cuckoo clock. So long Holly.'

And in Vienna they had the ideal setting for a classic film.

STEPHANSDOM

The latticework spire of this Gothic masterpiece rises high above the city and is a focal point for all visitors.

Stephansdom (St Stephen's Cathedral) was built on the site of a 12th-century church, and its remains – the Riesentor (Giant's Gate) and the Heidentürme (Towers of the Heathens) – are incorporated into the present building. Both features are Romanesque in style; the **Riesentor** (so named for the mammoth's tibia, mistaken for a giant's shin, that once hung there) is the main western entrance, and is topped by a tympanum of lattice patterns and statues. The church was re-created in Gothic style at the behest of Habsburg Duke Rudolf IV in 1359, who laid the foundation stone and earned himself the epithet of 'The Founder' in the process.

The dominating feature of the church is the skeletal **Südturm**, or south tower, nicknamed 'Steffl'. It stands 136.7m high and was completed in 1433 after 75 years of building work. Ascending the 343 steps will bring you to the cramped viewing platform for an impressive panorama (open 9 am to 5.30 pm; €2.20). It was to be matched by a companion tower on the north side, but the imperial purse withered and the Gothic style went out of fashion, so the half-completed tower was topped off with a Renaissance cupola in 1579. Austria's largest bell, the **Pummerin** ('boomer bell'), was installed here in 1952; it weighs 21 tonnes. The north tower, accessible by a lift, is open from at least 9 am to 6 pm daily; entry costs €2.95.

A striking feature of the exterior is the glorious **tiled roof**, showing dazzling chevrons on one end and the Austrian eagle on the

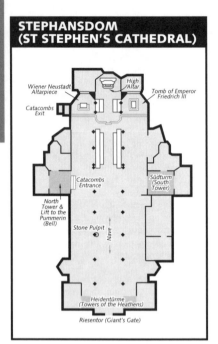

STEPHANSDOM
(ST STEPHEN'S CATHEDRAL)

Wiener Neustadt Altarpiece

High Altar

Tomb of Emperor Friedrich III

Catacombs Exit

Catacombs Entrance

Südturm (South Tower)

North Tower & Lift to the Pummerin (Bell)

Stone Pulpit

Nave

Heidentürme (Towers of the Heathens)

Riesentor (Giant's Gate)

other; a good perspective is gained from the north-east of Stephansplatz. The cathedral suffered severe damage during a fire in 1945, but donations flowed in from all over Austria and the cathedral was completely rebuilt and reopened in just three years.

Interior walls and pillars are decorated with fine statues and side altars. A magnificent Gothic piece is the **stone pulpit**, fashioned in 1515 by Anton Pilgram. The expressive faces of the four fathers of the church (saints Augustine, Ambrose, Gregory and Jerome) are at the centre of the design, yet Pilgram himself can be seen peering out from a window below. The baroque **high altar** in the main chancel shows the stoning of St Stephen. The left chancel has the winged Wiener Neustadt altarpiece, dating from 1447; the right chancel has the Renaissance red marble tomb of Friedrich III. Under his guidance the city became a bishopric (and the church a cathedral) in 1469. Don't forget to study

the decorations and statue groups on the outside of the cathedral: at the rear the agony of the Crucifixion is well captured, although some irreverent souls attribute Christ's pained expression to toothache.

The **Katakomben** (catacombs) in the cathedral are open daily, with frequent tours between 10.30 am and 4.30 pm (in English if there's sufficient demand; €2.95). The tour includes viewing a mass grave and a bone house, all that remains of countless plague victims. You also see rows of urns containing the internal organs of the Habsburgs. One of the many privileges of being a Habsburg was to be dismembered and dispersed after death: their hearts are in the Augustinerkirche in the Hofburg and the rest of their bits are in the Kaisergruft.

HOFBURG

The huge Hofburg (Imperial Palace) is an impressive repository of culture and heritage. The Habsburgs based themselves here for over six centuries, from the first emperor (Rudolph I in 1279) to the last in 1918 (Charles I). In that time new sections were periodically added, resulting in the current mix of styles and the massive dimensions. The palace now houses the offices of the Austrian president. The Spanish Riding School (see the Entertainment chapter) is also based in the Hofburg.

The oldest part is the **Schweizerhof** (Swiss Courtyard), named after the Swiss guards who used to protect its precincts. Dating from the 13th century and recently renovated, this small courtyard gives access to the Royal Chapel and the Imperial Treasury. The Renaissance Swiss Gate dates from 1553. It adjoins a much larger courtyard, **In der Burg**, with a large **monument** to Emperor Franz II at its centre. The buildings around it are all from different eras.

The most active phase of building was carried out from the second half of the 19th century to WWI. Sections created at this time include the impressive St Michael's domed entrance and the Neue Burg, from which Hitler addressed a rally during his triumphant 1938 visit to Vienna after the Anschluss. Plans called for the building of a further

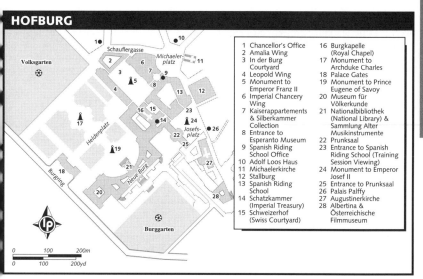

HOFBURG

1 Chancellor's Office	16 Burgkapelle
2 Amalia Wing	(Royal Chapel)
3 In der Burg	17 Monument to
Courtyard	Archduke Charles
4 Leopold Wing	18 Palace Gates
5 Monument to	19 Monument to Prince
Emperor Franz II	Eugene of Savoy
6 Imperial Chancery	20 Museum für
Wing	Völkerkunde
7 Kaiserappartements	21 Nationalbibliothek
& Silberkammer	(National Library) &
Collection	Sammlung Alter
8 Entrance to	Musikinstrumente
Esperanto Museum	22 Prunksaal
9 Spanish Riding	23 Entrance to Spanish
School Office	Riding School (Training
10 Adolf Loos Haus	Session Viewing)
11 Michaelerkirche	24 Monument to Emperor
12 Stallburg	Josef II
13 Spanish Riding	25 Entrance to Prunksaal
School	26 Palais Palffy
14 Schatzkammer	27 Augustinerkirche
(Imperial Treasury)	28 Albertina &
15 Schweizerhof	Österreichische
(Swiss Courtyard)	Filmmuseum

wing, the mirror image of this curving facade on Heldenplatz, but the Habsburg era ended before it could be instigated.

Augustinerkirche

The Augustinerkirche (Augustinian Church) is one of the older parts of the Hofburg, dating from the early 14th century. Although Gothic in style, the interior was converted to baroque in the 17th century, and its original appearance was restored in 1784. Important tombs include that of Archduchess Marie Christina, designed by Canova. In an inner sanctum are the hearts of the Habsburgs, but this room can only be visited by prior appointment (☎ 533 70 99; not Sunday).

Kaiserappartements

The 22 rooms in the Kaiserappartements (Imperial Apartments) are as opulent as you might expect, with fine furniture, hanging tapestries and bulbous crystal chandeliers. The dining room has a table for 20 laid out in suitably elegant fashion. Rooms in this part of the palace were occupied by Franz Josef I and Empress Elisabeth. They're worth seeing, though you might want to skip them if your appetite for such things is

limited, and take in the interior finery of Schloss Schönbrunn instead.

The adjoining **Silberkammer** collection is included in the entry price. Laying a table with some of this silver and porcelain would certainly impress the in-laws; the largest silver service here can take care of 140 dinner guests.

Opening hours are 9 am to 5 pm daily, and admission costs €6.95 (€5.45 for students under 26, ISIC card needed; €2.55 for children). Hourly guided tours are only in German; English-speakers can hire an audioguide (€2.95 either way).

Burgkapelle

This Gothic Burgkapelle (Royal Chapel) is where the Vienna Boys' Choir sings at Sunday Mass (see the Entertainment chapter). It has a vaulted roof and rich fittings around the altar, but is not particularly spectacular without the choir. Opening times are weekdays only, 11 am to 3 pm (to 1 pm on Friday); it's closed in July and August.

Schatzkammer

The Schatzkammer (Imperial Treasury) contains secular and ecclesiastical treasures of great value and splendour. The sheer wealth exhibited in the collection of crown jewels is staggering: Room 7 has a 2860-carat Colombian emerald, a 416-carat balas ruby and a 492-carat aquamarine. The imperial crown (Room 2) dates from the 10th century, and has eight gold plates; precious gems alternate with enamel plaques showing religious scenes. The private crown of Rudolf II (1602) is a more delicate piece, with gems interspersed by four beautifully engraved gold bas-reliefs, showing Rudolf in battle and at three of his coronations.

Room 5 contains mementoes of Marie Louise, the second wife of Napoleon; the best piece here is the cradle donated by the city of Paris to their son. The golden bees around the sides are a standard motif of Napoleonic state artefacts. Room 8 has two unusual objects formerly owned by Ferdinand I: a 75cm-wide bowl carved from a single piece of agate, and a narwal tusk (243cm long), once claimed to have been a unicorn's horn.

The religious relics include fragments of the True Cross, one of the nails from the Crucifixion, and one of the thorns from Christ's crown. Ecclesiastical vestments display delicate and skilled work.

This section also contains some rather more worldly artefacts, like the extremely elaborate Column of the Virgin Mary made from gilded silver, which stands over 1m tall and is encased with 3700 precious stones – a modest conversation piece fit for any mantelpiece.

The Treasury is open 10 am to 6 pm Wednesday to Sunday. The entry price of €7.30 (€5.10 concession) includes use of a hi-tech personal electronic guide (English available). Allow anything from 30 minutes to two hours to get around.

Prunksaal

This is a baroque hall of the national library (entrance at Josefsplatz) created by Johann Bernhard Fischer von Erlach and his son Joseph between 1723 and 1726. It was commissioned by Charles VI; his statue stands under the central church-like dome, which itself has a fresco depicting the emperor's apotheosis (by Daniel Gran). Leather-bound scholarly tomes line the walls, and the upper storey of shelves is flanked by an elegantly curving wood balcony. Rare ancient volumes (mostly 15th-century) are stored within glass cabinets, with pages opened to beautifully drawn sections of text. The hall is open 10 am to 4 pm daily (to 7 pm Thursday, 2 pm Sunday and holidays). From late October to early May, hours reduce to 10 am to 2 pm Monday to Saturday. Entry is €4.40 (€2.95 concession). The Esperanto Museum for artificial languages is also part of the library (entrance in St Michael's Gate; free).

Sammlung Alter Musikinstrumente

The Sammlung Alter Musikinstrumente (Collection of Ancient Musical Instruments) is the best part of the three-museums-in-one in the Neue Hofburg. Before you enter the first room, pick up the headphones (free from the desk. They're activated by infrared as you walk round, giving a relaxing and evocative musical accompaniment to the instruments on display. Instruments of all shapes and sizes are to be found, including horns shaped like serpents and violins with carved faces. There are some richly ornate pieces, such as the baroque cabinet incorporating a keyboard from the early 17th century (in Saal XI). Different rooms are dedicated to different composers (eg Haydn, Mozart and Beethoven), and contain instruments played by those notables.

The museum is open 10 am to 6 pm Wednesday to Monday and admission costs €4.40 (€2.95 concession). This includes entry to two adjoining collections. The **Ephesus Museum** has relief statues and a scale model of the famous archaeological site in Turkey. The **Hofjagd und Rüstkammer** (arms and armour) collection dates mostly from the 15th and 16th centuries and has some fine examples of ancient armour, note the bizarre pumpkin-shaped helmet from the 15th century.

Museum für Völkerkunde

The Museum für Völkerkunde (Ethnological Museum) expounds on non-European cultures, usually with the aid of temporary exhibitions. Its Mexican pre-Colombian exhibits are important. Opening hours are 10 am to 4 pm Wednesday to Monday; admission costs from €3.65 (€1.85 concession), depending upon exhibitions.

Albertina

The Albertina is a famous and extensive collection of graphic arts, comprising some 40,000 drawings. Only part of the collection is ever on display at one time. Its premises in the Hofburg (Albertinaplatz wing) are being renovated, and it is expected to reopen in September 2002.

Kaisergruft

Although not part of the Hofburg complex, this is where its residents ended up. The Kaisergruft (Imperial Burial Vault), opened in 1633, is beneath the Kapuzinerkirche (Church of the Capuchin Friars) on Neuer Markt. It was instigated by Empress Anna (1585–1618), and her body and that of her husband, Emperor Matthias (1557–1619), were the first to be placed here. Since then, all but three of the Habsburg dynasty found their way here, the last being Empress Zita in 1989.

It's interesting to observe how fashions change through the ages even in death; tombs range from the unadorned to the ostentatious. By far the most elaborate caskets are those portraying 18th-century baroque pomp, such as the huge double sarcophagus containing Maria Theresa and Francis I, with fine scenes engraved in the metal and plenty of angels and other ornamentation. The tomb of Charles VI is also striking and has been expertly restored. Both of these were the work of Balthasar Moll.

The only non-Habsburg of the 138 people here is the Countess Fuchs, a formative influence on the youthful Maria Theresa. The vault is open 9.30 am to 4 pm daily and entry costs €2.95 (€2.20 concession).

LIPIZZANER MUSEUM

This museum at 01, Reitschulestrasse 2 will show you everything you might want to know about Lipizzaner stallions and the antics they get up to in the Spanish Riding School and the stud farm where they're reared. There's English text, but the content is a little thin. Windows allow a view directly into the stallion stables, albeit obscured by thick glass and fine mesh. It's open 9 am to 6 pm daily, and entry costs €5.10 (€3.65 concession).

MINORITENPLATZ VICINITY

The **Minoritenkirche**, on Minoritenplatz, is a 14th-century church that later received a baroque facelift. Across the square to the south is the **Bundeskanzleramt** (Federal Chancellor's Office), 01, Ballhausplatz 2. It's notable mainly for its historical significance as a seat of power since the time of Maria Theresa. Prince Metternich had his offices here, and it is where Chancellor Dollfuss was murdered by the Nazis on 25 July 1934. In 2000 the square outside became the meeting point for demonstrations (every Thursday) against the inclusion of the FPÖ in the federal government (see Government & Politics in the Facts about Vienna chapter).

Take the short Leopold Figl Gasse east, to reach Herrengasse, and then turn left (north). On your right you'll pass **Palais Ferstal**, housing Café Central (see Coffee Houses in the Places to Eat chapter), and the Freyung Passage, an arcade containing elegant shops. On your left, as the road opens out into Freyung, you'll see the classic baroque facade of **Palais Kinsky**, built by Johann Lukas von Hildebrandt in 1716. Across Freyung is the **Schottenkirche** (Church of the Scots), which had its origins in the 12th century, though the present facade dates from the 19th century. There's an art and artefacts museum in the adjoining monastery (open Thursday to Sunday; €3.65).

AM HOF

The Babenberg rulers of Vienna once had a fortress on this square before moving to the Hofburg, and there are also Roman ruins here. On the north side at No 10 is the **former civic armoury** (16th century), with an impressively elaborate facade. The Mariensäule column in the centre of the square is dedicated to Mary and was erected in 1667. The **Kirche Am Hof**, on the south-east side, is baroque, adapted from its fire-damaged Gothic predecessor. Behind the church is Schulhof, where there's the **Uhren Museum** (see the boxed text 'Municipal Museums' later in this chapter) and the **Puppen & Spielzeug Museum** (Doll & Toy Museum; closed Monday; €4.40, €2.20 concession).

JUDENPLATZ

The old Jewish quarter, Judenplatz, is just off the north-east corner of Am Hof. Here you'll find an attractive square, underneath which are excavations of a medieval synagogue. At Judenplatz 8 a museum documenting Jewish life in Vienna is being prepared. In the centre of the square is a pale, bulky memorial to Austrian Jews who perished in the Holocaust, which received mixed reviews when it was unveiled in October 2000 (see the boxed text). On the north side of Judenplatz is the former **Böhmische Hofkanzlei** (Bohemian Court Chancery). Walk round to Wipplingerstrasse to see its striking facade by JB Fischer von Erlach; opposite is the plainer **Altes Rathaus**, where there's a museum and a courtyard fountain.

JÜDISCHES MUSEUM

The Jüdisches Museum (Jewish Museum) at 01, Dorotheergasse 11 uses holograms and an assortment of objects to document the history of the Jews in Vienna, from the first settlements at Judenplatz in the 13th century up to the present. The Jews in Vienna have had a tumultuous history. Jews were first expelled in 1420 (the 300 who remained were burned to death in 1421) and again in 1670. The darkest chapter in the story came with the arrival of the Nazis in 1938 and the consequent persecution and curtailment of Jewish civil rights. Violence exploded on the night of 9 November 1938, known as the *Reichskristallnacht*. All the synagogues except the **Stadttempel**, 01, Seitenstettengasse 4, were destroyed, and 7000 Jews were arrested and sent to concentration camps. Jews in Vienna now number 12,000, compared to 185,000 before 1938. The museum is open 10 am to 6 pm (9 pm Thursday) daily except Saturday, and entry costs €5.10 (€2.95 concession).

PETERSKIRCHE

Peterskirche (St Peter's Church; 1733), on Petersplatz, is another example of a fine baroque interior. The fresco in the dome was painted by JM Rottmayr. It is said that Charlemagne founded the first church that stood on this site, an event depicted in the exterior relief on the south-east side.

Holocaust Stories in 'Nameless Library'

When you reach Vienna's Judenplatz, you'll be confronted by the squat, boxlike structure that is Austria's first Holocaust memorial. Finally unveiled in October 2000 after several years of dispute, it pays homage to the 65,000 Austrian Jews who were killed during the Anschluss.

The stark, pale concrete sculpture doesn't offer the relief of a curved line or pleasing ornamentation. 'This monument shouldn't be beautiful,' said Nazi-hunter Simon Wiesenthal at the unveiling. 'It must hurt.' British sculptor Rachel Whiteread created the 'nameless library' to represent the untold stories of Holocaust victims. It has the names of Austrian concentration camps written across its base.

The monument sits on the site of a recently discovered medieval synagogue where dozens of Jews committed suicide in 1421, to escape forcible baptism by the Christians. This has brought objections to the monument from several members of the Jewish community, who claim it stands on a sacred site. And they're not the only ones – Viennese residents have expressed considerable criticism of the sculpture.

Vienna's mayor, Michael Haupl, said at the unveiling that the memorial is 'necessary for Austria', an unfortunate reminder that anti-Semitism has played such a role in the country's history. He said that no-one can any longer deny the atrocities that took place in Austria 60 years ago, and that the new memorial will 'send a message to the world'.

The neogothic splendour of the Rathaus

ohlmarkt by night ...

... and the Burgtheatre by tram

Relaxation and recreation on the blue Danube

Imperial palace as citizens' loungeroom – the Hofburg from Heldenplatz

ANKERUHR

The picturesque Art Nouveau Ankeruhr (Anker clock) at Hoher Markt 10–11 was created by Franz von Matsch in 1911. It's named after the Anker Insurance Co, who commissioned it. Over a 12-hour period, figures slowly pass across the clock face, indicating the time against a static measure showing the minutes. Figures represented range from Marcus Aurelius (the Roman emperor who died in Vienna in AD 180) to Josef Haydn, with Eugene of Savoy, Maria Theresa and others in between. Details of who's who are outlined on a plaque on the wall below. Tourists flock here at noon, when all the figures trundle past in succession, and organ music from the appropriate period is piped out.

FLEISCHMARKT

This street, formerly a meat market, has a distinctive **Greek Orthodox church** at No 3. Next door is a quaint and famous old tavern, the Griechenbeisl (see the Places to Eat chapter) at No 11. Farther along is a cluster of **Art Nouveau buildings**. No 14, built by F Dehm and F Olbricht between 1889 and 1899, exhibits gold and stucco embellishments. No 7 (Max Kropf; 1899) is where the film director Billy Wilder lived from 1914–24. Arthur Baron was responsible for Nos 1 and 3 (1910), now home to a bank and a Spar supermarket. A few steps to the north of Fleischmarkt is **Ruprechtskirche** (St Rupert's Church), Ruprechtplatz, the oldest church in Vienna, dating from around the 11th century.

POSTSPARKASSE

The celebrated Post Office Savings Bank building at 01, Georg Coch Platz was the work of Otto Wagner between 1904 and 1906 and from 1910 to 1912. The design and choice of materials were both innovative. Inside, note the sci-fi aluminium heating ducts and the naked stanchions – pared down functionality *par excellence*. The main savings hall can be perused during office hours (8 am to 3 pm Monday to Friday, to 5.30 pm Thursday), and there is an information counter. Compare the modern appearance of the Postsparkasse with the classical-looking former **Kriegsministerium** (Imperial War Ministry) on the Ring opposite, which was built around the same time.

DOMINIKANERKIRCHE

Dominikanerkirche (Dominican Church; 1634), 01, Postgasse 4, was built on the site of an earlier church and has a fine baroque interior, with white stucco, frescoes, and even the imperial double-headed eagle on the ceiling. The Dominicans first came to Vienna in 1226.

HAUS DER MUSIK

It's strange that this city of music should wait so long to get a House of Music (Haus der Musik), 01, Seilerstätte 30. Imaginatively presented, it opened in June 2000 and is well worth a visit.

There are three separate sections on three floors. Floor 2 explains the physics of sound, using fun interactive computer terminals. You can also play around with sampled sounds and record your own CD. Floor 3 has interesting rooms devoted to the great composers (hand-held commentary in English) – Haydn, Mozart, Beethoven, Schubert, Strauss, Mahler and the Viennese School. The 'virtual conductor' room allows you to conduct the Vienna Philharmonic (the recording responds to your movements). Floor 4 has experimental and electronic music, which you can also modify yourself.

You could easily spend three hours here. It's open 10 am to 10 pm daily and admission costs €8 (€5.85 concession).

On the 1st floor is a separate section devoted to the Vienna Philharmonic (€5.10, €4.05 concession), though it's rather brief and most visitors' appetite for things musical would have been satiated already.

Ringstrasse & Surrounds

Starting north-west of the Ring, these sights can be found in anticlockwise order around Ringstrasse.

JOSEPHINUM

The Josephinum (Map 3), 09, Währinger Strasse 25, is also known as the Museum of Medical History (Geschichte der Medizin). Go to the 1st floor in the right-hand wing. Opening hours are 9 am to 3 pm Monday to Friday (not public holidays) and admission costs €1.50 (€0.75 concession). It's a small museum but still fascinating, and a little bizarre.

The prime exhibits are the ceroplastic and wax specimen models of the human frame, created over 200 years ago by Felice Fontana and Paolo Mascagni. They were used in the Academy of Medico-Surgery, instigated by Josef II in 1785 to try to improve the skills of army surgeons who lacked medical qualifications. These models, showing the make-up of the body under the skin, were intended to give the students a three-dimensional understanding of the organs, bones, veins and muscles. Three rooms of this gory lot will make you feel like you've wandered onto the set of a tacky horror movie. One strange touch is the necklace they've put on the female model lying down in the first room. Why this ornamentation? She's hardly ready for a sophisticated night out, seeing that half her torso is missing.

The rest of the museum contains arcane medical instruments, photos of past practitioners, accounts of unpleasant-looking operations and ailments, and some texts (one book is thoughtfully left open on a page dealing with the dissection of eyeballs).

SIGMUND FREUD MUSEUM

Sigmund Freud is one of Vienna's most famous sons. This museum (Map 3) is housed at 09, Berggasse 19, in the apartments where he lived and psychoanalysed from 1891 to 1938 (until he fled from the Nazis). It contains furniture, Freud's possessions (such as his case embossed with the initials SF), letters, documents and photographs; very detailed notes (in English) illuminate the offerings. Students and Freud freaks could spend a while here; most casual observers would probably just saunter through the rooms and wonder to what extent Freud's theories were influenced by that terracotta votive offering of male genitals (exhibit 35 on the ornaments shelf in the waiting room). There's also a fairly dull home movie of Freud, narrated by his daughter Anna. The museum is open 9 am to 5 pm daily (to 6 pm in summer) and costs €4.40 (€2.95 concession).

VOTIVKIRCHE

In 1853 Franz Josef survived an assassination attempt when a knife-wielding Hungarian failed to find the emperor's neck through his collar – reports suggested that a metal button deflected the blade. The Votivkirche (Votive Church; Map 7) was commissioned in thanks for his lucky escape and is located at 09, Rooseveltplatz. Heinrich von Ferstel designed this twin-towered Gothic construction, which was completed in 1879. The tomb of Count Niklas Salm, one of the architects of the successful defence against the Turks in 1529, is in the Baptismal Chapel. The interior is bedecked in frescoes and bulbous chandeliers. Take note of the interesting stained-glass windows – one to the left of the altar tells of Nazism and the ravages of war. The church is open 9 am to 1 pm and 4 to 6.30 pm Tuesday to Saturday and 9 am to 1 pm Sunday.

UNIVERSITY

The new university building (Map 7) on Dr Karl Lueger Ring was constructed in the style of the Italian Renaissance during the Ringstrasse developments. The university itself actually dates from 1365 (hence the 1884 Ringstrasse site is only 'new' in comparison!); the original building still exists at 01, Bäckerstrasse 20.

RATHAUS

The impressive Rathaus (City Hall; Map 7) 01, Rathausplatz, is a neogothic structure completed in 1883 and built by Friedrich von Schmidt. The main spire soars to 102m if you include the pennant held by the knight at the top. It is built around an arcaded courtyard where concerts are sometimes held. Free guided tours of the building are conducted at 1 pm on Monday, Wednesday and Friday, except when the city council is session, or if there's fewer than five people (meet at the Rathaus information office).

Between the Rathaus and the Ring is the **Rathaus Park**, with fountains, benches and several statues. It is split in two by a wide walkway lined by statues of notable people from Vienna's past.

BURGTHEATER

Opposite the Rathaus is the **Burgtheater** (National Theatre; Map 7; ☎ 514 44-4140), which is one of the prime theatre venues in the German-speaking world. It was built in Renaissance style to designs by Gottfried Semper and Karl von Hasenauer, and had to be rebuilt after sustaining severe damage in WWII. The interior is equally grand and has stairway frescoes painted by the Klimt brothers, Gustav and Ernst. Guided tours in English are conducted at 3 pm on most days (€3.65/2.20 for adults/students).

VOLKSGARTEN

The Volksgarten (People's Garden; Map 7) is next to the Burgtheater. It's attractively laid out, with a riot of rosebushes and several statues (eg, to the playwright Franz Grillparzer). There's also the **Temple of Theseus**, an imitation of the one in Athens. The Volksgarten is open 6 am to 10 pm daily (8 pm from October to March).

PARLAMENT

The Parlament building (Map 7) is on the opposite side of the Ring to the Volksgarten, and was designed by Theophil Hansen. The building is in Greek revival style, with huge pillars and figures lining the roof. The beautiful **Athena Fountain** in the front was sculptured by Karl Kundmann. Grecian architecture was chosen, as Greece was the home of democracy; Athena is the Greek goddess of wisdom. It was hoped that both qualities would be permanent features of Austrian politics.

Parlament is the seat of the two federal assemblies, the Federal Council (Bundesrat) and the National Council (Nationalrat). Guided tours (except during sessions) are conducted Monday to Friday at 11 am and 3 pm (also at 9 and 10 am, 1 and 2 pm from

mid-July to mid-September). Admission costs €2.95.

On its southern side is the German Renaissance **Justizpalast** (Palace of Justice), home of Austria's Supreme Court.

NATURHISTORISCHES MUSEUM

The Naturhistorisches Museum (Map 7; Museum of Natural History), 01, Maria Theresien Platz, is the scientific counterpart of the Kunsthistorisches Museum (Museum of Fine Arts) opposite. The building is as grand but the exhibits aren't quite in the same league. There are still plenty of interesting things to see , particularly along the lines of minerals, meteorites and assorted animal remains in jars. Zoology and anthropology are covered in detail and there's a children's corner, some good dinosaur exhibits and a room with 3D projections of micro-organisms. The 25,000-year-old statuette from Willendorf is here (see the Danube Valley in the Excursions chapter) – though she's a mere youngster compared to the 32,000 BC statuette from Stratzing (the oldest figurative sculpture in the world).

Opening hours are 9 am to 6.30 pm Thursday to Monday (to 9 pm Wednesday). Admission costs €3.65 (students €1.85). Tours of the roof are possible (€5.85 extra).

KUNSTHISTORISCHES MUSEUM

The Kunsthistorisches Museum (Map 7; Museum of Fine Arts), 01, Maria Theresien Platz, is one of the finest museums in Europe and should not be missed. The Habsburgs were great collectors, and the huge extent of lands under their control led to many important works of art being funnelled back to Vienna.

Rubens was appointed to the service of a Habsburg governor in Brussels, so it is not surprising that the museum has one of the best collections of his work in the world. The collection of paintings by Pieter Bruegel the Elder is also unrivalled. The building itself is delightful and was designed to reflect the works it displays, with older architectural styles faithfully reproduced. No expense was spared in construction and all the marble here is genuine.

Ceilings are superbly decorated with murals and stucco embellishments.

Halfway up the stairway to the 1st floor you'll see Canova's sculpture *Theseus & the Minotaur*. On the walls above the arches are the portraits of some of the more important artists exhibited in the museum, such as Dürer, Rembrandt and Raphael. The murals between the arches were created by three artists, including a young Gustav Klimt (north wall), painted before he broke with classical tradition.

It's impossible to see the whole museum in one visit, so concentrate on specific areas. Temporary exhibitions (which may cost extra) sometimes cause reorganisation of rooms, and famous works are occasionally lent to other museums. Various guides and plans are for sale in the shops – you'll probably be able to make do with the *Kunsthistorisches Museum Vienna* booklet in English for €1.50, which includes a floorplan of the museum, and information on sister collections (eg, the Schatzkammer and Sammlung Alter Musikinstrumente in the Hofburg; the Wagenburg in Schönbrunn). Guided tours in English depart at 1 am and 3 pm except Monday (€2.20), and provide an interesting analysis of a handful of the main paintings. The museum is open 10 am to 6 pm Tuesday to Sunday, with the picture gallery closing at 9 pm on Thursday. Entry to the museum is usually €7.30 (€5.10 concession). See the Web site at www.khm.at.

Ground Floor

To the right (the west wing) upon entering is the Egyptian collection, including the burial chamber of Prince Kaninisut. Amid the many sarcophagi and statues in this section are the mummified remains of various animals (falcon, baboon, cat etc).

Next come the Greek and Roman collections, including sculptures, urns, vases and Etruscan art. One of the most impressive pieces is the *Gemma Augustea cameo* (Saal XV), made from onyx in AD 10, with delicately carved white figures on a bluish-brown background.

The east wing contains a collection of sculpture and decorative arts covering Austrian high baroque, Renaissance, mannerism and medieval art. There is some exquisite 17th-century glassware and ornaments, and unbelievably lavish clocks from the 16th and 17th centuries (Saals XXXV and XXXVII). But the prime item here (Saal XXVII) is the salt cellar (1543) by Benvenuto Cellini, made in gold for Francis I of France. It depicts two naked deities: the goddess of the earth, reclining on elephants, with a small temple by her side where the pepper was kept, and Poseidon, god of the sea, making himself comfortable on a team of sea horses with the salt in a bowl by his trident. Hidden beneath the base are small wheels, so the cellar could be pushed easily around the table. This beautiful work of art begs an envious question: if the humble cruet set looked as good as this, what did the rest of the dining room look like?

First Floor

The Gemäldegalerie (picture gallery) on this floor is the most important part of the museum – you could lose yourself for hours wandering round whole rooms devoted to works by Bruegel, Dürer, Rubens, Rembrandt, Van Dyck, Cranach, Caravaggio, Canaletto, Titian and many others. Some rooms have information cards in English giving a critique of particular artists and their work.

East Wing This is devoted to German, Dutch and Flemish paintings. Saal X contains the Bruegel collection, amassed by Rudolf II. A familiar theme in Pieter Bruegel the Elder's work is nature, as in his cycle of seasonal scenes, three of which are shown here. *The Hunters in the Snow* (1565) portrays winter; the hunters return towards a Dutch-like frozen lake with frolicking skaters, beyond which rise some very un-Dutch-looking mountains. The viewer's eye is drawn into the scene by the flow of movement – a device commonly exploited by Bruegel. This is also seen in the atmospheric *The Return of the Herd* (1565), illustrating a glowering autumnal day. Bruegel's peasant scenes are also excellent, such as *The Battle Between Carnival & Lent* (1559), where the centre and foreground are dominated by carnival tomfoolery, with the dour, cowled and caped figures in religious processions pushed to the edges of the scene.

The next gallery (Saal XI) shows Flemish baroque, in vogue some 80 years later, with warm, larger-than-life scenes such as *The King Drinks* by Jacob Jordaens (with the revellers raising their glasses to a motto in Latin that translates as 'None resembles a fool more than the drunkard') and *The Fishmarket* by Frans Snyders.

Albrecht Dürer (1471–1528) is represented in Room 16. His brilliant use of colour is particularly shown in *The Holy Trinity Surrounded by All Saints*, originally an altarpiece. The *Martyrdom of 10,000 Christians* is another fine work.

The paintings by the mannerist Giuseppe Arcimboldo in Room 19 use a device well explored by Salvador Dali – familiar objects arranged to appear as something else. But Arcimboldo did it nearly 400 years earlier! His series of four composite pictures *Summer*, *Winter*, *Water* and *Fire* (1563–66) cleverly show faces composed of objects related to those particular themes.

Peter Paul Rubens (1577–1640) was a very influential figure because of his synthesis of northern and Italian traditions. His works can be seen in Saals XIII and XIV and in Room 20. Try to spot the difference between those he painted completely himself (eg, note the open brushwork and diaphanous quality of the fur in *Ildefonso Altar*) and those that he planned and finished but were mostly executed by his students (like the vivid but more rigid *Miracle of Ignatius Loyola*, a dramatic baroque picture displayed along with Rubens' initial study for the scene).

Rembrandt has several self-portraits in Saal XV. Vermeer's *The Allegory of Painting* (1665–66) is in Room 24. It's a strangely static scene of an artist in his studio, but one that transcends the mundane by its composition and use of light.

West Wing Saal I has some evocative works by Titian, of the Venetian school. He uses colour and broad brushstrokes to create character and mood, rather than distinct outlines. In Room 2 is *The Three Philosophers* (1508), one of the few authenticated works by Giorgione.

In Room 4 is Raphael's harmonious and idealised portrait, *Madonna in the Meadow* (1505). The triangular composition and the complementary colours are typical features of the Florentine high Renaissance. Compare this to Caravaggio's *Madonna of the*

Museumsquartier

By the time the Museumsquartier on Museumsplatz (Map 7) is completed it will be one of the 10 largest cultural complexes in the world. It officially opens in summer 2001, though some things were moved there before then. For information, visit the Web site at www.mqw.at.

The **Leopold Museum** is expected to be the most popular collection on the premises. The big draw is the world's largest collection of works by Egon Schiele, though many other famous Austrian artists are represented – among them Klimt, Kokoschka, Loos, Hoffmann, (Otto) Wagner, Waldmüller and Romako (10.30 am to 7 pm Tuesday to Sunday, to 9 pm Tuesday and Thursday; €6.55/5.10 full/concession).

The **Museum moderner Kunst** (Museum of Modern Art) has the largest exhibition space. The various movements in 20th-century art are shown: expressionism, cubism, futurism, constructivism, surrealism, pop art, photo-realism, conceptual and minimal art, installations and Viennese Actionism. Well-known artists represented include Picasso, Klee, Warhol, Magritte, Ernst and Giacometti. Yoko Ono is represented by an all-white chess set – and you thought she could only sing badly! (10 am to 6 pm Tuesday to Sunday, to 10 pm Thursday; €5.10/4.05 full/concession).

The third main collection on site is the **Kunsthalle**, a showcase for international modern and contemporary art (11 am to 10 pm daily; €5.85/4.40 full/concession).

Rosary (1606) in Saal V, an example of new realism in early baroque; note the dirty soles on the feet of the supplicants. Caravaggio emphasises movement in this picture by a subtle deployment of light and shadow.

Susanna at her Bath (1555) by Tintoretto can be found in Saal III. It re-creates the Old Testament tale of Susanna being surprised at her ablutions by two old men. The picture successfully portrays both serenity and implicit menace. Tintoretto employs mannerist devices (contrasting light, extremes of facial features) to achieve his effect.

Saal VII has paintings by Bernardo Bellotto (1721–80), Canaletto's nephew. He was commissioned by Maria Theresa to paint scenes of Vienna, and several are shown here. Note the way landmarks are sometimes compressed to create a more satisfying composition; the view from the Belvedere is not a faithful reproduction. The pastoral view of Schönbrunn is in stark contrast to its urban situation today.

Room 10 has portraits of the Habsburgs. Juan Carreño's portrait of Charles II of Spain really shows the characteristic Habsburg features: a distended lower lip and jaw and a nose that would be more at home in an aviary. Most of the young women in Diego Velázquez's royal portraits are wearing dresses broad enough to fit around a horse, but the artist still manages to make the subjects come to life.

AKADEMIE DER BILDENDEN KÜNSTE

The Akademie der bildenden Künste (Academy of Fine Arts; Map 7), 01, Schillerplatz 3, has a smallish picture gallery. Hieronymus Bosch's impressive *The Last Judgement* altarpiece is here, as well as works by Guardi (scenes of 18th-century Venice), Cranach the Elder, Titian and Rembrandt. Flemish painters are well represented, particularly Rubens. Van Dyck and Jordaens also get a look-in. The building itself has an attractive facade and was designed by Theophil Hansen. It was this academy that turned down would-be artist Adolf Hitler, forcing him to find a new career (see the boxed text). In front there's a statue of Schiller.

The gallery is open 10 am to 4 pm daily except Monday; admission costs €3.65 (€1.50 concession).

Hitler's Vienna

Born in Braunau am Inn, Upper Austria, in 1899, with the name Adolf Schicklgruber, Adolf Hitler moved to Vienna when he was just 17. Six unsettled, unsuccessful, poverty-stricken years later he abandoned the city to make a name for himself in Germany. He later wrote in *Mein Kampf* that his Vienna years were 'a time of the greatest transformation which I have ever been through. From a weak citizen of the world I became a fanatical anti-Semite'. Hitler briefly returned in 1938 at the head of the German army, to be greeted by enthusiastic crowds.

Although Vienna would be happy for the world to forget about its association with Hitler, an increasing number of tourists are retracing the Vienna footsteps of the infamous fascist. He spent several years living in a small, dimly lit apartment at Stumpergasse 31, in the 6th district. It's a private block, but frequent visits by curious tourists have prompted plans (unrealised as yet) to turn the apartment into a museum.

Hitler was a regular visitor to the opera, and despite his penury, preferred to pay extra to stand in sections that were barred to women. Café Sperl (see Coffee Houses in the Places to Eat chapter) is another address on the Hitler itinerary: here he would loudly express his views on race and other matters. Among his gripes was probably the nearby Akademie der bildenden Künste (Academy of Fine Arts), which twice rejected an application by the would-be artist, dismissing his work as 'inadequate'. Although convinced that proper training would have made him into a very successful artist, these rejections caused Hitler to write to a friend that perhaps fate may have reserved for him 'some other purpose'.

Otto Wagner

Along with Adolf Loos, Otto Wagner (1841–1918) was one of the most influential *fin de siècle* Viennese architects. He was trained in the classical tradition, and became a professor at the Akademie der bildenden Künste (Academy of Fine Arts). His early work was in keeping with his education, and he was responsible for some neorenaissance buildings along the Ringstrasse. But as the 20th century dawned he developed an Art Nouveau style, with flowing lines and decorative motifs. Wagner joined the Secession in 1899 and attracted public criticism in the process, one of the reasons why his creative designs for Vienna's Historical Museum were never adopted. In 1905 Wagner, Klimt and

Stadt Pavillon

others split from the Secession. Wagner began to strip away the more decorative aspects of his designs, concentrating instead on presenting the functional features of buildings in a creative way.

SECESSION BUILDING

In 1897, 19 progressive artists broke away from the Künstlerhaus and the conservative artistic establishment it represented and formed the Vienna Secession. Their aim was to present current trends in contemporary art and leave behind the historicism that was then in vogue in Vienna. Among their number were Gustav Klimt, Josef Hoffman, Kolo Moser and Joseph M Olbrich (a former student of Otto Wagner). Olbrich was given the honour of designing the new exhibition centre of the Secessionists. It was erected just a year later at 01, Friedrichstrasse 12 (Map 7), and combined sparse functionality with stylistic motifs.

The building is certainly different from the Ringstrasse architectural throwbacks. Its most striking feature is a delicate golden dome rising from a turret on the roof that deserves better than the description 'golden cabbage' accorded it by some Viennese. Other features are the mask-like faces above the door with dangling serpents instead of earlobes, the minimalist stone owls gazing down from the walls, and the vast ceramic pots supported by tortoises at the front. The motto above the entrance asserts: *Der Zeit ihre Kunst, der Kunst ihre Freiheit* (To each time its art, to art its freedom).

The fourteenth exhibition (1902) held in the building featured the famous *Beethoven*

Frieze by Klimt. This 34m-long work was only supposed to be a temporary display, little more than an elaborate poster for the main exhibit, Max Klinger's Beethoven monument. Yet it was painstakingly restored and since 1985 has been on display in the basement. The frieze has dense areas of activity punctuated by mostly open spaces, reminiscent of something plastic partially melted and stretched out over a fire. It features willowy women with bounteous hair who jostle for attention with a large gorilla, while slender figures float and a choir sings. Beethoven would no doubt be surprised to learn that it is based on his ninth symphony.

The rest of this so-called 'temple of art' clings true to the original ideal of presenting contemporary art, though it may leave you wondering exactly where the altar is. 'Sometimes people just walk past the art, they think they're in empty rooms,' the lady at the desk once told us. You have been warned! It's open 10 am to 6 pm Tuesday to Sunday (to 8 pm on Thursday); entry costs €4.40 (students €2.95). The Secession also has an outside cafe.

MAJOLIKAHAUS

This Art Nouveau building at 06, Linke Wienzeile 40 (Map 5) was created by Otto Wagner in 1899. It's named after the majolica tiles he used for the flowing floral motifs on the facade. No 38 next door is also by Wagner; it features railings created from metal leaves and a brace of jester figures on the roof who look like they could be shouting abuse at the traditional Viennese buildings nearby. The golden medallions on the facade are by Kolo Moser. These buildings overlook the open-air **Naschmarkt**, an interesting place for a wander, especially on Saturday (see Markets in the Shopping chapter).

STADT PAVILLONS

Within Resselpark at Karlsplatz are Otto Wagner's Stadt Pavillons (Map 7). They were created for Vienna's first public transport system, which was built from 1893 to 1902. Wagner was in charge of the overall design for the metro lines, bridges and station buildings. Here he incorporated floral designs and gold trim on a steel and marble structure. When the new U-Bahn transport system was put in place, the west pavilion was used as an exit for the U4 line of the Karlsplatz station, and now also houses a small municipal museum (closed Monday). The east pavilion is now a cafe. There is also a municipal museum in Wagner's Stadt Pavillon at Hietzing, near Schönbrunn.

North of the park (east of Akademiestrasse) you can see two traditional Viennese buildings, the white **Künstlerhaus** and the rust-and-white **Musikverein**.

HISTORISCHES MUSEUM DER STADT WIEN

This museum (Map 7) at 04, Karlsplatz 5, by Karlskirche, is the biggest and best of those run by the city of Vienna (see the boxed text 'Municipal Museums'). It gives a detailed rundown on the development of Vienna from prehistory to the present day, and does a good job of putting the city and its personalities in context, without needing words. Exhibits occupy three floors and include maps and plans, artefacts, many paintings (eg, by Klimt, Schiele, and Biedermeier painters like Waldmüller) and reconstructed rooms from the homes of Adolf Loos and Franz Grillparzer. Two models (on the 1st and 2nd floors) of the Innere Stadt show the impact of the Ringstrasse developments, and there are

some good period photographs. It's open 9 am to 4.30 pm daily except Monday (€3.65)

KARLSKIRCHE

At the south-east corner of Resselpark is Karlskirche (St Charles' Church; Map 7) This imposing creation was built between 1716 and 1739, after a vow by Charles VI a the end of the 1713 plague. It was designed and commenced by Johann Bernhard Fischer von Erlach and completed by his son Joseph. Although predominantly baroque, i combines several architectural styles. The twin columns are modelled on Trajan's Column in Rome, and show scenes from the life of St Charles Borromeo (who helped plague victims in Italy), to whom the church is dedicated. The huge oval dome reaches 72m the interior of the dome features cloud-bound celestial beings painted by Johann Michael Rottmayr. The altar panel is by Sebastiano Ricci and shows the Assumption of the Virgin. In front of the church is a pond, complete with a Henry Moore sculpture.

About 200m north-east of the church is Schwarzenbergplatz. Here is the **Russian Monument**, a reminder that the Russians liberated the city at the end of WWII. It comprises a soldier atop a tall column. In front is a **fountain** (Hochstrahlbrunnen), and behind stands the **Schwarzenberg Palace**, cocreated by JB Fischer von Erlach and Johann Lukas von Hildebrandt.

STADTPARK

The Stadtpark (City Park; Map 7) adjoins Parkring. It was opened in 1862 and is an enjoyable recreation spot for strolling or relaxing in the sun. It has a pond, winding walkways and several statues. The **Kursalon**, in the south-west corner, hosts waltz concerts in the afternoon and evening from April to 1 November; nearby in the park is the **Johann Strauss Denkmal**, a golden statue of Johann Strauss under a white arch (this often appears in tourist brochures).

MUSEUM FÜR ANGEWANDTE KUNST

The Museum für angewandte Kunst (MAK; Museum of Applied Arts; Map 7), 01,

Municipal Museums

There are 20 municipal museums run by the city of Vienna, if you include the always accessible Roman ruins (free) on Michaelerplatz. A free booklet is available describing them.

Entry for the Historisches Museum der Stadt Wien (see entry in main text), the Uhren Museum and the Hermesvilla cost €3.65 for adults, €1.85 for seniors, €1.50 for students and €5.50 for families. All the rest cost €1.85 for adults or €0.75 for students (no senior/family reductions). A book of 10 entry tickets costs €11.65. All municipal museums are free for visits before noon on Friday, and they're all closed on 1 January, 1 May and 25 December.

The **Uhren Museum** (Clock Museum; Map 7), 01, Schulhof 2, on three floors (no lift), displays 1200 clocks and watches, ranging from the 15th century to a 1989 computer clock (open 9 am to 4.30 pm Tuesday to Sunday). The **Hermesvilla** (Map 2) is in the Lainzer Tiergarten (see Hiking under Activities later in this chapter); this former hunting lodge features the private apartments of Franz Josef and Empress Elisabeth.

Several municipal museums are based in the former residences of the great composers, and generally contain assorted memorabilia and furniture of their exalted former inhabitants. Most of the museums are open 9 am to 12.15 pm and 1 to 4.30 pm daily except Monday (exceptions are noted below). A visit may take up to 30 minutes. Locations include:

Eroica House (Map 3), 19, Döblinger Hauptstrasse 92 – this house was named after Beethoven's Symphony No 3, which was written here.

Haydn Museum (Map 5), 06, Haydngasse 19 – Haydn lived here for 12 years while composing most of the oratorios *The Creation* and *The Seasons*. He died here in 1809. The museum also has rooms devoted to Brahms.

Johann Strauss Residence (Map 7), 02, Praterstrasse 54 – Strauss composed the Blue Danube Waltz here.

Mozart's Apartment (Figaro House; Map 7), 01, Domgasse 5 – Mozart spent 2½ productive years here and his work included writing *The Marriage of Figaro*. It's open 9 am to 6 pm except Monday.

Pasqualati House (Map 7), 01, Mölker Bastei 8 – Beethoven lived on the 4th floor of this house from 1804 to 1814.

Schubert Commemorative Rooms (Map 5), 04, Kettenbrückengasse 6 – Schubert lived here briefly before his death in 1828 (open 1.30 to 4.30 pm Tuesday to Sunday). You can see his birth house (Map 3) at 09, Nussdorfer Strasse 54.

In addition, each district has its own *Bezirksmuseum* (district musuem), with free entry and limited opening times – check addresses in the telephone book.

Stubenring 5, provides a large display space for its permanent collection and temporary exhibitions, as well as having a popular cafe. The 1871 high Renaissance-style building offers some fine features in its own right, especially the ceilings. There are two main parts to the permanent collection: the exhibition rooms and the Study Collection.

Each of the **exhibition rooms** is devoted to a different style, eg, Renaissance, baroque, orient, historicism, empire, Art Deco, and the distinctive metalwork of the Wiener Werkstätte. Rooms are presented in an interesting way: the layout of each was

the responsibility of a specific artist, and their reasons for displaying the exhibits in a particular manner are explained; their justifications are sometimes pretentious but invariably illuminating. In the Biedermeier room, Jenny Holzer placed electronic signs near the ceiling so 'they can be ignored'; the aluminium sofa here is fun. A famous room is Barbara Bloom's display of Art Nouveau chairs; they're all back-lit and presented behind translucent white screens. There's a Klimt frieze upstairs, and some interesting pieces in the 20th-century design and architecture room (like Frank

Gehry's cardboard chair). Objects exhibited in these rooms encompass tapestries, lace, furniture, glassware and ornaments.

In the basement is the **Study Collection**, which groups exhibits according to the type of materials used: glass and ceramics, metal, wood and textiles. Actual objects range from ancient oriental statues to modern sofas. There are some particularly good porcelain and glassware pieces, with casts showing how they're put together.

MAK (☎ 711 36-0) is open 10 am to 6 pm (9 pm Thursday) daily except Monday. Admission costs €6.55 (€2.20 if no special exhibitions) for adults, €3.30 (€1.10) concession, or €10.90 (€3.65) for a family ticket. Entry is free on 14 April, 26 October and 24 December.

Schönbrunn & the West

The main sight in the west is Schloss Schönbrunn, one of the most popular attractions in Vienna.

SCHLOSS SCHÖNBRUNN

It may not look a modest dwelling, but this baroque palace (Map 5) is a much diminished version of the grandiose imperial centrepiece that was first planned.

The name comes from the beautiful fountain (Schöner Brunnen) built around a spring that Emperor Matthias (1557–1619) found while hunting. A pleasure palace was built here by Ferdinand II in 1637, but this was razed by the Turks in 1683. Soon after, Leopold I commissioned Johann Bernhard Fischer von Erlach to build a more luxurious summer palace. Fischer von Erlach came up with hugely ambitious plans for a palace to dwarf Versailles to be built on the hill where the Gloriette Monument now stands. However, the imperial purse felt unworthy of the venture and a 'less elaborate' building was constructed. It was finished in 1700.

Maria Theresa, upon her accession to the throne in 1740, chose Schönbrunn as the base for her family and her court. The young architect Nikolaus Pacassi was commissioned to renovate and extend the palace to meet the new requirements. Work was carried out from 1744 to 1749. The interior was fitted out in rococo style, and the palace then had some 2000 rooms, as well as a chapel and a theatre. Like most imperial buildings associated with Maria Theresa, the exterior was painted her favourite colour – yellow.

Napoleon lived in the palace in 1805 and 1809. In 1918 the last Habsburg emperor, Charles I, abdicated in the Blue Chinese Salon, after which the palace became the property of the new republic. Bomb damage was suffered during WWII, and restoration was completed in 1955. In 1992 the palace administration was transferred to private hands, whereupon further renovations commenced (and admission prices soared). These are still ongoing – a children's museum should open in newly restored rooms by 2002.

The palace can be reached by the U4 line; 'Schönbrunn' is the closest stop, though 'Hietzing' is better for the zoo and the western part of the gardens. You can visit the Web site at www.schoenbrunn.at.

Palace

The interior of the palace is suitably majestic with frescoed ceilings, crystal chandeliers and gilded ornaments. However, the endless stucco and gold twirls can seem overdone at times. Franz Josef evidently thought so too, for he had the rococo excesses stripped from his personal bedchamber in 1854.

The pinnacle of finery is reached in the **Great Gallery**. Gilded scrolls, ceiling frescoes, chandeliers and huge crystal mirrors create the effect. Numerous sumptuous balls were held here, including one for the delegates at the Congress of Vienna (1814–15).

The **Mirror Room** is where Mozart (then six) played his first royal concert in the presence of Maria Theresa and the royal family in 1762. His father revealed in a letter that afterwards young Wolfgang leapt onto the lap of the empress and kissed her. The **Round Chinese Room** is over-the-top ut rather ingenious too. Maria Theresa held secret consultations here: a hidden doorway led to her adviser's apartments and a fully laden table could be drawn up through the floor so the dignitaries could dine without being disturbed by servants.

The **Million Gulden Room** is so called because that's the sum that Maria Theresa paid for the decorations, comprising Persian miniatures set on rosewood panels and framed with gilded rocaille frames. The **Gobelin Salon** is named after its 17th-century Gobelin tapestries. An unusual item in the **Napoleon Room** is a stuffed crested lark, the favourite childhood bird of Napoleon's son, who died in this room.

The **Porcelain Room** and the **Miniatures Room** both display drawings by members of the imperial family. In the **Breakfast Room** the walls are decorated with embroideries made by Maria Theresa and her daughters.

Opening times are 8.30 am to 5 pm daily (4.30 pm from 1 November to 31 March). There are two self-guided tours, each including a personal audioguide in English. The Imperial Tour gives access to 22 rooms for €6.90 (€6.20/3.65 for students under 16/children); allow 45 to 60 minutes. The Grand Tour includes 40 rooms and costs €9.10 (€8/4.75 students/children); allow up to 1½ hours. Tickets are stamped with a departure time, and there may be a time-lag before you're allowed to set off in summer, so buy your ticket straight away and then explore the gardens. On the Grand Tour you have the option of paying an extra €1.85 for an English-speaking guide, but you have to hurry to the guide's schedule.

The **Bergl Rooms** were painted by Johann Wenzl Bergl (1718–89); his exotic depictions of flora and fauna attempt to bring the ambience of the gardens inside, with some success. These are not part of the ordinary tours, but they can be visited from April to October with the VIP pass, which can save you money if you plan to see everything. The VIP pass gives free access to the Grand Tour (with no waiting time), the Gloriette, the Maze and the imperial bakery. It costs €14.20 (€12.75/6.90 students/children).

Wagenburg

This is the Imperial Coach Collection of the Kunsthistorisches Museum, situated across the courtyard to the west of the palace. The horse-drawn carriages on display range from tiny children's wagons to great vehicles of state. The most ornate is the imperial coach of the court, built for Maria Theresa around 1765. It's extreme baroque on wheels, with fussy gold ornamentation and painted cherubs. Allow around 30 minutes to look around. It's open 9 am to 6 pm daily, or 10 am to 4 pm on Tuesday to Sunday from 1 November to 31 March; €4.40, €2.95 concession.

Gardens

The beautifully tended formal gardens, arranged in the French style, are a symphony of colour in the summer. The extensive grounds have many attractions hidden away in the tree-lined avenues, arranged according to a grid and star-shaped system between 1750 and 1755. From 1772 to 1780 Ferdinand Hetzendorf added the **Roman Ruins** (now the site of summer concerts), the **Neptune Fountain** (a riotous ensemble from Greek mythology), and the crowning glory, the **Gloriette Monument**, standing tall on the hill overlooking the gardens. The view from up here, looking back towards the palace with Vienna shimmering in the distance, is excellent. It's possible to go on the roof of the Gloriette (April to October only; entry €2.20), but the view is only marginally superior. A new attraction in the gardens is a 630m-long maze (€2.20). The palace grounds are open from 6 am until sunset.

On the west side of the grounds are the **Palmenhaus** (Palm House) and the **Tiergarten** (zoo). The palm house contains worldwide flora and is open from 9.30 am to at least 4.30 pm daily. Entry costs €3.30 (€2.20 for students under 27), or €10.15 (€8) for a combined ticket including the zoo. The Schönbrunn VIP pass gets you a discount.

The attractively laid out zoo is the oldest zoo in the world, dating from 1752. The once-cramped animal cages have now (mostly) been improved. There's every sort of animal you'd expect, though no lions at present. Walkways radiate out from a central pavilion, painted in Maria-Theresa yellow. Opening times are 9 am to 4.30 pm (November to January), to 5 pm (February), 5.30 pm (March and October), 6 pm (April) and 6.30 pm (May to September). Feeding times are interesting – displayed maps tell you who's dining when. Admission costs €8.75 (€5.85 seniors, €4 students under 27, €2.90 children).

KIRCHE AM STEINHOF

This distinctive Art Nouveau creation (Map 2) was the work of Otto Wagner from 1904 to 1907. Kolo Moser chipped in with the mosaic windows. The roof is topped by a copper-covered dome that earned the nickname *Limoniberg* (lemon mountain) from its original golden colour. The design illustrates the victory of function over ornamentation prevalent in much of Wagner's work, even down to the sloping floor to allow good drainage. It's at 14, Baumgartner Höhe 1, near the end of bus No 48A. The church is on the grounds of the Psychiatric Hospital of the City of Vienna, and the interior can be seen on Saturday at 3 pm.

About 2km west is Hüttelbergstrasse. Here you will find two **villas**, at Nos 26 and 28, designed by Wagner. The most unusual (No 26) was built in 1888 and is now a small Ernst Fuchs private museum (☎ 914 85 75-14). In the gardens (visible from the road) are some interesting statues, ceramics and the ornate **Brunnenhaus** created by Fuchs. The villas are near the Wien West camp site (take bus No 148 or 152).

KIRCHE ZUR HEILIGSTEN DREIFALTIGKEIT

The remarkable Kirche zur Heiligsten Dreifaltigkeit (Holy Trinity Church; Map 2), sometimes called the Wotrubakirche, looks like a collection of concrete blocks haphazardly stacked together. It was designed by Fritz Wotruba and completed in 1976. It's a long way to the south-west of the city, at the intersection of Georgsgasse and Rysergasse in district 23, near the Kaserngasse stop of bus No 60A.

Other Outlying Attractions

Starting in the south, sights are describe moving in an anticlockwise direction, ending in the north-east.

SCHLOSS BELVEDERE

This splendid baroque palace (Map 6) wa built for Prince Eugene of Savoy, conqueror of the Turks in 1718 and hero of many other conflicts. It was designed b Johann Lukas von Hildebrandt. The Unteres (Lower) Belvedere was built fir (1714–16), with an orangery attached, an was the prince's summer residence. Connected to it by a long, landscaped garden the Oberes (Upper) Belvedere (1721–23 the venue for the prince's banquets an other festivities.

Considered together, the Belvedere res dences were at the time almost more mag nificent than the imperial residence, th Hofburg. This was something of an irrita tion to the Habsburgs, especially as th prince was able to look down onto the cit

Prince Eugene

One of Austria's greatest military heroes wasn't even a native of the country. Prince Eugene of Savoy (1663–1736) was born in Paris. After being informed he was too short to be accepted into the French army he left France in 1683 to join the Habsburg forces. Eugene was just in time to help beat off the Turkish forces besieging Vienna. He was given his own regiment and within 10 years was promoted to field marshal. His skills as a military strategist showed in his victories against the Turks at Zenta in 1697, and during the campaign in the Balkans from 1714 to 1718, which finally drove the Turks out of all but a small corner of Europe. His capture of the fortress at Belgrade in 1718 was instrumental in concluding that war. Prince Eugene's skills as a statesman were also employed in the War of the Spanish Succession, where he negotiated with his former homeland.

from the elevated vantage point of the Oberes Belvedere. It was therefore with some satisfaction that Maria Theresa was able to purchase the Belvedere after the prince's death. It then became a Habsburg residence, most recently occupied by the Archduke Franz Ferdinand who started a court there to rival his uncle's (Franz Josef) in the Hofburg. Ferdinand was assassinated in 1914, an event that sparked off WWI.

The Belvedere is now home to the **Östereichische Galerie** (Austrian Gallery); the baroque section is in the Unteres Belvedere (entrance via 04, Rennweg 6A; take tram No 71) and 19th- and 20th-century art is in the Oberes Belvedere (entrance via 04, Prinz Eugen Strasse 27; take tram D). Opening hours are 10 am to 5 pm Tuesday to Sunday; entry for both is €6.55 (€4.40 concession). You don't have to visit both parts on the same day, and the ticket is also good for entry to the Gustinus Ambrosi Museum at 02, Scherzergasse 1a.

Oberes Belvedere

This houses the most important collection. The baroque interior provides a diverting setting for the drift into modern art. An elaborate fresco depicts the apotheosis of Prince Eugene, and there are Herculean figures supporting columns in the entrance lobby. You can rent headphones with a commentary in English for €3.30.

The 1st floor has paintings from the turn of the 19th century, particularly the work of Hans Makart (1840–84) and Anton Romako (1832–89), who both influenced the later Viennese Art Nouveau artists. But the 20th-century section of this floor has the gallery's best exhibits. Gustav Klimt (1862–1918) was one of the founders of the Secessionist Art Nouveau school. His later pictures (such as the two portraits of Adele Bloch-Bauer) employ a harmonious but ostentatious use of background colour (much metallic gold and silver) to evoke or symbolise the emotions of the main figures. One of the best known but also one of the most intriguing works here is Klimt's The Kiss (1908). It shows a couple embracing within what looks like a yellow overcoat,

surrounded by the usual Klimt circles and rectangles. The man's neck is twisted unnaturally as he strains towards her; her face is half turned away and enclosed within his hands. Nobody knows quite how to interpret this scene: is she demurely and willingly proffering her cheek, or is she trying to avoid his advances? Some of Klimt's impressionist landscapes are also on display.

Egon Schiele (1890–1918) produced intense, melancholic work. Notice the hypnotic and bulging eyes on the portrait of his friend, *Eduard Kosmack* (1910). Schiele's bold, brooding colours and unforgiving outlines are in complete contrast to Klimt's golden tapestries and idealised forms. He lived with one of Klimt's models for a while – Schiele's portraits of her were very explicit, bordering on the pornographic. Some critics are fond of trying to explain his obsessions with sex and desperate subjects by looking at Schiele's upbringing: his father went insane from syphilis and destroyed the family's stocks and bonds in a fire. Schiele's last work is *The Family*. He added the child between the woman's legs when he found out his own wife was pregnant; however, she died of Egyptian flu before the child was born. Schiele died of the same illness before this painting was completely finished (look closely and you'll see the imprecision of the male's left hand).

Other artists represented include Herbert Boeckl, Anton Hanak, Arnulf Rainer and Fritz Wotruba. There are several examples of the output of the influential expressionist, Oskar Kokoschka (1886–1980). The gallery also has some exhibits from non-Austrian artists such as Munch, Monet, Van Gogh, Renoir and Cézanne.

The top (2nd) floor has a display of 19th-century paintings from the Romantic, classical and Biedermeier periods. In particular, this section has work by the Biedermeier painter Georg Waldmüller, showing to very good effect his very precise portraits and rural scenes.

Unteres Belvedere

The baroque section offers some good statuary, such as the originals from Donner's

Neuer Markt fountain and *The Apotheosis of Prince Eugene*. Eugene was presumably suffering delusions of grandeur by this time, for he commissioned the latter work himself; the artist, not to be outdone, depicted himself at the prince's feet. Paintings include those of Maria Theresa and her husband, François of Lorraine. A room is devoted to the vibrant paintings by Franz Anton Maulbertsch (1724–96).

The **Orangery** has a collection of Austrian medieval art. This comprises religious scenes, altarpieces and statues. There are several impressive works by Michael Pacher (1440–98), a Tirolean artist who was influenced by both early Low Countries art and the early Renaissance of northern Italy.

Gardens

The long garden between the two Belvederes was laid out in classical French style and has sphinxes and other mythical beasts along its borders. South of the Oberes Belvedere is a small **Alpine Garden**, which has 3500 plant species and a bonsai section. It's open during the flowering season (April to July) from 10 am to 6 pm daily and entry costs €2.95 (students €2.55). North from here is the much larger **Botanic Gardens** belonging to the Vienna University. These are open 9 am to one hour before dusk daily from April to October and admission is free.

CEMETERIES

Numerous famous composers have memorial tombs in the **Zentralfriedhof** (Central Cemetery; Map 2), 11, Simmeringer Hauptstrasse 232–244, including Gluck, Beethoven, Schubert, Brahms and Schönberg. Mozart has a monument here, but he was actually buried in an unmarked mass grave in the **St Marxer Friedhof** (Cemetery of St Mark; Map 6), 03, Leberstrasse 6–8. No body quite knows where; his wife, Constanze, searched in vain for the exact location. A poignant memorial (Mozartgrab) made from a broken pillar and a discarded stone angel marks the area where he was most likely buried. For St Mark's, take tram No 71 to Landstrasser Hauptstrasse then follow the signs (10 minutes).

From the Landstrasser Hauptstrasse stop you can take tram No 71 or 72 on to the Central Cemetery, open 7 am to 6 pm daily

---

Corpse Disposal, Viennese Style

It is said that nowhere are people so obsessed with death as in Vienna. Songs performed in wine taverns often deal with the subject, and the city has a unique museum dealing with coffins and the undertakers' craft, the **Bestattungsmuseum** (Map 6; ☎ 501 95-4227), 04, Goldeggasse 19; visits noon to 3 pm weekdays by arrangement only.

The country as a whole has one of the highest suicide rates in the world. Being able to afford a lavish funeral at death is a lifetime ambition for many Viennese. Joseph II caused outrage in the 1780s with his scheme to introduce false-bottomed, reusable coffins.

In 1784 the huge Central Cemetery was opened as there was simply no more space in the city cemeteries. To try to persuade the populace that their future dear departed would rest better in this new location, they shipped out the coffins of the famous composers where they now rest together in group 32A. An unusual method was contemplated for transporting bodies to the suburban site: engineers drew up plans for a tube, many kilometres long, down which coffins would be fired using compressed air. However, the high cost of this scheme (one million florins) led to its abandonment.

At dawn, before the public are admitted to the Central Cemetery, special hunters are employed to shoot male pheasants, hares and wild rabbits. The reason is that these inconsiderate creatures have a tendency to eat or disturb the carefully arranged flowers around the graves. Meanwhile, you won't find any cemeteries for pets in Vienna. Animals are expressly forbidden from being buried in the soil, as the high water table might be contaminated by seepage of chemicals used in inoculations and putting the pets down. Pet cremations are now big business, although they are strictly controlled.

Get off at gate (Tor) two for the graves of the composers and other famous Viennese figures. There's a cemetery plan at the gate. Postwar Austrian presidents are entombed in front of the memorial church. Behind the church, at the far end of the cemetery, are the simple plaques devoted to those who fell in the world wars. These are in contrast to the ostentatious displays of wealth in the mausoleums of the rich, who couldn't take it with them but certainly tried. Most graves are neat, well tended and garlanded with fresh flowers. For a further contrast, wander around the old Jewish section, where the tangle of broken headstones and unfettered undergrowth is a reminder that few relatives are around to maintain these graves.

A visit to the **Namenlosen** cemetery can be poignant. It contains unidentified, 'nameless' corpses washed up on the shores of the Danube. It's south-east of the city at 11, Alberner Hafen, and is reached by bus No 6A, but only some of the buses go that far.

KUNSTHAUSWIEN

This art gallery (Map 4) at 03, Untere Weissgerberstrasse 13, looks like something out of a toy shop. It was designed by

Peace Empire & a Hundred Waters

Friedensreich Hundertwasser was born as Friedrich Stowasser on 15 December 1928. In 1943, 69 of his Jewish relatives on his mother's side were deported to Eastern Europe and killed. He died of a heart attack in February 2000 while on the way back from Australia to Europe on the *Queen Elizabeth II*. Though Hundertwasser achieved little international notice, he was a major national figure.

MARK HONAN

In 1948, he spent three months at the Akademie der bildenden Künste (Academy of Fine Arts), and the following year adopted his new name, meaning 'peace empire' and 'a hundred waters'. Environmental themes were present even in his early work, eg, *People (Complement to Trees)* from 1950. (This is now displayed in the KunstHausWien, which Hundertwasser also designed; pictured above.) His paintings employ vivid colours, metallic silver and spirals, which are sometimes reminiscent of Gustav Klimt's ornamental backgrounds.

Hundertwasser felt that 'the straight line is Godless'. He faithfully adhered to this principle in all his building projects, proclaiming that his uneven floors 'become a symphony, a melody for the feet, and bring back natural vibrations to man'. He believed that cities should be more harmonious with their surrounding (natural) environment: buildings should be semisubmerged under undulating meadows, homes should have 'tree tenants' that pay rent in environmental currency.

Hundertwasser was always something of an oddity to the Viennese establishment, and he complained that his more radical building projects were quashed by the authorities. Nevertheless, he was commissioned to re-create the facade of the Spittelau incinerator (Map 3). This was opened in 1992; it's the most unindustrial-looking heating plant you'll ever see (it's just north of Franz Josefs Bahnhof: take U3 to Spittelau). Hundertwasser stated that man is shielded from nature by three levels of insulation: cities, houses and clothes. He tried to limit the effect of the first two levels with his building projects. His proposed solution to the third was to go naked, and he did make a couple of public speeches in the nude in the 1960s.

To the end, Hundertwasser was one of Vienna's most idiosyncratic inhabitants. Whether organising a campaign to retain Austria's traditional car number plates, designing postage stamps, redesigning national flags, or simply painting pictures, he was always passionate, sometimes irritating and usually challenged established thinking.

Friedensreich Hundertwasser; his innovative buildings feature coloured ceramics, uneven floors, patchwork paintwork, irregular corners and grass and trees on the roof (see the boxed text).

The contents of the KunstHausWien are something of a paean in honour of Hundertwasser, presenting his paintings, graphics, tapestry, philosophy, ecology and architecture. His vivid paintings are as distinctive as his diverse building projects. Hundertwasser's quotes are everywhere; some of his pronouncements are annoyingly didactic or smack of old hippiedom ('each raindrop is a kiss from heaven'), but they're often thought-provoking. There are even a couple of films about him. The gallery also puts on quality temporary exhibitions featuring other artists. Opening hours are 10 am to 7 pm daily; the cafe around the back is open 10 am to midnight daily. Entry costs €6.95 (€5.10 concession) for the Hundertwasser collection, and the same again for the exhibitions, with a combination ticket costing €11.65 (€8.75). Monday is half-price day (unless it's a holiday).

While you're in the area, walk down the road to see **Hundertwasserhaus** (Map 6), a block of residential flats designed by Hundertwasser on the corner of Löwengasse and Kegelgasse. It is now one of Vienna's most prestigious addresses, even though it only provides rented accommodation and is owned by the city of Vienna. Opposite is the **Kalke Village**, also the handiwork of Hundertwasser, created from an old Michelin factory. It contains a cafe, souvenir shops and art shops, all with Hundertwasser's trademark uneven surfaces and colourful ceramics. It's open from 9 am to 5 pm daily (to 7 pm in summer).

WIENER KRIMINALMUSEUM

The Wiener Kriminalmuseum (Crime Museum; Map 4), 02, Grosse Sperlgasse 24, gives a prurient, tabloid-style look at crimes and criminals in Austria. It dwells with particularly grisly relish on murders in the last 100 years or so, though there are skulls of earlier criminals, and even an 18th-century head pickled in a jar. Accompanying text is copious, but it's only in German. Opening hours are 10 am to 5 pm Tuesday to Sunday; admission is €4.40 (€3.65 concession, €2.20 for kids). Axe murderers get in free (as an exhibit rather than as a visitor).

Flak Towers

MARK HONAN

Several unsightly relics from WWII survive in Vienna. These bare monolithic blocks are flak towers (*Flacktürme*), built from 1943 to 1944 to defend against air attacks. And they were built to last – the 5m-thick walls of reinforced concrete mean that they are quite difficult to pull down. So they remain standing as an uncomfortable reminder of the Nazi era, featureless but for four circular gun bases at the top corners (these protrusions are strangely reminiscent of Mickey Mouse's ears).

Two flak towers can be seen in Augarten in the 2nd district (Map 4). Another, just off Mariahilfer Strasse in Esterházy Park (Map 5), is the only one that has been put to any use (unrealised plans for the others have included converting them to a casino, art gallery, car park and helicopter launch pad). It contains the **Haus des Meeres** (open 9 am to 6 pm daily; €6.90), exhibiting a moderate collection of sharks, crocodiles and snakes. The outside walls are used for climbing exercises organised by the Österreichischer Alpenverein (☎ 587 47 48); not in winter, €3.65 for two hours. Also in Esterházy Park, underground in a former air-raid shelter, is the **Museum of Torture** (Folter Museum), open 10 am to 7 pm daily.

Athena announces the neoclassical Parlament

Brunnenhaus, Fuchs' fantastic fountain house

Johann Strauss and empty coffee house

The Riesenrad – where Harry met Holly

tephansplatz from the top of Haas Haus

Fresh produce aplenty at the Naschmarkt

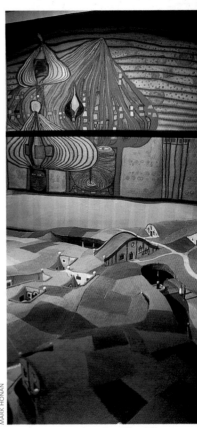

At Haas Haus, the future is colourful

Vienna can look different from a fiacre

Amusement park faces at the Prater

Hundertwasser style at KunstHausWien

PRATER

At the western end of the Prater (Map 4) is a large amusement park, often known as the Volksprater or Wurstelprater. It's dominated by the giant **Riesenrad** (Ferris wheel) built in 1897. This achieved celluloid fame in *The Third Man*, in the scene where Holly Martins finally confronts Harry Lime. The wheel rises to almost 65m and has a total weight of 430 tonnes. It rotates slowly, allowing plenty of time to enjoy the view from the top during the 10-minute ride. The wheel operates as late as midnight in the summer (€4).

The amusement park has all sorts of funfair rides, ranging from gentle children's merry-go-rounds to stomach-twisting big dippers. There are also bumper cars, go-karts, haunted houses, games rooms, minigolf, a mini-train and plenty of places to eat and drink. Rides cost €1.10 to €4.

Even if you don't like fairground rides, it's a great place just to wander and soak up the atmosphere. As you walk, you're liable to bump into one of the colourful metal sculptures depicting humans caught up in strange hallucinogenic happenings. Some are rather witty. Look for them on Rondeau and Calafattiplatz.

Sharing the same building in the park are the **Planetarium** (show in German only; Sunday except in summer; €3.65) and the **Pratermuseum**, a municipal museum that traces the history of the Wurstelprater and its woodland neighbour, the Grüner Prater (closed Monday; €1.85). Joseph II first opened up the Prater (former royal hunting grounds) to the public in 1766.

DONAUPARK

The **Donauturm** (Danube Tower; Map 4) in Donaupark, 22nd district, is the tallest structure in Vienna – the antenna reaches to 252m. (Next highest is the newly built Millennium Tower at 202m.) Two revolving restaurants at 170m and 160m allow you to enjoy a fine panorama. Go up to watch the sun set behind the Wienerwald. Meals in the restaurants cost €6 to €20. Admission costs €5.10 (€3.65 for children).

Nearby is **UNO City** (☎ 269 60), home to international organisations, which is leased to the UN for a rent of AS1 (€0.08) per annum. It has extraterritorial status, so take your passport when visiting. Guided tours are conducted weekdays.

Activities

There are plenty of opportunities for visitors to participate in sporting activities such as basketball, tennis, squash, sailing, swimming, judo, ice hockey etc. However, apart from a couple of leaflets listing city-owned indoor and outdoor swimming pools *(Bäder)*, neither the tourist office nor the city information desk in the Rathaus has much sports information. The best place to contact is the Sportamt (Map 6; ☎ 4000-84111), Ernst-Happel-Stadion, 02, Meiereistasse 7. In addition, good hotels will be able to tell you about local facilities, or you can check the newspapers, or get addresses from the phone book.

The Prater, a large area between the Danube and the Danube Canal, is an important location for sports. It has tennis courts, a bowling alley (Map 4; 02, Hauptallee 124), horse riding, sports stadia and swimming pools. A more compact sports complex is the Stadthalle (Map 5; ☎ 98 100), 15, Vogelweidplatz 15, which has a swimming pool, ice rink and bowling alley.

HIKING

To the west of the city, the rolling hills and marked trails of the Wienerwald are perfect for walkers. The Prater also has a wood with walking trails. The *Wander bares Wien* leaflet from the Sportamt has maps of trails close to the city and explains how to get there by public transport (city travel passes are valid).

A good trail to try is the one starting in Nussdorf (take tram D from the Ring) and reaching **Kahlenberg** for a fine view over the city. On your return to Nussdorf you can undo all that exercise by imbibing a few at a Heuriger. The round trip is an 11km hike, or you can save your legs by taking the Nussdorf-Kahlenberg 38A bus in one or both directions.

For information on farther-flung parts of the Wienerwald, see the Excursions chapter.

Another place to roam around is the **Lainzer Tiergarten** animal reserve, open from mid-February to mid-November between 9 am and dusk (free entry). You can get there by tram No 62 to Hermesstrasse and then bus No 60B to the last station.

GUIDED WALKING TOURS

Vienna tourist guides conduct around 40 different guided walking tours, covering everything from Art Nouveau architecture to Jewish traditions in Vienna. The monthly *Wiener Spaziergänge* leaflet from the tourist office details all of these, also giving the various departure points and indicating those conducted in English. Tours last about 1½ hours and cost €10.20 (€5.85 for those under 18).

The Third Man Tour, conducted in English by Dr Brigitte Timmermann (☎ 774 89 01), departs at 4 pm Monday and Friday; the meeting place is the U4 Stadtpark station, Johannesgasse exit, and you should have a torch and good footwear. The tour takes in all the main location spots used in the film. That includes the underground sewers, home to 2½ million rats. You'll discover that the sewers are not linked together, so it is impossible to cross the city underground as Harry Lime did in the film. Other places included are Harry Lime's apartment at Josefsplatz and the doorway on Schrevogelgasse where he was first spotted by Holly Martins.

For information on other organised tours (by bus, tram and boat), see the Getting Around chapter.

CYCLING

Cycling is a pleasant and popular activity, especially along the banks of the Danube. See the Getting Around chapter for more information.

SWIMMING

There are plenty of swimming options. A few swimming pools are privately owned, though many more are city owned. For information on the latter call ☎ 60112-8044, 7.30 am to 3.30 pm Monday to Friday.

City-owned pools and bathing complexes all have the same entry fees: €3.65 per adult, or €2.95 after noon and €1.85 after 4 pm (all including a locker). If you want a cabin instead of a locker, you pay €5.10, or €3.65 after noon. In the city-owned pools, kids under six get free entry; those aged six to 15 get free entry during the summer holidays.

Many places are open-air and these open only from May to mid-September, such as the Stadionbad (Map 7; ☎ 720 21 02), a large privately owned complex of pools in the Prater. Bus No 80B runs there from the U3 stop Schlachthausgasse. Other outdoor pools include the city-owned Krapfenwaldbad (Map 2; ☎ 320 15 01), 19, Krapfenwaldgasse 65–73, in the north (bus 38A), a small pool with a view of the city.

Some swimming baths also have sauna facilities (in which senior citizens get reductions), such as Ottakringer Bad (Map 3; ☎ 914 81 06), 16, Johann Staud Strasse 11, and Amalienbad (Map 6; ☎ 607 47 47), 10, Reumannplatz 23. Both of these city-owned places are open year-round.

There are plenty of beaches too, but don't expect to see much sand. Swimming spots (easy access to the water, no charges) are on both banks of the New Danube (Neue Donau). Some of these are for nude bathing; they're marked FKK *(Freikörperkultur)* on maps and signs, and are mostly near the edge of the city. The Reichsbrücke locality is a fun area – to the south are grassy slopes ideal for sunbathing, and to the north are plenty of outdoor bars and restaurants.

The Old Danube (Alte Donau; Map 4) also has various places where you can just jump in, or you can turn to the city-owned bathing complexes which are open approximately from May to September. There are several places north of Kagraner Brücke on the south bank giving access to the Old Danube, though of these only Strandbad Alte Donau has outdoor swimming pools as well as lake access. The biggest bathing complex is Gänsehäufel, an island jutting out in the Old Danube. It is also city owned, and has a nude section, swimming pools and lake access.

WATER SPORTS

Both the Old Danube and the New Danube provide opportunities for sailing, boating, windsurfing and water skiing. On the east bank of the New Danube by the Reichsbrücke bridge (U3 to Donauinsel) there's sailing, rowing and sailboard hire.

The Old Danube is the favoured area for sailing. Hofbauer (Map 4; ☎ 204 34 35, fax -36), 22, Obere Alte Donau 186, rents sailing boats and also has a rental kiosk at Kagraner Brücke and a branch on the New Danube at the Reichsbrücke bridge. Several other rental places are along the peninsula under the Kagraner Brücke, such as Kukis (Map 4; ☎ 263 33 93), where hourly rates rentals cost: surfboard €8.75, rowing boat €5.45, peddle boat €8.75, sailing boat €12.25, motorboat €11.80. For more outlets look in the Yellow Pages under *Boote/Vermietung* or contact the Österreichischer Segel-Verband (Austrian Sailing Federation; ☎ 662 44 62, fax 662 15 58), 23, Zetsche-gasse 21.

Language Courses

Many places offer German courses, and they can usually offer the option of accommodation for the duration.

Inlingua Sprachschule (Map 7; ☎/fax 512 94 99) 01, Neuer Markt 1, charges €415 for a minimum two weeks (20 lessons per week), with additional weeks costing around €160 each. There are monthly starts and a limit of eight students per class. It also does individual tuition and evening classes.

The Internationales Kulturinstitut (Map 7; ☎ 586 73 21, fax 586 29 93, e office@ ikivienna.at), 01, Opernring 7, has intensive courses (15 hours per week, €357 for four weeks; monthly starts) and evening classes (four hours per week, €306 for 10 weeks; starting in January, April and October). There are 10 to 16 students per class. Check the Web site at www.ikivienna.at.

You could also try Berlitz (☎ 512 82 86) at 01, Graben 13 and elsewhere. The tourist office can give you advice about other places where you can learn German.

Places to Stay

TYPES OF ACCOMMODATION

As in the rest of Austria, there has been a general move towards providing higher-quality accommodation at higher prices (eg, rooms where guests use hall showers are gradually being upgraded and fitted with private showers). This makes life more difficult for budget travellers, who may be forced to rely on hostels.

Breakfast is included in hostels, pensions and hotels listed in this chapter, unless stated otherwise; in the more expensive places this will be a substantial breakfast buffet instead of a continental breakfast. Prices quoted here are summer prices; most mid-range and top-end hotels reduce prices in winter (usually 1 November to 31 March, except over Christmas and New Year).

Hostels

Vienna offers a choice of private hostels or hostels affiliated with Hostelling International (HI). In the former, no membership is required. In HI hostels, nonmembers pay a guest surcharge of €2.95 per night for a guest card; after six nights the guest card counts as a full membership card.

The name for youth hostel in German is *Jugendherberge*. Austria has two youth hostel organisations. Hostels affiliated with the worldwide HI network are linked to either one or the other; this is something of a historical legacy and makes no difference to how the hostels are run. Either head office can give information on all Vienna's HI hostels. The Österreichischer Jugendherbergsverband (ÖJHV; Map 4; ☎ 533 53 53, fax 535 08 61, ✉ oejhv@chello.at) is at 01, Schottenring and the Österreichischer Jugendherbergswerk (ÖJHW; Map 7; ☎ 533 18 33, fax -85, ✉ oejhw@oejhw.at) is at 01, Helferstorferstrasse 4. Each has a travel agency on the premises, and the ÖJHW also sells hiking equipment.

Some hostels accept reservations by telephone, and in two of them (Myrthengasse and Brigittenau) you can prebook via the worldwide computer reservations system. Hostel prices average around €12 per night, though private hostels usually charge extra for breakfast. Unless otherwise stated, hostel prices are quoted per bed. Vienna's HI hostels may impose a three- to eight-night maximum stay in busy times.

Hotels & Pensions

Hotels and pensions are rated from one to five stars depending on the facilities they offer, though as respective criteria vary you can't assume a three-star pension is equivalent to a three-star hotel. Pensions tend to be smaller than hotels, and usually provide a more personal service and less standardised fixtures and fittings; often they're located on a few floors of an apartment block. Pensions generally offer a better size and quality of room for the price than hotels. Where they usually can't compete is in back-up services (eg, room service, laundry service) and on-site facilities (such as private parking, bar and/or restaurant). If none of that matters to you, stick with the pensions.

With very few exceptions, rooms in Vienna are clean and adequately appointed. Expect to pay a minimum of around €24/40 for a single/double with hall shower or €30/48 with private shower. In budget ac-

---

Getting Vienna's Numbers

In a Vienna address, the number of a building within a street *follows* the street name. Any number *before* the street name denotes the district.

In this book fax numbers are presented as extensions (eg, fax -30) of the phone numbers that they follow. To send a fax, dial the main phone number and add the fax extension.

Throughout Vienna you'll also see telephone numbers presented with extensions. For an explanation of this system see the Post & Communications section in the Facts for the Visitor chapter.

---

commodation, a room with a private shower may mean a room with a shower cubicle rather than with a proper *en suite* bathroom.

If business is slow, mid-range and top-end hotels (and, to a lesser extent, pensions) are willing to negotiate on prices. It's always worth asking for a special deal as prices can come down quite substantially. Some places, especially the five-star hotels, offer special weekend rates, or 'two nights for the price of one' packages. Even in budget places, ask for a special price if you're planning to stay for more than a few days. Cheaper places rarely accept credit cards, and some may close for a few months in winter.

Other Types of Accommodation

Vienna has five camping grounds, mostly in the western and southern suburbs. They all take caravans. From July to September student residences are converted to hotels, giving a much-needed boost to beds at the lower end of the market. A few rooms in private homes are on offer, mostly in the suburbs; expect a three-day minimum stay. Apartments are available through accommodation agencies, and hotels sometimes have self-contained apartment rooms.

FINDING SOMEWHERE TO STAY

Vienna can be a nightmare for budget backpackers who arrive without reservations. Even visitors who can afford to consider a range of options may find their choices full, especially in summer. Book ahead, especially at Christmas and Easter and between June and September. Reservations are binding on either side and compensation may be claimed by the hotel if you do not take a reserved room, or by you if the room is unavailable.

Accommodation Agencies

Several agencies can help with accommodation. Tourist offices (see the Facts for the Visitor chapter) charge a commission of around €3 per reservation, irrespective of the number of rooms being booked. They can help find private rooms but don't have lists to give out. What they can give you instead is a pamphlet detailing camping grounds and youth hostels, or the *Hotel Guide* covering hotels and pensions. Both are free and are revised annually.

Ökista (see Travel Agents in the Getting There & Away chapter) charges €10.90 to find hotel rooms (three-star and above) for a minimum of three nights. For stays of at least two weeks it can find a room in a family house from €14.55 per night B&B (€58.15 commission). The Odyssee Mitwohnzentrale (☎ 402 60 61, fax -11, @ mitwohnzentrale@ odyssee.vienna.at), 08, Lau-dongasse 8, finds private rooms from €25.50/ 47.25 for a single/double, including commission. Monthly rates for furnished apartments start at €475 per month (€365 in summer). The office is open 10 am to 2 pm and 3 to 6 pm Monday to Friday and commission is 25% of the rent for one month, reducing proportionately for longer stays.

Choosing a Location

Staying within the Innere Stadt is convenient for the sights, though inevitably you have to pay more for what you get. Many hotels and pensions are between the Ring and the Gürtel; these are better value and still within easy striking distance of the centre. Places in the suburbs have the lowest prices, though they have a cost in terms of accessibility; these are more of a viable option if you're not too bothered about late-night attractions in the city. Businesspeople will probably want the convenience of a central location, though conferences can be held at a number of locations around the city, including many of the top-end hotels.

If you have a car, staying in the city centre becomes even more expensive; parking is restricted in the Innere Stadt and adjoining districts, meaning you will end up paying high parking fees (typically around €11 to €26 for 24 hours, whether in public or hotel garages). A better option would be to find somewhere farther out where you can safely leave your car, and then rely on public transport. Even if you want a late night and have to take a taxi home, the taxi fare will still be less than a day's garage fees. Hotels outside the Innere Stadt with private garages charge around €8 to €18 for 24 hours; the farther

PLACES TO STAY

from the centre the cheaper it gets. Street parking is no problem in the suburbs.

PLACES TO STAY – BUDGET
Camping
Camping Wien West (Map 2; ☎ 14 23 14, e west2@vie.at; 14, Hüttelbergstrasse 80) is open all year except February. It costs €4.95/2.95 per adult/tent, or €5.45/3.30 in July and August. Two-/four-person bungalows cost from €18.20/29.10. To get there, take U4 or the S-Bahn to Hütteldorf, then bus No 148 or 152. *Camping Neue Donau (Map 2; ☎/fax 202 40 10; 22, Am Kleehäufel)* is the same price but doesn't have bungalows and is only open from mid-May to early September. It's the closest site to the city centre and the only one east of the Danube. Take U1 to Kaisermühlen, then the No 91A bus.

Camping Rodaun (Map 2; ☎/fax 888 41 54; 23, An der Au 2) is open from late March to early November and charges €5.30/4.40 per adult/tent. Take S1 or S2 to Liesing then bus No 60A.

Beyond the city limits to the south is the largest site, *Campingplatz Schloss Laxenburg (☎ 02236-713 33)*, on Münchendorfer Strasse. It has a swimming pool, restaurant and supermarket but there's no convenient public transport into Vienna. Charges are €5.45/2.95 for an adult/tent, or €6/3.30 in July and August (open 1 April to 31 October).

Hostels
Near the Centre No hostels invade the imperial elegance of the Innere Stadt. One of the nearest is HI *Jugendherberge Myrthengasse (Map 5; ☎ 523 63 16, fax 523 58 49, e hostel@chello.at; 07, Myrthengasse 7)*. Based in two buildings, it's convenient, busy and offers daytime check-in. All rooms have a private shower and bedside lights. Beds are €14.55 in six- or four-bed dorms or €16.75 in double rooms. Rates drop by €1.10 in winter, except over Christmas/New Year. Lunch or dinner is €4.75 and laundry is €3.65 per load. Telephone reservations are accepted and strongly advised.

Believe it or Not (Map 5; ☎ 526 46 58; 07, Apartment 14, Myrthengasse 10) is a small private hostel opposite the Myrthen-

gasse hostel. The only sign outside is on the doorbell. It has a sociable atmosphere, but one room has triple bunks and can get hot in summer. There's no breakfast; use the kitchen facilities instead. Beds are €12 in summer or €8 from November to Easter, and you get your own key so there's no curfew. *Panda Hostel (Map 5; ☎ 524 78 88, e VIENNAhostelPANDA@chello.at; 07, 3rd floor, Kaiserstrasse 77)* has the same prices and a similar set-up, with a TV in every room and around 20 beds. It's linked to Lauria (see under Hotels & Pensions).

Hostel Zöhrer (Map 3; ☎ 406 07 30, fax 408 04 09, e zoehrer@compuserve.com; 08, Skodagasse 26) is a private hostel close to the Ring, and is reasonable value. Six- to eight-bed dorms are €12.40 and doubles (bunk beds) are €33.45, all with private shower. There's a kitchen, courtyard and own-key entry; reception is open from 7.30 am to 10 pm.

Turmherberge Don Bosco (Map 6; ☎ 713 14 94; 03, Lechnerstrasse 12), southeast of the Ring in a church tower, has the cheapest beds in town – €5.85 plus a one-off payment of €1.85 for sheets if required. However, the place hasn't been modernised since the 1950s – some rooms are cramped and have few lockers (no locks). Breakfast is not included though there are basic kitchen facilities. It has 50 beds and is open from 1 March to 31 November. Curfew is 11.45 pm; reception closes at noon and you can only check in once it reopens at 5 pm (telephone reservations accepted).

Two hostels, both open 24 hours, are near Westbahnhof. *Hostel Ruthensteiner (Map 5; ☎ 893 42 02, fax 893 27 96, e hostel .ruthensteiner@telecom.at; 15, Robert Hamerling Gasse 24)* is one block south of Mariahilfer Strasse. Large dorms are €10.55 (€9.45 with seasonal deals), plus a one-off €1.45 if you need sheets. Sheets are provided in the three- to five-bed rooms (€12.30) and the basic singles/doubles for €17.80/34.20. Breakfast costs €2.15 and there's a kitchen and shady rear courtyard.

Wombat's (Map 5; ☎ 897 23 36, fax 897 25 77, e wombats@chello.at; 15, Grangasse 6) is a friendly, newly built non-HI hostel, with a pub and courtyard garden. Dorms/doubles are €12.75/35.65 and breakfast is €2.55. It's about a 10-minute walk from Westbahnhof and you can book online at the Web site: www.wombats.at.

Kolpingsfamilie Meidling (Map 5; ☎ 813 54 87, fax 812 21 30, e office@wien12.kolping.at; 12, Bendlgasse 10–12) is near the Niederhofstrasse U6 stop, south of Westbahnhof. Beds are from €9.45 (eight- to 10-bed dorms) to €13.10 (four-bed dorms). All dorms have private shower and some have WC; the four-bed dorms have a balcony. There are lockers (no keys) and a patio round the back. Non-HI members pay €2.95 extra, which is a bit of a cheek as they don't provide the guest card stamp. Breakfast/dinner costs €3.30/ 4.75. Curfew is at midnight, but reception is open 24 hours.

In the Suburbs *Jugendgästhaus Brigittenau* (Map 4; ☎ 332 82 94, fax 330 83 79, e jgh1200@chello.at; 20, Friedrich Engels Platz 24) is an HI hostel with 434 beds in a modern, multistorey building just a couple of minutes' walk from the Danube (trams N, 31 and 33 stop outside). Beds in a 24-bed dorm are €10.90, or in a room with two to six beds you pay €15.65 with shower and WC, €13.45 without. Prices drop by €1.10 in winter. Dinners are €4.75, and there's also a cafe, games room and garden. Reception is open 24 hours though rooms are closed from 9 am to 1 pm.

Jugendgästhaus Hütteldorf-Hacking (Map 2; ☎ 877 02 63, fax -2, e jgh@wigast.com; 13, Schlossberggasse 8) is an HI hostel with a total of 285 beds. Different-sized dorms, some with shower, cost from €13.45 in summer or €11.65 in winter, and there are three single rooms (€9.85 surcharge). Meals are €5.25, and laundry costs €5.10. There's a games lounge, and doors are locked from 9.30 am to 3 pm. Curfew is 11.45 pm but you can buy a key card (€2.20) for late entry. It's far from the centre of town, but only a five-minute walk from both the U4 Hütteldorf station and the N49 nightbus route.

Another HI hostel is the *Schlossherberge am Wilhelminenberg* (Map 2; ☎ 485 85 03-700, fax -702, e shb@wigast.com; 16, Savoyenstrasse 2), in the grounds of the Schloss Wilhelminenberg. Four-bed dorms with shower and WC are €16.40 per person and a double room is €54. Reception is open from 7 am to 11 pm and there's no curfew. The great view includes Vienna and some vineyards but it's a long way from the centre: bus Nos 46B and 146B link to citybound trams J, 44 and 46.

Student Residences

These *Studentenheime* are available to tourists from 1 July to 30 September, while the students are on holiday. In their student incarnations they usually have a kitchen and dining room on each floor, but when they reinvent themselves as seasonal hotels these useful facilities often remain locked ('fire risk' is the usual excuse). Rooms are perfectly OK but nothing fancy. Expect single beds (perhaps placed together in doubles), a work desk, a wardrobe and bare walls stripped of their term-time posters. Cheaper places have institutional-style ablutions blocks; pricier places offer private shower and WC and are all but indistinguishable from conventional hotels. Most are outside the Innere Stadt but are still reasonably convenient for the centre.

Blue House Hostel (Map 3; ☎ 369 55 85-0; 19, Peter Jordan Strasse 29) is an excellent choice – small-scale and friendly, with free Internet access, a washing machine, and kitchens that stay open. Singles/doubles with hall shower are €16/26.20, and breakfast is €3.30.

Porzellaneum (Map 3; ☎ 317 72 82, fax -30, e office@porzellaneum.sth.ac.at; 09, Porzellangasse 30) is also very cheap. Small singles and doubles are only €13.85 per person without breakfast, and reception is open 24 hours. Those of a modest disposition may be concerned that some of the hall showers are in open (ie, unpartitioned) rooms.

Gästehaus Pfeilgasse (Map 5; 08, Pfeilgasse 4–6) has singles/doubles/triples for €20.35/36.35/45.80 with shower and WC in the corridor. It shares the building and the reception (open 24 hours) with *Hotel Avis*, where rooms have private shower and WC

PLACES TO STAY

and cost €45.10/59.60. Opposite is *Academia (Pfeilgasse 4–6)*, offering the same deal as Hotel Avis. For all three places, contact ☎ 401 76, fax 401 76-20, e acahot@ academia-hotels.co.at.

Auersperg (Map 7; ☎ *406 25 40; 08, Auerspergstrasse 9)* has singles/doubles from €27.30/45.10, or €37.80/62.50 with private shower and WC. It's near the Ring and has 24-hour reception. Unless you're inquiring only a few days ahead, make advance reservations via Albertina Hotels Austria (☎ 512 74 93, fax 512 19 68), 01, Führichgasse 10.

Music Academy (Map 7; ☎ *514 84-48; fax -49,* e *jagersberger@mhsw.ac.at; 01, Johannesgasse 8)* is the only place inside the Ring. It has singles/doubles costing from €35.65/68.35 with private bath and WC or from €32/56.70 without, while triples/ quads are €63.25/75.60 with sink. Prices are reduced for students in September. All rooms have a fridge, and a phone for incoming calls. It also has a washing machine and 24-hour reception, and one room and one apartment (inexpensive) are available year-round.

Auge Gottes (Map 3; ☎ *319 44 88-10, fax -11; 09, Nussdorfer Strasse 75)* will reopen in 2002, following extensive renovations and upgrading.

Hotels & Pensions
Near the Centre *Lauria (Map 5;* ☎ *522 25 55,* e *VIENNAapartmentsLAURIA@ chello.at; 07, 3rd floor, Kaiserstrasse 77)* is in a residential building, close to transport and shops. It has friendly staff, own-key entry, kitchen facilities (no breakfast), TVs and thoughtful, homy touches. Some rooms have large pictorial scenes on the wall. Doubles are €40/54.50 (€32.70 with bunk beds) without/with private shower. Triples (€54.50/65.40), quads (€65.40/76.30) and large apartments (€126.30 to €192.50, sleeping four to nine people) are also available. There may be a two-day minimum stay for reservations, and credit cards are accepted.

Pension Wild (Map 7; ☎ *406 51 74, fax 402 21 68; 08, Langegasse 10)* is a central, gay-friendly, everyone-friendly place. 'Wild' is the family name, not a description. Singles/ doubles are €35.65/42.90 and singles/ doubles/triples with private shower are €42.90/57.45/76.35. On the top floor are new rooms with shower, toilet and cable TV for €50.15/71.95/89.40. There are kitchens and reception is open 24 hours. A gay massage/sauna centre shares the building.

Auer (Map 3; ☎ *406 21 21, fax -4; 09, Lazarettgasse 3)* is also friendly and pleasant, and feels very Viennese. Singles/doubles start from €26.90/40.70 with hall shower; doubles/triples with private shower are €45.80/60.35. This pension has 14 rooms and reception is on the 1st floor (no lift).

Hotel Westend (Map 5; ☎ *597 67 29, fax -27; 06, Fügergasse 3)* is close to Westbahnhof and has reasonable singles/doubles for €25.80/45.45 (€29.45/54.15 with shower). However, telephone ahead as the new owner may make changes.

Not far away, *Fünfhaus (Map 5;* ☎ *892 35 45, fax 892 04 60; 15, Sperrgasse 12)* has a range of clean rooms – some of them are new, fresh and large. Singles/doubles are €37.10/53.10 with shower and WC, or €29.10/43.65 without. Courtyard parking costs €3.65, and it's closed from mid-November to 1 March.

Pension Kraml (Map 5; ☎ *587 85 88, fax 586 75 73; 06, Brauergasse 5)* is on the bus No 13A route. Small, friendly and family run, it has singles/doubles for €24.75/46.55 and large doubles with private shower for €53.80, or €61.05 with WC also. Triples start at €61.05, and there are also family apartments from €74.15. Unusually for a budget place, breakfast is buffet style, though you can subtract €2.20 per person and skip it.

Kolping-Gästehaus (Map 7; ☎ *587 56 31-0, fax 586 36 30,* e *reservierung@ wien-zentral.kolping.at; 06, Gumpendorfer Strasse 39)* has its entrance on Stiegengasse. It has singles/doubles with shower, toilet and TV for €52.35/71.25, and a few singles without for €21.85. The rooms are reasonable value, though this place is also a student residence and even the hotel section has something of an institutionalised aura about it.

Close to the centre is **Quisisana** (Map 7; ☎ 587 71 55, fax 587 71 56-33, ⓔ office@ quisisana-wien.co.at; 06, Windmühlgasse 6), with a cafe-restaurant on site and variable but good-value rooms. It charges from €29.10/48 for rooms with shower or €24.45/40.70 without. Also a good deal is **Pension Miklos** (Map 6; ☎ 587 51 61, fax 587 27 50; 05, Schönbrunner Strasse 41), near the Naschmarkt and transport routes. Simple singles with hall shower are €18.20; singles/doubles with private shower and toilet cost €32.75/42.20, and there are also family rooms. Rooms are rather basic conversions from residential flats, but most are large, with a lounge area. Add €3.30 for breakfast. There's no lift.

Pension Esterházy (Map 5; ☎ 587 51 59; 04, Nelkengasse 3), just off Mariahilfer Strasse, has decent-sized rooms (many singles) for €24.75/38.55 without breakfast. It's not a bad deal, despite the fact that some rooms are drab and the exterior needs renovating. Showers and toilets are down the hall, though a couple of rooms with private facilities are planned.

Pension Hargita (Map 5; ☎ 526 19 28, fax 526 04 92, ⓔ pension-hargita@magnet .at; 07, Andreasgasse 1) has 19 clean, quaint rooms but no lift. Singles/doubles are €32.75/50.90 with shower, €29.10/43.65 without. Breakfast is €2.95.

Pension Falstaff (Map 3; ☎ 317 91 86, fax -4, ⓔ majidi_s@hotmail.com; 09, Müllnergasse 5) has singles/doubles for €29.80/48.70 (with an irksome fee of €2.20 to use the hall shower) or €37.10/56 with private shower. Prices are around €7.30 lower in winter, and furnishings are ageing but adequate. It's convenient for tram D to the Ring and Nussdorf.

Praterstern (Map 7; ☎ 214 01 23, fax 214 78 80, ⓔ hotelpraterstern@aon.at; 02, Mayergasse 6), east of the Ring, has a garden. Singles/doubles are €24/42.55, or €35.65/53.80 with shower and toilet. Some readers have complained about the attitude of one or two of the staff, but they've always been fine when we've made our (anonymous) visits.

A 10-minute walk from Südbahnhof is **Hotel Kolbeck** (Map 6; ☎ 604 17 73, fax 602 94 86, ⓔ hotelkolbeck@chello.at; 10, Laxenburger Strasse 19). Rooms with hall shower are €29.10/50.90; those with private shower, WC and cable TV are €50.90/79.95. Reception is open 24 hours.

Down the road is **Cyrus** (Map 6; ☎/fax 604 42 88; 10, Laxenburger Strasse 19), with a range of rooms, all with shower and satellite TV. Singles are €21.85 to €36.35 and doubles are €43.65 to €65.45; prices depend on the size, furnishings and whether they have private toilet.

Nearby is **Pension Caroline** (Map 6; ☎ 604 80 70, fax 602 77 67, ⓔ fruehstueck spension.caroline@netway.at; 10, Gudrunstrasse 138), convenient for local transport. Attractive, renovated rooms with shower, WC and satellite TV are €37.80/61.05.

Pension Bosch (Map 6; ☎ 798 61 79, fax 799 17 18; 03, Keilgasse 13) is in a traditional building in a residential street. Rooms (€32.75/54.50 without shower, €42.15/64 with, €43.65/71.25 with shower and WC) have personal touches and satellite TV; most have old-fashioned furnishings. Reception is on the 1st floor (there's a lift).

At **Pension Ani** (Map 3; ☎ 405 65 53, fax 408 10 82; 09, Kinderspitalgasse 1), rooms cost from €40/54.55 with shower, cable TV and phone, or you can pay €43.65/65.45 for bigger rooms with WC. Prices are sometimes negotiable – call ahead to ask for the best deal.

In the Suburbs **Jugendgästehaus Hernals** (Map 3; ☎ 480 79 16; 17, Sautergasse 34) is a former student residence and offers standardised rooms with two or three single beds. Tram No 43 (stop: Wattgasse) goes to the Ring. Singles/doubles/triples are €19.65/32/48, or €18.20/29.10/43.65 in winter. It's the same price for the few rooms with private shower. Unless you're inquiring only a few days ahead, make advance reservations via Albertina Hotels Austria (☎ 512 74 93, fax 512 19 68), 01, Führichgasse 10.

Matauschek (Map 5; ☎/fax 982 35 32; 14, Breitenseer Strasse 14) is opposite the Hütteldorfer Strasse U3 stop and has 25

PLACES TO STAY

variable rooms with TV. Singles/doubles cost €25.45/43.60 with hall shower, or €36.35/58.15 with private shower and toilet. The simple restaurant is closed on Wednesday and Thursday, though reception stays open.

Rustler (Map 5; ☎/fax 982 01 62; 14, *Linzer Strasse 43*) is an efficiently run place close to Schönbrunn (or take tram No 52 from Westbahnhof). It has a pretty garden (complete with garden gnomes), double glazing and a small bar-breakfast room. Rooms with satellite TV are €54.50/74.15 for a single/double with shower and WC, €41.45/60.35 with shower, or €29.10/48 using the hall shower. There are triples too. It's closed from around November to March, except over Christmas/New Year.

PLACES TO STAY – MID-RANGE
Innere Stadt

You tend to get less for your money in the Innere Stadt. The following can all be found on Map 7 (the area code is 01).

Pension Nossek (☎ 533 70 41, fax 535 36 46; *Graben 17*) is good value for its ideal situation. Clean, comfortable, baroque-style singles (€47.25 to €61.80) and doubles (€90.85 to €116.30) are priced depending on the size, view and private facilities. Book weeks ahead during high season.

Schweizer Pension Solderer (☎ 533 81 56, fax 535 64 69, **e** *schweizer.pension@ gmx.at; Heinrichsgasse 2*), run by Swiss sisters, is very clean. It offers singles/doubles from €34.50/54.15 with shower in the hall only, €50.55/64.95 with private shower, and €58.60/75.80 with shower and WC. Most rooms have cable TV and ornamental ceramic stoves. You get a key to operate the old-fashioned lift, and there's street parking for €5.10. Reserve well in advance.

Pension am Operneck (☎ 512 93 10; *Kärntner Strasse 47*) has big rooms with private shower, toilet and TV (Austrian channels only) for €45.10/65.45. There are just six rooms so you usually need to reserve months ahead. Reception is open from 7 am to 7.30 pm.

Hotel Orient (☎ 533 73 07, fax 535 03 40; *Tiefer Graben 30*) has a *fin-de-siècle* hallway and facade, and rooms decked out in a variety of interesting styles. Scenes from *The Third Man* were shot here. Rooms with private shower start at €50.90/65.45 for a single/double. Some rooms are rented by the hour for discreet liaisons, but it's by no means a seedy place.

Hotel Post (☎ 515 83-0, fax -808, **e** *office@hotel-post-wien.at; Fleischmarkt 24*) has renovated rooms in bright colours. Singles/doubles are €69.80/107.60 with shower and WC. Rooms without a shower are €40.70/65.45 – a good deal for the Innere Stadt. All rooms have satellite TV, and prices go down in winter.

Hotel Wandl (☎ 534 55-0, fax -77, **e** *reservation@hotel-wandl.com; Petersplatz 9*) is a family-run hotel with many of its 138 rooms arranged around inner courtyards. Guests get free Internet access. Modern rooms in pale colours start at €71.22/123.55, or there are a few cheaper rooms without shower, including an elegant double (€87.25) with historic frescoes. Prices drop by about 10% in winter.

Near the Centre

Alla Lenz (Map 5; ☎ 523 69 89-0, fax -55, **e** *alla-lenz@magnet.at; 07, Halbgasse 3–5*) is an excellent, top-of-the-range pension with a rooftop swimming pool (free to guests), a cafe, and a garage next door (€10.90 daily). Doubles start at €85.80 (lower in winter, and for stays of two nights or more) and have air-con, private shower and WC, telephone and cable TV. There are singles, which aren't such a good deal at €71.25, and apartments too.

Nearby, *Pension Atrium* (Map 5; ☎ 523 31 14, fax -9; 07, Burggasse 118) has clean, renovated rooms from €48/68.35 with shower, WC and TV, plus one apartment for €78.50. Also close by is *Pension Carantania* (Map 5; ☎ 526 73 40, fax -6, **e** *pension .carantania@chello.at; 07, Kandlgasse 35–7*). Big singles/doubles with shower, WC and cable TV are €52.35/71.95, and most have old-style furnishings.

Altwienerhof (Map 5; ☎ 892 60 00, fax -8, **e** *altwienerhof@netway.at; 15, Herklotzgasse 6*) is a small, family-run hotel offering good-value, decent-sized rooms and a quality restaurant. Stylish singles/doubles are €50.90/84.30 and have a shower, WC, TV and phone. Half or full board is possible.

Pension Continental (Map 5; ☎ 523 24 18, fax 523 26 30, e hotel.continental@chello.at; 07, Kirchengasse 1) has variable rooms (the newer ones are nicer) starting at €54.55/79.95 with bath or shower, WC and cable TV. It enjoys a convenient location overlooking Mariahilfer Strasse and has private parking for €7.30.

Hotel Cryston (Map 5; ☎ 813 56 82, fax 812 37 01-70, e hotel.cryston@netway.at; 12, Gaudenzdorfer Gürtel 63) is close to U-Bahn (U4) and tram stops. It has good rooms from €50.90/85.80 with shower, WC, satellite TV and double-glazed windows. There's also free private parking and a breakfast buffet. Rooms for €30.55/47.25 have a sink but don't have TV, shower or WC. There's a nominal €0.75 charge to use the hall showers.

Hotel Fürstenhof (Map 5; ☎ 523 32 67, fax -26, e reception@hotel-fuerstenhof.com; 07, Neubaugürtel 4), opposite Westbahnhof, is a typical Viennese family-run hotel. Rooms with TV are €63.95/101.05 with shower and WC or €40.70/61.05 without. Inquire about any discounts that may be available.

All rooms in the following places have shower and WC, cable or satellite TV, and other amenities.

Hotel Donauwalzer (Map 3; ☎ 405 76 45, fax -999, e hotel.donauwalzer@gmx.at; 17, Ottakringer Strasse 5) has characterful rooms that vary in quality and style (anything from baroque to oriental). Prices start at €42.90/64.70. The cafe-bar has live music on Friday and Saturday nights, and is a favourite among residents of Polish descent.

Hotel Maté Dependance (Map 3; ☎ 404 66, fax 404 55; 17, Bergsteiggasse 22) charges €61.80/93.05 for singles/doubles, or €56/71.95 in winter. Rooms are average, but there's free tea and coffee, and guests can also use the good facilities in the main Hotel Maté (see Places to Stay – Top End).

Hotel Adlon (Map 7; ☎ 216 67 88, fax -116, e hoteladlon@netway.at; 02, Hofen-

edergasse 4)* has a relaxing ambience, and white rooms with fake flowers for €61.80/90.90 (€52.35/80 in winter). There's a sauna (€7.30, including a drink) and a funky aquarium around the reception desk.

Hotel Congress (Map 6; ☎ 505 55 06, fax 505 23 40; 04, Wiedner Gürtel 34–36) is convenient for Südbahnhof and offers Art Nouveau touches in the decor. Rooms are €64.70/108.30 (€57.45/86.50 from November to March).

In the Suburbs

Hotel Victoria (Map 5; ☎ 877 18 98, fax 877 20 42, e hotel.victoria@magnet.at; 13, Eduard Klein Gasse 9) is near Schloss Schönbrunn. It has a range of double rooms with shower, WC and TV, costing from €58 for unrenovated rooms up to €116 for large rooms with a view. Single occupancy costs about 25% less.

West of the city in the Wienerwald is *Sophienalpe (Map 2; ☎ 486 24 32, fax 485 16 55-12, e sophienalpe@hotels.or.at; 14, Sophienalpe 13)*, with an indoor swimming pool and a restaurant. The yellow Bundesbus (No 243) from the end of tram No 43 goes within 500m of the hotel, but as it runs infrequently and not in the evening, you really need a car to stay here. Singles/doubles with private shower and WC are €40/58.20, with bigger doubles going for €65.45. From 1 November to 31 March check-in is only at weekends (daily otherwise).

Schloss Wilhelminenberg (Map 2; ☎ 485 85 03, fax 485 48 76, e schloss.wilhelminenberg@austria-trend.at; 16, Savoyenstrasse 2) is also convenient for the Wienerwald and has a big garden, stately appearance and fine views from the terrace cafe. Prices start at €65.45/98.15 for rooms with very high ceilings, cable TV, shower and WC. Bus Nos 46B and 146B stop outside and link to city-bound trams J, 44 and 46. There's plenty of parking.

Beyond the Central Cemetery, at the terminus of tram No 71, is *Pension Weber (Map 2; ☎ 769 10 82, fax -40; 11, Kaiserebersdorfer Strasse 283)*. It offers singles/doubles with shower, WC and cable TV for €52.35/71.25. There's lots of parking.

PLACES TO STAY

There are only a few places east of the Danube, mainly because this area has less character and is less convenient for the tourist sights. You might save a euro or two staying in the farther-flung places on this side, but it probably isn't worth considering this option. An exception is **Strandhotel Alte Donau** (Map 4; ☎ 204 40 94, fax -40, **e** strandhotel@alte-donau.at; 22, Wagramer Strasse 51), on the east bank of the Alte Donau and a five-minute walk from the U1 line. It has two sections, with the larger, newer rooms situated across the (free) car park. Singles/doubles with shower, WC, TV and telephone start from €54.50/76.35, while those without toilet are €34.90/50.90. Rooms without shower or WC are €32/47.25. There's also a garden with private swimming access.

PLACES TO STAY – TOP END

You can expect that rooms in this category will have, as a minimum, private shower or bath, WC, cable TV, direct-dial phone, minibar and radio. These hotels will have all the facilities business visitors might require.

Innere Stadt

The following can all be found on Map 7 (the area code is 01).

Hotel am Schubertring (☎ 717 02-0, fax 713 99 66, **e** aschu@atnet.at; Schubertring 11) is a good choice. The maze-like corridors lead to well equipped singles/doubles with Biedermeier or Art Nouveau furniture. Prices start from €105.40/134.45, or from €90.84/119.95 in winter.

Good value **Hotel Austria** (☎ 515 23, fax -506, **e** office@hotelaustria-wien.at; Am Fleischmarkt 20) is down a quiet cul-de-sac. You can rent pleasantly furnished rooms for €92.30/134.50, or €61.80/88.70 in winter.

Appartement Pension Riemergasse (☎ 512 72 200, fax 513 77 78, **e** otto@otto.at; Riemergasse 8) can arrange parking for €14.55 a day. A variety of apartments are available, all with kitchenette, telephone, cable TV, toilet and bath or shower. Prices for the smallest apartments range from €90.85 single occupancy to

€174.45 for four people. Larger apartments sleep up to seven people (€305.25). Breakfast costs €4.80 per person. Credit cards are not accepted.

Hotel zur Wiener Staatsoper (☎ 513 12 74, fax -15, **e** office@zurwienerstaatsoper .at; Krugerstrasse 11) has an attractive stuccoed facade. Singles/doubles (€76.35/101.75) are quiet and have white fittings, but are perhaps a little too compact for ideal comfort. Garage parking is discounted to €16 per day.

The relatively plain frontage of **Hotel Kaiserin Elisabeth** (☎ 515 26, fax -7, **e** kaiserin@ins.at; Weihburggasse 3) belies its pleasant interior and long history (Mozart stayed here). Nicely decorated rooms are €109/185.35, though there are a few small singles for €72.70 with bath instead of shower.

Hotel am Stephansplatz (☎ 53 405-0, fax -711, **e** hotel@stephansplatz.co.at; Stephansplatz 9) is the closest you can sleep to Stephansdom without building a nest in the belfry. Comfortable, sizable singles/doubles cost €116.30/188.95 or less.

The rest of the places in this section are five-star hotels. Standard or 'economy' (something of a misnomer in this category) rooms are comfortable and with all the expected fittings and facilities, but they're not necessarily much better than those in a good four-star hotel. You're really paying the premium for the ambience, reputation, better service levels and the grandeur of the reception and lobby areas. They all also offer 'superior' rooms and suites. Breakfast generally costs extra, but may be included in special, lower weekend rates.

At **Hotel Sacher** (☎ 51 456-0, fax -810, **e** hotel@sacher.com; Philharmonikerstrasse 4), elegance and tradition go hand in hand. Rooms with Baroque furnishings and genuine 19th-century oil paintings start at €182/288.

Hotel Imperial (☎ 501 10-333, fax -440, **e** Hotel_Imperial@Sheraton.com; Kärntner Ring 16) is a truly palatial and expensive period hotel that usually attracts visiting bigwigs. Singles/doubles cost from €320/400.

Similarly impressive is **Hotel Bristol** (☎ 51 516-536, fax -550, e Hotel.Bristol@ westin.com; Kärntner Ring 1), where rooms start at €298/386. Nearby, **Ana Grand** (☎ 515 80-0, fax 515 13 13, e reservation@ anagrand.com; Kärntner Ring 9) was rebuilt during the 1990s. There's a new 24-hour fitness centre, and rooms from €262/335.

Hotel Marriott (☎ 515 18-0, fax -6736, e reservations@marriott.com; Parkring 12a) has large, air-con rooms for €262 (single or double). The fitness room, sauna and 13m swimming pool are free for hotel guests, and the harmonious, galleried lobby shelters shops, cafes and a waterfall tumbling down fake rocks.

Hotel Ambassador (☎ 961 610, fax 513 29 99, e reservations@ambassador.at; Kärntner Strasse 22) reopened in 2000 following extensive renovations. Rooms cost from €169/211.

Near the Centre

Hotel Maté (Map 3; ☎ 404 55, fax -888, e mate@point.at; 17, Ottakringer Strasse 34–36) has standard four-star rooms but the hotel has five-star facilities, including a swimming pool, sauna and fitness room (all free for guests) as well as a solarium (€5.85). Prices start at €71.25/122.10, or €64.70/93.05 in winter.

Thüringer Hof (Map 3; ☎ 401 79-0, fax -600, e thuehof@via.at; 18, Jörgerstrasse 4–8) rents out a variety of rooms from €75.60/99.60 (€59.60/79.25 in winter); some are very spacious and have impressive chandeliers. There's parking for €5.85 and a rooftop terrace.

Attaché (Map 6; ☎ 505 18 17, fax -232, e attachehot@aol.com; 04, Wiedner Hauptstrasse 71) is a pension charging €79.95/ 122.85 or less, depending on the season. Many of its 23 rooms have period furniture, including Art Nouveau style.

Hotel Tyrol (Map 7; ☎ 587 54 15, fax -9, e reception@hotel-tyrol-vienna.com; 06, Mariahilfer Strasse 15) is a smallish hotel with rooms from €71.25/93.05, some with large, oval baths. Renovations are planned by the new owner. The entrance is around the side on Königsklostergasse.

Reither (Map 5; ☎ 893 68 41, fax 893 68 35, e Hotel.Reither@aon.at; 15, Graumanngasse 16) is a Best Western B&B hotel tucked away in a nondescript side street. Rooms with the usual amenities start from €80/123.50, and the sauna and indoor swimming pool are free for guests.

Hotel Arkadenhof (Map 3; ☎ 310 08 37, fax 310 76 86, e management@arkaden hof.com; 09, Viriotgasse 5) is a comfortable, stylish, small hotel that opened in 1992. Rooms have all facilities, including air-con, and cost €107.60/143.90 (€93.05/ 122.10 in winter).

A comparable place is the **Theater-Hotel** (Map 3; ☎ 405 36 48, fax 405 14 06, e chwien@cordial.co.at; 80, Josefstädter Strasse 22), which has an Art Nouveau aura about it. Published room rates are €116.30/182.40, or €101.75/150.45 in winter, though they seem to be amenable to offering special deals here.

Located in a typically grand Viennese building, the **Hotel Atlanta** (Map 3; ☎ 405 12 30, fax 405 53 75, e hotel.atlanta@ cybertron.at; 09, Währinger Strasse 33) is a good four-star hotel. Rooms are reasonably spacious, and well furnished with elegant touches. Singles/doubles go for €79.95/116.30 and triples are €138.10. From November to March prices are reduced by about €15 per person.

Hotel Boltzmann (Map 3; ☎ 316 12-0, fax -816, e boltzmann@arcotel.co.at; 09, Boltzmanngasse 8) has renovated rooms in cheerful colours. Singles/doubles cost €109.05/145.35.

Close to the Theater an der Wien, the theatrical connection of **Hotel-Pension Schneider** (Map 7; ☎ 588 38-0, fax -212, e hotel-schneider@netway.at; 06, Getreidemarkt 5) is obvious when you enter the lobby and see the signed photos of the actors and opera stars who have stayed here. Singles cost €71 to €101, doubles cost €125, and there are excellent self-contained two-person apartments for €160. Prices are slightly lower in the winter.

Aphrodite (Map 7; ☎ 211 48, fax -15; 02, Praterstrasse 28) is a four-star hotel with a unique extra: beauty treatments for both

PLACES TO STAY

men and women (eg, a three-day program costs €400). You'll be dazzled by the many mirrors in the rooms, presumably there so you can admire your progress. There's also a rooftop terrace, swimming pool, sauna and fitness room, all of which are free to guests. Singles/doubles cost from €83.60/163.55, with reductions in winter.

Albatros (Map 3; ☎ *317 35 08, fax -88,* ℮ *albatros@austria-trend.at; 09, Liechtensteinstrasse 89)* is a modern hotel which has renovated but quite plain rooms with air-con. Singles/doubles are €105.40/136.65. There's also a sauna and solarium on site (charge payable), and free tea and coffee in the lobby.

Another modern hotel in the same hotel chain is *Favorita (Map 6;* ☎ *601 46-0, fax -720,* ℮ *favorita@austria-trend.at; 10, Laxenburger Strasse 8–10)*. Rooms cost €101.75/126.45 and the sauna and steam bath are free for guests.

The five-star *Inter-Continental (Map 7;* ☎ *711 22-0, fax 713 44 89,* ℮ *vienna@interconti.com; 03, Johannesgasse 28)* ajoins the Innere Stadt, and overlooks the Stadtpark. It has a huge stylish lobby and ballroom, and rooms from €189/226 with traditional furnishings. The solarium, sauna and fitness room are free for guests.

Schwarzenberg (Map 6; ☎ *798 45 15, fax 798 47 14,* ℮ *palais@schwarzenberg .co.at; 03, Schwarzenbergplatz 9)* is a small five-star hotel in the Palais Schwarzenberg. Rooms with period furniture start at €219/248. There are extensive private grounds with a swimming pool and tennis courts, and free parking.

In the Suburbs

Celtes (Map 2; ☎ *440 41 51, fax -116; 19, Celtesgasse 1)* is in the Neustift am Walde Heurigen area (take bus No 35A from Spittelau). The rooms are average but reasonably priced (€65.45/101.75 for singles/doubles) and there's a bar and a garden.

Parkhotel Schönbrunn (Map 5; ☎ *87 804, fax -3220,* ℮ *parkhotel.schoenbrunn@austria-trend.at; 13, Hietzinger Hauptstrasse 10–20)* is easily accessible from the centre by U4 (get off at the Hietzing stop).

It was built partially with money from Emperor Franz Josef, who considered it his guesthouse. The lobby and grand ballroom all have the majesty of a five-star place, and many rooms surround a large garden with sun lounges, trees and grass. There's also a 12m swimming pool, fitness room and sauna (all free for guests). Rooms start at €86.50/123.60, or €101.10/144.70 for deluxe 'business rooms' with a modem connection.

Also on the U4 line (stop: Meidling Hauptstrasse) is *Renaissance (Map 5;* ☎ *85 102-0, fax -100,* ℮ *renaissance.vienna .viehw@renaissancehotels.com; 15, Ullmannstrasse 71)*, the only suburban five-star hotel. Modern in style, it has a rooftop swimming pool and rooms starting at €145/167.

LONG-TERM RENTALS

Viennese looking for accommodation turn to *Bazar* magazine (€1.85). It's packed with advertisements for all sorts of things, including ads placed by people seeking or offering houses or flats to share. It's free to place ads. The time scale of places on offer may range from indefinite rental, to occupation of a flat for a month or so while the resident is on holiday abroad. The *Falter* events magazine also carries accommodation ads, as does *Austria Today*.

The accommodation agencies mentioned earlier under Finding Somewhere to Stay can arrange long-term accommodation for you, either in apartments or private rooms. Another approach is to ask around the universities and the student residences, and check university notice boards – those in the main university building and in the technical university are good bets. There's quite a swift turnover of student-type accommodation so you'll be able to find something. Monthly prices start at about €255/290 for a single/double in a shared apartment or from €470 for a complete apartment sleeping two to four people.

Some of the places already listed under Places to Stay – Budget (Hotels & Pensions) can offer monthly rates. *Lauria* offers long-term apartment or room rental from November to Easter. There's also ***Kolping-Gästehaus***, charging about €725 per person per month for a single/double with private shower, toilet, telephone and cable TV, or €220 for old singles using hall shower. They also have student rooms that are available to everyone during the summer, with meals an optional extra: singles/doubles are €271/378 with shower and toilet or €200/292 without. To get these student rooms you need to contact the Hausbewohnerbüro (☎ 587 56 31-117) on the 1st floor, not the main hotel reception.

For more luxurious living, ***Hotel-Pension Schneider*** (see Top End – Near the Centre) is just one of a number of top-end hotels which offer apartments. ***Appartement Pension Riemergasse*** (see Top End – Innere Stadt) offers fully furnished apartments at nightly or monthly rates. At ***Singerstrasse Apartments*** (☎ 514 49-0, **e** apartments@ singerstrasse2125.at; 01, Singerstrasse 21–25) there are serviced apartments ideal for businesspeople, from €560/1999 per week/month – see the Web site at www .singerstrasse2125.at for details.

Places to Eat

There are thousands of restaurants to choose from in Vienna, covering all budgets and all styles of cuisine. Coffee houses *(Kaffeehäuser)* and wine taverns *(Heurigen)* are a defining characteristic of Vienna, and are great places to eat. *Beisl* is a common Viennese name for a small tavern or restaurant. If you haven't the time or the money for a sit-down meal, there are many takeaway places, including the *Würstelstande* that are another Viennese institution; they provide a quick snack of sausage and bread for around €1.45 to €2.55 (see the boxed text).

The main meal is taken at midday, when you'll commonly hear the term *Mahlzeit* when the food is served, which basically means 'enjoy your meal'. In the evenings you'll hear *Gutenappetit*. Most restaurants have a set meal or menu of the day *(Tagesteller, Tagesmenü or Mittagsmenü)* that gives the best value for money: a lunch menu with soup can sometimes cost as little as €4 to €5.10. Chinese restaurants are particularly good value in this respect. For reasons of space only a few have been mentioned in this chapter, but they're well worth looking out for. Pizzerias are numerous and also offer good value.

The cheapest sit-down food is generally in the university restaurants *(Mensas)*. These are open to everyone, though they usually only serve weekday lunches. Expect to find two or three different daily specials, including a vegetarian choice. Students may be able to get a discount of €0.30 or so if they show an ISIC card. Mensas are good places to meet students (who usually speak English well) and find out about the new 'in' places around town.

The main train stations all have several options for a cheap meal. Branches of the Wienerwald chain of restaurants offer unremarkable but reasonably priced chicken dishes, either on an eat-in or takeaway basis. Nordsee is its fishy equivalent.

The Schnitzelhaus chain is excellent for fast food on a schnitzel theme, especially good for soaking up excess alcohol from the night before. Prices are low: a schnitzel with fries or potato salad costs €3.30, a cordon bleu is €4.30, and the grandaddy schnitzel, 'Bigone Gusto Fonso', is €6.20. There are nearly 30 branches around town and all are open 10 am to 10 pm daily. It's a bit like an Austrian version of McDonald's but without the red-haired clown.

Heurigen are deeply entwined in the Viennese way of life. Traditionally set up to allow farmers to sell their home-made wine, they are now found throughout the city, still selling local wine and providing hearty buffet-style food at affordable prices. For details about Heurigen in Vienna, see the Entertainment chapter.

For expensive dining, five-star hotels invariably have a gourmet restaurant. Pricier

A Culinary Institution

The *Würstelstande* (sausage stand) is a familiar Viennese institution and may sell up to a dozen types of sausage. Each comes with a chunk of bread and a big dollop of mustard *(Senf)* – which can be sweet *(süss* or *Kremser Senf)* or hot *(scharf)*. Tomato ketchup and mayonnaise can be requested. The thinner sausages are served two at a time, except in the less expensive 'hot dog' version, when the sausage is placed in a bread stick.

Types of sausage include: the *Frankfurter*, a standard thin, boiled sausage; the *Bratwurst*, a fat, fried sausage; and *Burenwurst*, the boiled equivalent of Bratwurst. *Debreziner* is a thin, spicy sausage from Hungary. *Currywurst* is Burenwurst with a curry flavour, and *Käsekrainer* is a sausage infused with cheese. *Tiroler Wurst* is a smoked sausage. If you want to surprise and perhaps impress the server, use the following Viennese slang to ask for a Burenwurst with sweet mustard and a crust of bread: *'A Hasse mit an Sóassn und an Scherzl, bitte'*. But you probably won't get it – crusts are reserved for regular customers.

restaurants usually add a cover charge *(Gedeck)*, typically around €1.85 at lunch and €3.30 in the evening.

Dogs, an integral part of many Viennese lives, are taken everywhere – including restaurants and bars. So don't be surprised to see a wagging tail, occasional dogfight or canine tantrum over your Wiener Schnitzel and Krügerl.

VIENNESE CUISINE

Traditional Viennese food is generally quite heavy and hearty with meat strongly emphasised. Even so, many places now offer at least one vegetarian dish, and there has been a noticeable move towards providing light, healthy meals (eg, a *Fitnessteller*), especially in the summer.

Wiener Schnitzel is Vienna's best-known culinary concoction, and it is consumed everywhere. It's a cutlet covered in a coating of egg and breadcrumbs and fried. The cutlet is veal *(Kalb)* or, less expensively, pork *(Schwein)*; occasionally you can get variations like turkey *(Puten)*.

Goulash *(Gulasch)* is also very popular. It's a beef stew with a rich sauce flavoured with paprika. Paprika pops up in various other dishes too, though note that *Gefüllte Paprika* is a bell pepper (capsicum) stuffed with rice and meat. Dumplings *(Knödel)* are an element of many meals, and can appear in soups and desserts as well as main courses. *Nockerl* is a home-made pasta with a similar taste to Knödel. Chicken may be called variously *Geflügel* (poultry), *Huhn* (hen) or *Hähnchen* (small cock). A great variety of sausage *(Wurst)* is available, and not only at the takeaway stands. Beef *(Rindfleisch)*, lamb *(Lamm)* and liver *(Leber)* are mainstays of many menus.

Potato will usually appear as French fries, boiled, roasted, as *Geröstete* (sliced small and sauteed) or in salads, such as *Petersilkartoffel* (potatoes with parsley). A typical side salad to the Wiener Schnitzel is *Kartoffelsalat* or *Erdapfelsalat*, both names for potato salad. Tagliatelli-like pasta *(Nudeln)* is a common substitute. *Sauerkraut* is sour-tasting cabbage. You can sometimes find regional Austrian dishes

such as *Tiroler Bauernschmaus*, a selection of meats served with sauerkraut, potatoes and dumplings.

The most famous Austrian dessert is the *Strudel*, baked dough filled with a variety of fruits – usually apple *(Apfel)* with a few raisins and cinnamon. *Salzburger Nockerl* (an egg, flour and sugar pudding), although a Salzburg speciality, also makes an appearance on menus. *Palatschinken* are a thinner version of the common pancake and are another popular dessert, but are often eaten as a main dish as well. Vienna is renowned for its excellent pastries and cakes, which are very effective at transferring bulk from your moneybelt to your waistline.

DRINKS
Nonalcoholic Drinks

Coffee is the preferred hot beverage, rather than tea. Mineral or soda water is widely available, though tap water is fine to drink (Vienna's water comes from the Alps via 100km-long pipes). Apple juice *(Apfelsaft)* is also popular. *Almdudler* is a soft drink found all over Austria; it's a sort of cross between ginger ale and lemonade. Nonalcoholic drinks are generally expensive (usually around the same price as beer) – taking a water bottle with you while sightseeing could help your budget.

Alcohol

Austrian wine comes in various categories that designate quality and legal requirements in the production, starting with the humble *Tafelwein*, through to *Landwein*, *Qualitätswein* and *Prädikatswein*; the latter two also have subgroups. See the Heurigen section in the Entertainment chapter for more information on wine.

Austria is also known for its fine beer; some well-known brands include Gösser, Schwechater, Stiegl, Ottakring and Zipfer. It is usually a light, golden colour *(hell)*, though you can sometimes get a dark *(dunkel)* version too. *Weizenbier* (wheat beer), or *Weissbier*, has a distinctive taste, slightly sweeter than normal beer. It can be light or dark, clear or cloudy, and is usually served with a slice of lemon straddling the

Reading Addresses

In a Vienna address, the number of a building within a street *follows* the street name. Any number *before* the street name denotes the district.

glass rim. Draught beer *(vom Fass)* comes in a 500mL or 300mL glass, called respectively a *Krügerl* (sometimes spelled *Krügel)* and a *Seidel*. A *Pfiff* is only 125mL and is a bit of a waste of time and money.

Austria produces several types of rum. *Obstler* (not a rum) is a spirit created from a mixture of fruits, and *Sturm* is made from fermenting grapes. Sturm is only available in early autumn, and can be quite deceptive, tasting like grape juice but having a kick like a mule. *Schnapps* is also a popular spirit, and often taken after a big meal to try and settle the stomach. Farmers often sell their home-made schnapps in the markets around town.

PLACES TO EAT – SELF-SERVICE & BUDGET
Innere Stadt
The following places to eat can all be found on Map 7 (the area code is 01).

If you only want a snack, try one of the many Würstel stands, or you could go to *McDonald's* (there's one on the corner of Johannesgasse and Singerstrasse).

Vienna's most famous Würstel stand is *Würstelstand am Hoher Markt* (Map 7), which is frequented by people from all walks of life. It stocks a wide selection of sausages and beer, and always seems to be open, only closing between 5 and 7 am daily. If you're going to eat one sausage while in town, make sure it's a *Käsekrainer*, a sausage stuffed with lumps of cheese. It's heavy and filling, and can sometimes be a messy affair, as with each bite you're never too sure if the melted cheese will come spurting out. In their typically morose way, the Viennese have nicknamed a Käsekrainer served with the end of a bread loaf *'Eitrige mit an Buckl'*, which loosely translates as 'a hunchback full of pus'. How appetising!

Nordsee (☎ 512 73 54) has a branch at Kärntner Strasse 25, open 9 am to 8 pm daily.

The *University Mensa* (☎ 406 45 94, *Universitätsstrasse 7)* has dishes from a mere €3.05 and opens 11 am to 2 pm weekdays. Take the continuous lift (which is worth the trip itself) to the 6th floor then walk up one storey. The cafe adjoining the Mensa has the same meals and longer hours (8 am to 6 pm weekdays), and it stays open over summer.

In the next block is *Café Bierkeller Zwillings Gewölb* (☎ 408 53 15, *Universitätsstrasse 5)*, also popular with students. It features daily specials from about €3.65 in a maze of subterranean rooms. It's open 10 am to 1 am Monday to Friday and 9.30 am to 2 am Saturday.

Nearby, the *Katholisches Studenthaus Mensa* (☎ 408 35 85, *Ebendorferstrasse 8)* opens 11.30 am to 2 pm Monday to Friday (closed August to mid-September). Tagesteller starts at €4.30, mains are under €2.90.

The *Academy of Applied Art Cafeteria* (*Oskar Kokoschka Platz 2)*, open 9 am to 6 pm (to 3 pm Friday) weekdays, is a place where you'll be able to get cheap snacks and light meals.

The most central university cafeteria is the *Music Academy Mensa* (☎ 512 94 70, *Johannesgasse 8)*. Lunch is between 11 am and 2 pm Monday to Friday (to 1.30 pm Monday to Friday during the summer holidays), though you can also have coffee and snacks from 7.30 am to 2.30 pm weekdays. Main meals cost €3.05 to €4.50 and breakfast for €2.10 is served until 10.30 am.

Nearby at No 3 is *Zur Fischerin Capua* (☎ 512 62 45), with fishing trophies on the walls and good weekday menus (till about 4 pm) from €4.95 to €6.55 including soup. There are tables on the 1st floor above the small bar area (open 8 am to 2 am daily).

Trzesniewski (☎ 512 32 91, *Dorotheergasse 1)* is open 8.30 am to 7.30 pm Monday to Friday and 9 am to 1 pm Saturday. It's a basic deli bar where you stand in line and choose your food from the counter. Open sandwiches with a variety of toppings are about €0.65 each; they're quite tiny (two bites and they're gone), but this is a famous Viennese institution and you may want to sample a few, if only to follow in Kafka's mouthfuls (he was a regular here). Beer comes in the tiny Pfiff (125mL) measures. There is also a Trzesniewski in the 3rd district (☎ *712 99 64, Landstrasser Hauptstrasse 97–101*) and the 6th district (☎ *596 42 91, Mariahilfer Strasse 95*).

Rosenberger Markt Restaurant (☎ *512 34 58, Maysedergasse 2*) is a downstairs buffet place offering a fine array of meats, drinks and desserts to enable you to compile a meal for around €7.30, but watch out for extras (like bread and butter) that can be pricey. If you really want to save some euros, concentrate on the salad or vegetable buffet: some people unashamedly pile a Stephansdom-spire-shaped food tower on small plates (from €2.35) for a filling feast. It's open from 10.30 am to 11 pm daily, and has free lockers for your bags.

Restaurant Marché Mövenpick (☎ *512 50 06*) is in the Ringstrassen Galerien shopping complex, Kärntner Ring 5–7. It's almost the same as Rosenberger except the small salad/vegetable bowls are only €1.90. Another good feature is the pizza for €4.75, where you can help yourself to a variety of toppings. It's open 8 am to 8 pm Monday to Saturday, and noon to 7 pm Sunday and holidays.

Sushi bars have sprung up all over Vienna in recent years. *Akakiko* (☎ *533 85 14, Heidenschuss 3*) has sushi from €1.80 per piece, or complete lunchboxes from €6.05; it opens 10 am to midnight daily. There's another branch next to McDonald's at Singerstrasse 4.

Pizzerias are scattered around too, and are generally reasonable value. ***Pizza Bizi*** (☎ *513 37 05, Rotenturmstrasse 4*) is a convenient self-service place open 11 am to 11.30 pm daily. Pasta with a choice of sauces is €4.75, pizzas are €4.35 to €5.45 (or €2.20 for a slice) and there are salad and vegetable buffets. Pizza Bizi also has a takeaway counter at Franz Josefs Kai 21 and at Mariahilfer Strasse 22–24 in the 7th district.

Brezel Gwölb (☎ *533 88 11, Ledererhof 9*) serves Austrian food from €4.95 to €12.75 in a cobbled courtyard or an atmospheric, cellar-like interior, complete with background classical music. It's open 11.30 am to 1 am daily.

East to West (☎ *512 91 49, Seilerstätte 14*) is one of the better Chinese restaurants in town, with a good selection of dishes and Mittagsmenüs from €4.95 to €7.15. The atmosphere is calm and relaxing, and there is a nice little outdoor seating area out front. It's open 11.30 am to 2.30 pm and 5.30 to 11 pm daily.

China Restaurant Turandot (☎ *535 43 87, Vorlaufstrasse 2*) is open 11.30 am to 2.30 pm and 6 to 11 pm daily. The three-course weekday lunch specials are €5.75; there's also an all-you-can-eat lunch buffet for €6.20 (€7.65 on weekends and weekday evenings).

Weekday Chinese all-you-can-eat buffets start at €5.70 at ***Restaurant Siam*** (☎ *533 52 35, Krugerstrasse 6*), which is open 10.30 am to 3 pm and 5.30 to 11.30 pm daily.

Naschmarkt is a buffet-style restaurant chain, offering a good choice of meals, including a three-course lunch menu for €5.15 (€5.90 on weekends). There's also a branch at Schottengasse 1 (☎ *533 51 86*) open 10.30 am to 9 pm Monday to Friday and to 3.30 pm weekends and holidays, and there's another (with an outside terrace) at Schwarzenbergplatz 16 (☎ *505 31 15*) open from 6.30 am to 10.30 pm Monday to Friday and from 9 am on weekends.

Restaurant Smutny (☎ *587 13 56, Elisabethstrasse 8*) serves typical Viennese food in a room with wall tiles and colourful lightshades. Dishes are filling and reasonably priced (from €4.10) and it's open 10 am to midnight daily.

The North-West

All these places can be found on Map 3.

There are numerous inexpensive places to eat to the north and west of the university. The Afro-Asiatisches Institut (AAI), 09, Türkenstrasse 3, has a ***Mensa*** (☎ *310 51 450*) with meals for about €3.60, and courtyard eating in the summer. It's open 11.30 am to 4.30 pm weekdays (2 pm in July and August). The cafe on the 1st floor is open daily and carries *Newsweek* magazine.

PLACES TO EAT

Tunnel (☎ 405 34 65; 08, Florianigasse 39) is another student haunt. It's open from 9 am to 2 am daily, and the food is satisfying and easy on the pocket. You can get a great breakfast for €2.50, lunch specials start at €5 and prices don't top €8.75 in the evenings. Bottled beer costs from €2.10 for 500mL. Tunnel also has a cellar bar with live music (see the Entertainment chapter).

Vegi Rant (☎ 425 06 54; 09, Währinger Strasse 57) has a three-course daily menu for €7.70, and dishes like *Gluten Schnitzel* for €6.70; it's open 11.30 am to 2.30 pm Sunday to Friday. There is a health food shop next door. Good vegetarian lunches (€5.10) are also available at *Kräuterdrogerie* (☎ 405 45 22; 08, Kochgasse 34), a health food and Ayurvedic remedies shop.

If you're sick of schnitzel, make the effort to get to the friendly *Avocado American Diner* (☎ 407 51 30; 17, Hernalser Hauptstrasse 64). The food is fresh and delicious, with wonderful concoctions like chicken and avocado pita (€4.95) and avocado burger (€6.70). It's open 11.30 am to midnight for food, and does takeaway.

One of the best value-for-money pizzerias in town is *Ruffinio* (☎ 406 45 40; 08, Josefstädter Strasse 48). Not only are the pizzas good and cheap (€4 to €12.35), but they are enormous. Fortunately, it's possible to organise a doggy bag for your leftovers. Ruffinio is open 11 am to midnight daily and fills up early in the evening.

The South-West

Würstel stands are all over the place, and many sport signs proclaiming *'mein Kunde ist Kaiser'* (my customer is emperor), like the one at the Ring end of Mariahilfer Strasse. Another sign that can be found on the stands around town states *'mein Kunde ist König'* (my customer is king). The nearby Naschmarkt has plenty of places to eat, from quality restaurants to hearty takeaway food stalls. The Turkish influence is very evident in this market, with Turkish breads and cheeses for sale; filling kebabs for around €2.55 are a popular choice for lunch.

Near the Innere Stadt end of the Naschmarkt is *Indian Pavillon* (Map 7; ☎ 587 85 61; 04, Naschmarkt 74–75), a small eatery serving up nice spicy Indian food. Tagesteller ranges from €6.20 to €6.90 and mains stop at €6.90. Munch on your poppadoms and rogan josh while listening to classic Indian music from 10.30 am to 6.30 pm Monday to Friday, and till 5.30 pm Saturday.

Farther into the tangle of the Naschmarkt is *Toko Ri* (Map 7; ☎ 587 26 16; 04, Naschmarkt 263–264), a Japanese takeaway restaurant. The popular *Mittagsbox* (lunchboxes) range from €6.90 to €8.75, and it's open 11 am to 10 pm Monday to Saturday.

The *Technical University Mensa* (Map 7; ☎ 586 65 02; 04, Resselgasse 7–9) can be found inside the university building; find the yellow area and then go upstairs to the 1st floor. Good weekday lunches (11 am to 2.30 pm) are only €3.55 to €4.30, with several choices.

There are *Schnitzelhaus* branches (Map 5) at (☎ 817 35 14) 06, Otto Bauer Gasse 24 and (☎ 586 17 74) 05, Kettenbrückengasse 19.

Schnitzelwirt Schmidt (Map 5; ☎ 523 37 71; 07, Neubaugasse 52) is a great place for schnitzels and prides itself on its enormous portions (from €4.90). This informal, often hectic place is something of an institution among travellers – you really have to visit to see the size of these things. Unless you have a huge appetite, share one (they're used to supplying two plates) and just get extra garnishes (around €1.75 each). Many variations on the basic schnitzel are offered: the 'Schnitzel Don Carlos' (€7.95) is a good choice – it comes with a piled serving of rice, capsicum and ham. They can wrap leftovers to take away. Service is sometimes sloppy; get your drinks order in first (these are from a different server) – it's no fun chomping through a mountain of schnitzel with a parched throat. Opening hours are 11 am to 10 pm (closed Sunday and holidays).

A good pizzeria is *Il Mare* (Map 5; ☎ 523 74 94; 07, Zieglergasse 15). It's open noon to 2.30 pm and 6 to 11 pm (closed Sunday and holidays). The pictures on the wall betray a definite fondness for nautical themes, as befits the name. Pizzas are thin but with tasty toppings (€4.35 to €10.90; most are around €6.20).

Gaunkerl *(Map 5; ☎ 523 95 76; 07, Kaiserstrasse 50)* serves typical Viennese food, from about €5.45. It's open 11 am to midnight Monday to Saturday and also 11 am to 2 pm Sunday from November to March. The decor in the front room creates the illusion that you're sitting outside, complete with glowing stars and witches on broomsticks flying overhead. The illusion becomes more convincing after a couple of beers.

The Spittelberg quarter, an historic area with restored Biedermeier houses, has a number of interesting shops and bars, and hosts a wonderful Christmas market in December. The following four places are all situated in cobblestoned Spittelberg (Map 7).

Amerlingbeisl *(☎ 526 16 60; 07, Stiftgasse 8)* attracts mainly young people, both as a good eating (€4.50 to €7.65) and a drinking (beer €2.75 a Krügerl) venue. It's open from 9 am to 2 am daily. On balmy nights the roof slides back for those who are able to cram into the popular rear courtyard.

The basement **Plutzer Braü** *(☎ 526 12 15; 07, Schrankgasse 2)* is a popular haunt of a cross section of people. The ever-changing Mittagsmenü is great value at €5.55 for soup and a main. It has outdoor seating in summer and is fairly subdued during the day but has a lively atmosphere in the evenings, helped along by happy hour from 5 to 7 pm and midnight to 1 am, when every cocktail is €4.40. It opens 11.30 am to 2 am daily, with food till 11.45 pm.

Around the corner from Plutzer Braü is another cheap eatery, **Centimetre II** *(☎ 524 33 29; 07, Stiftgasse 4)*. Bread with spreads is ordered by the centimetre, €0.10 for cold and €0.15 for warm toppings. Huge mains are between €3.55 and €5.75. Opening hours are 10 am to 2 am Monday to Friday, from 11 am on Saturday and 11 am to midnight Sunday. It's also not a bad spot for a drink. There's another branch in the 8th district *(☎ 405 78 08, Lenaugasse, 11)*. Nearby there's a cheap pizzeria, **La Gondola** *(☎ 526 40 02; 07, Burggasse 15)*, with pizzas ranging in price from €4.25 to €7.85, open 11 am to midnight daily.

K&K Bierkanzlei *(Map 7; 06, Windmühlgasse 20)* is small, cheap and typically Viennese. Filling and straightforward daily menus cost from €4.30 (several choices, with soup). Its opening hours are 11 am to 10 pm Monday to Friday and to 6 pm Saturday. There are many images of Franz Josef and Elisabeth around – their faces even appear on the salt and pepper pots. The K&K in the name, which you'll come across elsewhere, stands for *König und Kaiser* (king and emperor), and refers to the Austro-Hungarian dual monarchy.

Schutzhaus am Ameisbach *(Map 5; ☎ 914 61 55; 14, Braillegasse 1)* is great value, and has many tables in a large garden, plus a play area for kids. A popular choice is spare ribs: the full serving for €10.20, including sauces and baked potato, will feed two (a half-portion is €5.80). Take bus No 51A from Hietzing to Braillegasse. It only opens in summer, from 9 am (3 pm Tuesday) to midnight (11 pm Sunday) though the kitchen closes at 9.30 pm, or 9 pm on Sunday.

Farther out, **Prilisauer** *(Map 2; ☎ 979 32 28; 14, Linzer Strasse 423)* is a typical Viennese Gasthaus, with meals starting at about €5.85. There's a garden and several beers on tap. It is near the last stop on tram No 49; it's open 9 am to 11 pm Wednesday to Sunday and 4 to 11 pm Tuesday.

From Prilisauer, you could take bus No 150 or 151 to the Badgasse stop, where you'll find **Hawei** *(Map 2; ☎ 979 12 63; 14, Hadersdorfer Hauptstrasse 62)*. This place has good food and a garden and is nice for escaping the city, but its main novelty is that the beer prices fluctuate according to demand – monitor the price on screens above the bar. It calls itself *Erste Wiener Bierbörse* (Vienna's first beer stock exchange) and is open 4 pm to 2 am daily (from 11 am on Sunday).

The South

Opposite Südbahnhof is **Kristall** *(Map 6; ☎ 504 63 27; 10, Wiedner Gürtel 4)*, open 7 am to 4 am daily. Meals start at about €4.35 (English menu) and there is a decent selection. The food is surprisingly good for the price and there's plenty of it.

Mona Lisa (Map 6; ☎ 603 95 83; 10, Gudrunstrasse 136), near Südbahnhof, has cheap pizzas from €5.10, including special lunchtime deals (closed Sunday).

The East

Wien Mitte station has several places for cheap and quick eating, like the *Interspar* supermarket, which has a self-service restaurant upstairs (meals €4.35 to €6.55), which closes at 7 pm weekdays and 5 pm Saturday.

A good Indian restaurant is *Zum Inder* (Map 4; ☎ 216 21 96; 02, Praterstrasse 57), where you can get dishes from about €6.55 and a *Mittagsbuffet* for €5.75. Its opening hours are 11 am to 3 pm and 6 to 11 pm daily.

PLACES TO EAT – MID-RANGE
Innere Stadt

All the following places are on Map 7 (the area code is 01).

La Crêperie (☎ 512 56 87, Grünangergasse 10) has different rooms with varied and creative decor ranging from arty odds and ends and ancient books to a pseudo circus tent complete with clowns' faces. Meat and fish dishes are €10.55 to €17.80, beer is €2.75 a Krügerl (500mL) and wine is €1.75 an Achterl (125mL). If you stick to its speciality, crepes, a light meal can be inexpensive. These are available with sweet or savoury fillings; the Florentine (€7.15) is a good combination of spinach, ham, cheese and egg with a dollop of sour cream. It has outside seating down the side street (Nikolaigasse) and is open 4 pm to midnight Monday to Friday and from 11 am on weekends.

Zu den 3 Hacken (☎ 512 58 95, Singerstrasse 28) is a down-to-earth place with outside tables and a small room devoted to Schubert (despite the anachronistic WWII radio). It serves typical Austrian food for around €6.25 to €16, and opens 9 am to midnight Monday to Saturday.

Wrenkh (☎ 533 15 26, Bauernmarkt 10) is a fairly upmarket vegetarian restaurant, open 11.30 am to 3 pm and 6 pm to midnight daily. Mittagsmenü starts at €7.15, with a three-course evening menu for €14.20. A bar next door serves the same meals, and opens 11 am

to midnight daily. Wrenkh has a smaller *restaurant* (☎ 892 33 56; 15, Hollergasse 9), open the same times as the main restaurant, which also serves vegetarian food.

Definitely not for squeamish vegetarians is *Zum Weissen Rauchfangkehrer* (☎ 512 34 71, Weihburggasse 4), because of the many hunting trophies on the wall. Meat specialities are served up for around €8.75 to €16.75 (plus a €2.20 cover charge). It's an atmospheric place, mostly partitioned into small booths, and has live piano music nightly from 7 pm (open 11.30 am to 3 pm and 6 pm to midnight daily).

Figlmüller (☎ 512 61 77, Wollzeile 5) reputably serves the biggest schnitzels in town (€11.35). It's generally packed and has a distinctly touristy feel, but is entertaining nonetheless (open 11 am to 10.30 pm daily; closed August).

Grotta Azzurra (☎ 586 10 44, Babenbergerstrasse 5), open noon to 3 pm and 6.30 to midnight daily, provides good Italian food with most dishes above €10.55 (plus €2.55 cover charge). A popular starter is the antipasto buffet (€11.25/12.75 a small/large plate), which is selected by the server.

Wiener Rathauskeller (☎ 405 12 10, Rathausplatz 1) is in the Rathaus, and the entrance is on the north-east corner. Enjoy the atmosphere in the arcaded Rittersaal, where the walls are filled with murals and floral designs. Live harp music (after 7 pm, extra charge of €1.10) adds to the ambience. Down the corridor, the *Grinzinger Keller* is similar if sparser. From 8 to 11 pm Tuesday to Saturday, 1 April to 31 October, it puts on a dinner show for €32.70, comprising music, waltzing and a three-course meal. Otherwise, the same Viennese and international dishes are offered in both halls; most choices are above €10.55 (open 11.30 am to 3 pm and 6 to 10.30 pm, closed Sunday).

The North-West

Die Fromme Helene (Map 3; ☎ 406 91 44; 08, Josefstädter Strasse 53) is a small place with a cluttered salon look and good Viennese food. Although midday dining is not too expensive (menus from €5.45 with soup), evening dishes stop at €18.20. It's open

PLACES TO EAT

11.30 am to 2.30 pm and 6 pm to midnight weekdays, and 6 pm to midnight Saturday.

Feuervogel (Map 3; ☎ 317 53 91; 09, Alserbachstrasse 21) is a Russian restaurant that has been run by the same family of Ukrainians for over 78 years. The colourful decor matches the conversational gambits (in English) of the surviving generations. The food is hearty rather than refined, but it's tasty nonetheless. Main courses cost from €10.20 to €16 and there's sometimes live music on the weekend. It's open 6 pm to 2 am, but closed Sunday.

The main attraction of *Salettl (Map 3; ☎ 479 22 22; 19, Hartäckerstrasse, 80)* is its outdoor seating and view of the Wienerwald north-west of Vienna. The breakfasts (served 6.30 am to 2 pm) are popular, even though they are on the steep side, ranging from €5.70 to €14.20. It's also a pleasant place in summer for an evening meal or just for a drink; opens 6.30 am to 1.30 am daily.

The South-West

These places can all be found on Map 5.

Ungar-Grill (☎ 523 52 38; 07, Burggasse 97) is a Hungarian restaurant with a patio area and live Hungarian music every night. Fish, chicken, grills and other dishes are €7.30 to €10.90, and there's a €0.80 cover charge. Opening hours are 6 pm to midnight Monday to Saturday. Reserve ahead as it's popular with tour groups.

Another place to try nearby is *Sobieski (☎ 523 13 96; 07, Burggasse 83A)*, a small restaurant serving Polish and Austrian food. It has a good Tagesmenü for €5.45; mains are more expensive. It's open 11 am to 3 pm and 5 to 11 pm weekdays and noon to 10 pm Sunday (Saturday closed).

The attentive staff at *Beim Novak (☎ 523 32 44; 07, Richtergasse 12)* serve up traditional Austrian food (mostly over €7.30) with good explanations of each dish in the English menu. It's open 11.30 am to 3 pm and 6 pm to midnight weekdays and 5 pm to midnight Saturday; closed August.

The South

Oxen Steak (Map 6; ☎ 504 71 21; 04, Prinz Eugen Strasse 2) is carnivore territory, with ox skulls on the walls and schnitzels, steaks, grills and spare ribs (€6.20 to €15.15) on the menu. It's open 11.30 am to 2 pm and 6 to 11 pm daily.

The East

All these places to eat are on Map 4.

The Prater is home to *Schweizerhaus (☎ 728 01 52; 02, Strasse des Ersten Mai 116)*, famous for its roasted pork hocks *(Hintere Schweinsstelze)*. A meal consists of a massive chunk of meat on the bone (about 750g minimum at €13.55 per kilogram – expect to be rolled away from the table after finishing one by yourself), best served with mustard (€1.10) and freshly grated horseradish (€0.75). Chomping your way through vast slabs of pig smacks of medieval banqueting, but it's very tasty when washed down with draught Budweiser (the Czech stuff). It's a bit of an institution in summer, when the huge outdoor seating area is jam-packed with locals and tourists alike, or when an international football game is being played at the nearby Ernst-Happel-Stadion (see Spectator Sports in the Entertainment section). It's open 10 am to 11 pm daily, mid-March to 31 October only.

Café-Restaurant Luftberg (☎ 729 49 99), nearby on Walsteingarten Strasse, offers a similar meat orgy, and opens 11 am to midnight daily (closed in October).

Vegetarians will have better luck in the Prater at *Estancia Santa Cruz (☎ 728 03 80; 02, An der Prater Hauptallee 8)*, a large place with many outside tables in a shady garden. Latin American and Tex-Mex food costs from €5.95 to €10.35, including several nonmeat choices. It's open 4 pm to 1 am Monday to Friday and from noon on weekends, March to October.

Gasthaus Hansy (☎ 214 55 72; 02, Praterstern 67) serves Viennese food for €5.70 to €13.45. It's fairly bare inside but the food is reliably good, and there are outside tables (open 9 am to 11 pm daily).

PLACES TO EAT – TOP END
Innere Stadt

The following places are all on Map 7 (the area code is 01).

Situated in the modern building right by Stephansdom, **DO & CO** *(☎ 535 39 69-0, Stephansplatz 12, Haas-Haus)* provides a good view of the cathedral. It serves up international, including Asian, cuisine for €13.45 to €17.80. The food is superb – gourmet quality – but it's so busy that the service can be a little tardy (you should book ahead). It is open noon to 3 pm and 6 pm to midnight daily, and there's an adjoining cafe-bar (9 am to 2 am). There's also another DO & CO **restaurant** *(☎ 512 64 74, Akademiestrasse 3)*.

Zum Kuckuck *(☎ 512 84 70, Himmelpfortgasse 15)* is a tiny one-room place with a vaulted ceiling. Viennese dishes start at €12.75 or you can opt for multicourse gourmet menus from €16. The kitchen is open noon to 2.30 pm and 6 to 11 pm Monday to Saturday.

For Japanese food, try **Yugetsu Saryo** *(☎ 512 27 20, Führichgasse 10)*. On the ground floor is a sushi bar, or go upstairs to have the food cooked in front of you on a large hotplate built into the table. Lunch menus start at €8, otherwise expect to pay above €14.55 per person, plus drinks. Evening set menus start at €26.15. The kitchen is open from noon to 2.30 pm and 6 to 11 pm daily.

Another quality option for Asian dishes is **Yohm** *(☎ 533 29 00, Petersplatz)*, a stylish restaurant overlooking Peterskirche. Mains range from €11.25 to €18.55, but there are cheaper options for lunch. It's open 11 am to 2.30 pm and 6 to midnight daily.

Korso *(☎ 515 16-546, Mahlerstrasse 2)* features wood-panelled elegance and opulent chandeliers. Viennese and international specialities are €19.65 to €28.35 and there is a vast wine cellar. Its proximity to the opera leads it to offer a light three-course meal (€48) for those who are replete with culture but depleted of cuisine. Opening hours are noon to 3 pm and 6 pm to 1 am Sunday to Friday and 6 to 11 pm Saturday (closed Saturday and at lunchtime Sunday in July).

Drei Husaren *(☎ 512 10 92, Weihburggasse 4)* is in the same price range and is similarly formal and elegant, with soothing live piano music to aid digestion. There's a huge selection of excellent hors d'oeuvres, which are priced according to season and selection. The New Year's menu is only small change at €247.10. This traditional Viennese restaurant is open noon to 3 pm and 6 pm to midnight daily.

Livingstone *(☎ 533 33 93, Zelinkagasse 4)* calls itself a Californian restaurant, which means its dishes range from Japanese to Mexican. It's quite modern and new, with mains starting around the €13.80 mark. You could be cheeky and order a couple of side dishes for under €7.30, but this is frowned upon. Livingstone is open 5 pm to 4 am daily and is joined to Planter's Club (see Bars & Pubs – Innere Stadt in the Entertainment chapter).

The North-West

Restaurant Sailer *(Map 3; ☎ 479 21 21; 18, Gersthofer Strasse 14)* serves traditional Viennese dishes from €12.35 to €18.90, but with refined touches. The quality and service are exceptional for the price. There's a garden and a cellar area serving snacks, sometimes to musical accompaniment. It's open noon to 3 pm and 6 pm to midnight daily.

The South-West

The **Hotel Altwienerhof** *(Map 5; ☎ 892 60 00; 15, Herklotzgasse 6)* has a huge wine cellar and an elegant restaurant serving quality French and international cuisine for around €17.45 to €21.80. It's well known for the quality of its food and opens noon to 2 pm and 6 to 11 pm Monday to Friday and evenings only Saturday.

The East

Steirereck *(Map 6; ☎ 713 31 68; 03, Rasumofskygasse 2)* is gourmet territory. In fact, it's rated one of the best restaurants in Austria. Different parts of the restaurant have a different ambience, but it's formal throughout. Even the toilets are stylish. Tempting main courses all top €21.80 (choose from lobster, rabbit, pigeon, venison etc), but you still have to book days in advance for the evening. The three-course

PLACES TO EAT

lunch menu is €28.70; in the evening, the multi-course menu is €65.05, or €103.95 including wine with each course. It's open 11.45 am to 3 pm and 7 pm to midnight Monday to Friday.

SELF-CATERING

Supermarkets are dotted around the city. Only a few have been marked on the maps in this book, but anywhere you stay you should be reasonably close to one. *Hofer*, *Mondo* and *Zielpunkt* supermarkets are acknowledged as the cheapest; *Billa*, *Spar*, *Löwa* and *Merkur* will sometimes have discounted ranges. The few *Julius Meinl* supermarkets around the city are the most expensive. Typical opening hours are 7.30 or 8 am to 6 or 7.30 pm Monday to Friday, and to either noon or 5 pm Saturday.

Outside normal shopping hours you can stock up with groceries at the main train stations and petrol stations (for the basics), though prices are considerably higher. Westbahnhof has a large shop (with alcohol) in the main hall, open 6 am to 10.50 pm daily. Wien Nord station has a Billa supermarket open 7 am to 6.30 pm Monday to Saturday (to 8 pm Friday, to 2 pm Saturday), and several small provision shops open from 5.30 am to 9 pm daily. Wien Mitte has a large Interspar supermarket (standard hours) and a reasonably sized provisions store open 5.30 am to 9.50 pm daily. There are also supermarkets in Südbahnhof and Franz Josefs Bahnhof. Near the S-Bahn exit in the airport is a Billa supermarket, open 7.30 am to 10 pm daily.

See the Shopping chapter for information on markets.

BEISLN

The Beisl, from the Yiddish for 'little house', is an institution in Vienna. The decor and furniture are generally simple and wooden, and it's rare to hear any music being played. Traditional Viennese cuisine is the order of the day and the food is hearty, filling, and the portions usually too big to comfortably finish in one sitting. They make good places to mix with the locals and to practise your drawled Viennese dialect. Table football (*Tischfussball*, or *Wüzeln* in Viennese dialect) is a popular pastime in Vienna and many Beisln have tables.

Griechenbeisl (Map 7; ☎ 533 19 41; 01, Fleischmarkt 11) is a famous old tavern (it's been here since 1457!) once frequented by Beethoven, Schubert and Brahms. Choose from the many different vaulted rooms pierced by hanging antlers, or sit in the plant-fringed front garden. Viennese main dishes range from €11.65 to €17.45, and it's open 11.30 am to 11.30 pm daily, and also has live piano music from 7.30 pm.

Around the corner is another quality Beisl, *Beim Czaak* (Map 7; ☎ 513 72 15; 01, Postgasse 15). It has recently been renovated and no longer has the traditional Beisl look and clientele, but the food is good nonetheless and typically Viennese (Wiener Schnitzel €12.20, Tagesmenü €5.80). It's open 8.30 am to midnight Monday to Friday and from 11 am Saturday.

Legend has it that some customers at *Zu den zwei Lieseln* (Map 5; ☎ 523 32 82; 07, Burggasse 63) have been consumed by their Wiener Schnitzels rather than the other way around. And when you receive the *riesige* (huge) portions it's half-believable. Even though the decor may not look inviting (the exterior definitely needs a paint job!), the food is. It's quite cheap (mains from €3.65) and there is a good selection of schnitzels on offer; opening hours are 10 am to 10 pm Monday to Saturday.

Altes Fassl (Map 5; ☎ 544 42 98; 05, Ziegelofengasse 37) is another Beisl that serves large schnitzels. There's a good Mittagsmenü for €5.70 and vegetarian dishes are also available if you've had enough of pork and breadcrumbs. Opening hours are 11.30 am to 3 pm and 6 pm to 1 am (kitchen to 11.30 pm) daily (evenings only Saturday).

And yet again, riesige schnitzels are the standard at *Ubl* (Map 5; ☎ 587 64 37; 04, Pressgasse 26). The quiet, relaxed atmosphere and tree-shaded summer terrace helps to appease your groaning stomach. Mains range between €5.80 and €10.20. Ubl is open noon to 2.30 pm and 6 pm to midnight (kitchen till 10.30 pm) daily.

Quell (Map 5; ☎ 893 24 07; 15, Reindorfgasse 19) is about as untouristy as

PLACES TO EAT

you can get, situated in a neighbourhood far removed from the open-air museum that is the Innere Stadt. A smattering of German would be helpful in this typically Viennese Beisl, and mains range from €4.35 to €9.45. Quell opens 11 am to midnight Monday to Friday.

Although a cafe by name, *Cafe Benno* (Map 3; ☎ 406 67 35; 08, Alser Strasse 67) is more a Beisl. It's popular with a young crowd and has enough games to keep everyone happy even when it's completely packed. Along with schnitzel and the like, it offers a good selection of baguettes (all €3.35), but beware the garlic-drenched 'Vampirbaguette' if you plan on talking to anyone else that night. A Krügerl €2.75. It's open 11.30 am to 2 am daily.

COFFEE HOUSES

The coffee house is an integral part of Viennese life. There are hundreds of them, and they are a great place for observing the locals in repose and recovering after a hard day's sightseeing. Small/big coffees cost about €1.75/2.75. Although that's expensive, the custom is to take your time. You can linger as long as you like and enjoy the atmosphere or read the cafe's newspapers – some places stock British and other foreign titles (saving you €2.20 or so on purchase price). Traditional places will serve a glass of water with your coffee.

Coffee houses basically fall into two types, though the distinction is rather blurred nowadays. A *Kaffeehaus*, which is traditionally preferred by men but enjoyed

---

Types of Coffee

Legend has it that coffee beans were left behind by the fleeing Turks in 1683, and it was this happy accident that resulted in today's plethora of coffee establishments. Vienna's first coffee house opened in 1685, but it could have been emulating successful establishments already opened in Venice (1647 – the first in Europe), Oxford (1650), London (1652), Paris (1660) and Hamburg (1677), rather than having anything to do with the Turks.

Austrian coffee consumption was modest in the ensuing centuries, and it was only after WWII that it really took hold among the population at large. Austrians now drink more coffee than any other beverage, gulping down 221L per person per year (next in line comes beer at 120L, followed by milk at 104L, soft drinks at 84L, mineral water at 76L, black tea at 39L and wine at 33L). Only Finland, Sweden and Denmark consume more coffee per person.

Different types of coffee you'll come across are:

Mocca (sometimes spelled *Mokka*) or *Schwarzer* – black coffee

Brauner – black but served with a tiny jug of milk

Kapuziner – with a little milk and perhaps a sprinkling of grated chocolate

Melange – served with milk, and maybe whipped cream too

Einspänner – with whipped cream, served in a glass

Masagran (or *Mazagran*) – cold coffee with ice and Maraschino liqueur

Wiener Eiskaffee – cold coffee with vanilla ice cream and whipped cream

Waiters normally speak English (and can often be gruff and grumpy) and can tell you about any specialities available. In particular, various combinations of alcohol may be added (eg, *Mozart* coffee with Mozart liqueur, *Fiaker* with rum, *Mocca gespritzt* with cognac, *Maria Theresa* with orange liqueur). Some people find the basic coffee too strong, so there's the option of asking for a *Verlängerter* ('lengthened'), a *Brauner* weakened with hot water. Traditional places will serve the coffee on a silver tray and with a glass of water. Some types of coffee are offered in small (*kleine*) or large (*grosse*) portions. According to an old Viennese tradition, if the waiter fails to give you the bill after three requests you can walk out without paying (three instantaneous requests don't count!).

by everyone, offers games such as chess and billiards and serves wine, beer, spirits and light meals. A *Café Konditorei* attracts more women and typically has a salon look with rococo mouldings and painted glass. *Aida* is a particularly popular chain of Konditorei, a totally pink affair where you can discuss your latest operation or the neighbour's new driveway with the old ladies at the next table. A wide variety of cakes and pastries is usually on offer.

Café Museum (Map 7; ☎ 586 52 02; 01, Friedrichstrasse 6) is open 8 am to midnight daily and has chess, many newspapers and outside tables. The building was created by Adolf Loos in 1899 but has since been renovated.

Café Bräunerhof (Map 7; ☎ 512 38 93; 01, Stallburggasse 2) has classical music on weekends and holidays from 3 to 6 pm, and British newspapers. It's open 7.30 am to 9 pm weekdays, to 7 pm Saturday and 10 am to 7 pm Sunday.

Café Central (Map 7; ☎ 533 37 63-26; 01, Herrengasse 14) has a fine ceiling and pillars, and piano music from 4 to 7 pm. Trotsky came here to play chess. Say hello to the plaster patron with the walrus moustache near the door – a model of the poet Peter Altenberg. Opening hours are 8 am to 8 pm Monday to Saturday, 10 am to 6 pm Sunday and holidays; coffee costs from €2.15.

Close to the archways of the Hofburg is *Café Griensteidl (Map 7; ☎ 535 26 92; 01, Michaelerplatz 2)*, a good place to people-watch or flick through the large selection of international newspapers. It's open 8 am to 11 pm daily.

Café Hawelka (Map 7; ☎ 512 82 30; 01, Dorotheergasse 6) is one of the more famous coffee houses in Vienna. At first glance it's hard to see what the attraction is: scruffy pictures and posters, brown-stained walls, smoky air, cramped tables. At second glance you see why – it's an ideal location for people-watching. The gamut of Viennese society comes here, from students to celebrities. It's also a traditional haunt for artists and writers (such as the Vienna Group in the 1950s and 60s). After 10 pm it gets busy. You're constantly being shunted

up to accommodate new arrivals at the table, the organising elderly Frau seizing any momentarily vacant chair (curtail those toilet visits!) to reassign it elsewhere. Café Hawelka is open 8 am to 2 am (from 4 pm on Sunday and holidays); closed Tuesday.

Alt Wien (Map 7; ☎ 512 52 22; 01, Bäckerstrasse 9) is a rather dark coffee house, attracting students and arty types. At night it becomes a lively drinking venue; beer is €2.50 for a Krügerl. Also well known for its goulash (€5.80 large, €4 small, but it is quite small), it is open from 10 am to 2 am daily (to 4 am Friday and Saturday).

After a hard night drinking or dancing, greet the dawn at *Café Drechsler (Map 7; ☎ 587 85 80; 06, Linke Wienzeile 22)*, where you'll rub shoulders with traders at the Naschmarkt. Opening hours are 3 am to 8 pm (to 6 pm Saturday, closed Sunday). There are billiard tables (the pocketless variety), and meals are €6.20.

Café Sperl (Map 7; ☎ 586 41 58; 06, Gumpendorfer Strasse 11) has been well established since 1880 (it was Hitler's favourite coffee house). Features include the *Times* newspaper, Jugendstil fittings, pocketless billiard tables, outdoor seating and influxes of people from the nearby Theater an der Wien. It's open 7 am to 11 pm daily (from 3 pm Sunday and holidays).

Café Restaurant Landtmann (Map 7; ☎ 532 06 21; 01, Dr Karl Lueger Ring 4) has outside tables overlooking the Burgtheater. This elegant, upmarket cafe has English newspapers, coffee from €2.05, meals above €9.10 and a selection of cakes (open 8 am to midnight daily).

Café Schwarzenberg (Map 7; ☎ 512 89 98; 01, Kärntner Ring 17) is another traditional coffee house with seating inside and out. It's popular with all ages and open 7 am to midnight daily (from 9 am Saturday). There's live piano music on Friday from 8 to 10 pm, and weekends from 4 to 7 pm and 8 to 10 pm.

Farther north from Café Schwarzenberg on the Ring is *Café Prückel (Map 7; ☎ 512 43 39; 01, Stubenring 24)*. High ceilings and grand chandeliers help produce a beautiful interior, and from 7 to 10 pm on Friday you

PLACES TO EAT

Sacher Torte – More Than Just a Cake

The Sacher Torte is a cake with a torrid history. Two vicious 'wars' were fought between Hotel Sacher and the Demel cafe, in 1938 and 1953, over the origin of the cake. The 1953 war turned on a vital question: should the apricot jam be directly under the icing or in the middle of the cake?

In 1887, 200 to 400 of them were baked daily in the kitchen of Hotel Sacher for distribution as far afield as Berlin, Paris and London. These days, 12 pastry chefs produce 500 to 600 a day, and as many as 3000 during Christmas.

So what's the big deal? Sacher Torte is basically just a rich chocolate cake with apricot jam in it. But Hotel Sacher claims that Japanese spies have infiltrated the kitchen in attempts to uncover the mysteries of the cake – what are the four chocolates used in the cake's mixture? And what is the secret of the jam? (The hotel says the jam used in its cake is 68% fruit.)

If you're still wondering where that jam should be placed, here's a recipe for Sacher Torte:

Ingredients:

130g butter	6 eggs (separated)	15ml butter
110g icing sugar	130g cooking chocolate	120g chocolate
vanilla	130g flour	90ml strong brewed coffee
	apricot jam	180g sugar

Method:

1. Preheat oven to 325°F (165°C); have all ingredients at room temperature.

2. Melt the cooking chocolate in a double boiler over hot water.

3. Lightly warm the butter, cream it together with icing sugar and vanilla until light and fluffy. Beat the egg yolks in gradually until light in colour.

4. Gently whisk in the melted, cooled chocolate.

5. Beat the egg whites with castor sugar until stiff and fold into the mixture. Slowly fold in flour.

6. Line the base of a 22 to 24cm round baking tin with greaseproof paper; spoon in mixture.

7. Bake at 325°F for 50 to 60 minutes. Allow to cool completely before turning out from tin. Slice cake in half horizontally and spread with apricot jam. Reassemble and pour hot apricot jam over cake. Let stand for four to five hours, then ice.

8. To make Sacher Torte icing: mix the 15ml butter and 120g chocolate in a double boiler. Add the coffee and beat well. Add the sugar and some vanilla to taste. Spread the warm icing over the top and sides of the torte, and leave to cool for several hours.

can hear live piano music. Coffee is from €1.85, and Melange is €2.85. It opens 9 am to 10 pm daily.

Café Sacher (Map 7; ☎ 512 14 87; 01, Philharmonikerstrasse 4), behind the Staatsoper, is the very picture of opulence with chandeliers, battalions of waiters and rich, red walls and carpets (open 8 am to 11.30 pm daily). It's famous for its chocolate apricot cake, Sacher Torte (€4 a slice; coffee from €2.35); see the boxed text to learn more about this acclaimed confection.

Its main rival in terms of Torte is the elegant, equally expensive, mirrored environ-ment of *Demel (Map 7; ☎ 535 17 17; 01, Kohlmarkt 14)*. It's the archetypal Konditorei establishment, open 10 am to 7 pm daily.

The modern equivalent of the traditional coffee house is the *Coffeeshop Company (Map 7; ☎ 531 08 44; 01, Krugerstrasse 6)*. It has an American 'Starbucks' coffee shop look, but still retains the relaxed atmosphere of coffee houses in Vienna where you can sit undisturbed for hours. Espresso is the drink here, rather than Melange or Brauner, and you need to order at the counter. It's open 7 am to 11 pm Monday to Saturday and 10 am to 10 pm Sunday.

A fine local Kaffeehäus outside the Innere Stadt is **Café Hummel** *(Map 3; ☎ 405 53 14; 08, Josefstädter Strasse 66)*. There's a large selection of foreign-language papers on offer and an excellent outdoor seating area perfect for watching the world go by. Sip your Melange (€2.20) 7 am to 2 am daily (from 8 am Sundays and holidays).

Café Gloriette *(Map 5; ☎ 879 13 11; 13, Gloriette)* probably has one of the best views in all of Vienna. Sitting high on a hill behind Schloss Schönbrunn, it offers a sweeping vista of the Schloss and its magnificent gardens. After the climb up the hill it makes for a welcome pit stop. It's open 9 am to 1 am daily.

If you've had it with coffee and you want a good cup of tea, head to **Haas & Haas** *(Map 7; ☎ 513 19 16; 01, Stephansplatz 4)*. Choose from a vast array of teas and chomp through an English breakfast (€6.90) while admiring the back of Stephansdom. Opening hours are 9 am to 10 pm Monday to Friday and till 6.30 pm Saturday (closed Sunday).

PLACES TO EAT

Entertainment

The tourist office produces a monthly listing of events covering theatre, concerts, film festivals, spectator sports, exhibitions and more; see also its seasonal magazine, *Vienna Scene*. Weekly magazines with extensive listings include *City* (€0.75) and *Falter* (€2.05). If your German is limited *City* is probably better, even though *Falter* is more comprehensive.

The *Neue Kronen Zeitung* newspaper (€0.70) has daily listings of DJs, concerts and venues. Its Thursday edition includes the 'Wiener Stadt Krone' pull-out section which provides a rundown on the week's cultural, sporting and entertainment events. For informative online information on happenings around town go to www.falter.at or www.vienna-night.at. FM4, a local radio station, has the lowdown on events in English between 10 am and noon Monday to Saturday. Check with the tourist office for free events around town. For information on a variety of different cultural events throughout Vienna, see the Public Holidays & Special Events section in the Facts for the Visitor chapter.

Classical music is still the sound that dominates the Viennese streets. The program of musical events is unceasing, and as a visitor you'll continually be accosted by Mozart lookalikes in the city centre trying to sell you tickets for concerts or ballets (at some events the musicians wear historical costumes too). Even some of the buskers playing along Kärntner Strasse and Graben are classical musicians.

For entertainment on the move, DDSG Blue Danube (☎ 588 80, English service) offers Evergreen Dance Evenings on the Danube Canal from mid-May to late August (€16), departing at 8 pm and returning at 11 pm from Schwedenplatz on Friday and Saturday.

See the Places to Eat chapter for information on coffee houses – fine places to relax in a typically Viennese environment. Many of the restaurants listed in the Places

to Eat chapter are also good for a night ou as the distinction between bar and restau rant is quite often blurred in Vienna.

Vienna is one of the safest cities in th world, so if you get the urge to walk hom after a night out don't think twice about it. T be on the safe side though, avoid the Prate at night, along with Mexikoplatz (Map 4 both well known for their drug trade.

CLASSICAL MUSIC & OPERA

Productions in the *Staatsoper (Map 7; 0 Opernring 2)* are lavish affairs, and shoul not be missed. Seats cost anything fro €5.10 to €254.40. *Stehparterre* (standing room tickets; €3.65) put you in a good po sition at the back of the stalls, whereas th €2.20 tickets leave you high up at the rea of the gallery. The Viennese take their oper very seriously and dress up accordingl Wander around the foyer and refreshmer rooms in the interval to fully appreciate th gold and crystal interior. Opera is not per formed here in July and August, but th venue may be used for other events.

The other main venue for opera is th *Volksoper (Map 3; ☎ 514 44 3670; 0 Währinger Strasse 78)*, close to the Gürt and the U6 line. It includes kitsch operett and musicals in its repertoire. Seats rang from €3.65 to €65.40, while standing room tickets are either €1.45 or €2.20.

The famous Vienna Philharmonic O chestra performs in the Grosser Saal (larg hall) in the *Musikverein (Map 7; ☎ 505 8 90, fax 505 81 94, ☒ tickets@musikve ein.at; 01, Bösendorferstrasse 12)*, which said to have the best acoustics of any co cert hall in Austria. The interior is suitab lavish and can be visited on the occasion guided tour. Standing-room tickets in th main hall cost €3.65; no student ticket Smaller-scale performances are held in th Brahms Saal, for which the cheapest ticke (€4.35) have no view. The ticket office open 9 am to 7.30 pm Monday to Frida and 9 am to 5 pm Saturday (closed July ar

August). Tickets can be ordered over the Internet at www.musikverein.at.

Another major venue is the **Konzerthaus** *(Map 7; ☎ 712 12 11, fax 712 28 72, ☎ ticket@konzerthaus.at; 03, Lothringerstrasse 20)*, which can put on up to three simultaneous performances, in the Grosser Saal, the Mozart Saal and the Schubert Saal. Most programs are classical, but you can hear anything from ethnic music to gospel, pop or jazz. Tickets for performances range from €11.65 to €59.60. Student tickets (for those under 27 with an ISIC) are half-price. The Konzerthaus Tageskasse (ticket office) is open 9 am to 7.45 pm Monday to Friday and 9 am to 1 pm Saturday, or book online at www.konzerthaus.at. The Konzerthaus is closed in July and August except when it hosts Summer of Music events.

There are sometimes free concerts round town, such as at the Rathaus or in one of the churches; check with the tourist office. Schloss Schönbrunn (Map 5) is the site of outdoor classical concerts in the summer, and year-round Mozart concerts in the **Orangery** *(☎ 812 50 040)* at 8.30 pm; tickets cost from €28.34.

The **Kursalon** *(Map 7; ☎ 713 21 81)* in the Stadtpark offers a so-so Waltz Show in the evening from Easter to mid-October. At the time of writing it was closed for refurbishment and due to reopen in mid-2001. Call for more information or check with the tourist office.

Buying Tickets

Cheap standing-room *(Stehplatz)* tickets for the Staatsoper (€2.20 and €3.65) and Volksoper (€1.45 and €2.20) go on sale one hour before the performance, as they do at the Burgtheater (€1.45) and Akademietheater (€1.45). Queue up at the venue concerned. For major productions you may have to allow two or three hours; for less important works, you can often get tickets with minimal queuing. Once you get inside, reserve your place by tying a scarf or sweater to the rail, then go for a wander round. People also queue for student tickets: at these four venues they are the same price as the cheapest tickets (ie, €5.10 to €8.75 for the Staatsoper) for any seats left unsold, and they are available to students under age 27 who can show both a university ID and an ISIC card. They are available 30 minutes (operas) or one hour (theatres) before productions start.

The state ticket office, charging no commission, is the Bundestheaterkassen (Map 7; ☎ 514 44-7880), 01, Goethegasse 1, open 8 am to 6 pm weekdays and 9 am to noon weekends and holidays (to 5 pm first Saturday of every month). It only sells tickets for the four federal venues mentioned above and closes from 1 July to the last week in August, as all these places are closed in July and August.

Tickets are available here in the month prior to the performance and credit cards are accepted (for September performances at the Staatsoper, apply in June); credit card sales can also be made by telephone (☎ 513 15 13). For postal bookings at least three weeks in advance, apply to the Bundestheaterverband (☎ 514 44-2653, fax -2969), 01, Goethegasse 1, 1010 Wien, Austria. You pay only after your reservations are confirmed. The four venues also have their own box offices.

Last-minute tickets are available the day before a performance at the Staatsoper for €29.10 from the ticket office from 9 am to noon. Call ☎ 514 44-2950 for information.

Tickets to all sorts of performances and events are available from various agents around town, but beware of hefty commission rates (20% to 30%!). Wien Ticket (☎ 588 85), in the hut by the Oper, is linked to the city government and charges either no commission or up to 6% (open 10 am to 7 pm daily).

Many of the other theatre and music venues around town offer cheap standing-room and/or student tickets (eg, the Theater an der Wien has €2.55 standing-room tickets, and €10.90 last-minute tickets for students under 25 who show an ISIC card).

THEATRE

You can see plays in English at the **English Theatre** *(Map 5; ☎ 402 12 60; 08, Josefsgasse 12)*. Plays are cast and rehearsed in

ENTERTAINMENT

London before the company is flown to Vienna. There's a range of ticket prices, from €13.80 to €35.60; students (under 27) pay from €9.10 for last-minute leftovers or receive 20% discount on normal priced tickets.

The smaller *International Theatre (Map 3; ☎ 319 62 72; 09, Porzellangasse 8)*, with its entrance on Müllnergasse, has a mainly American company living locally; tickets cost €18.25 to €20.35, or €10.20 for students (under 26) and senior citizens. It closes for around five weeks at the beginning of August, and has a linked venue, Fundus, at 09, Müllnergasse 6A.

Mime performances (generally avant-garde) are at the *Serapionstheater im Odeon (Map 7; ☎ 216 51 27; 02, Taborstrasse 10)*.

If you can follow German, the prime place to go is the *Burgtheater (Map 7; ☎ 514 44 221-8; 01, Dr Karl Lueger Ring 2)*, though there are plenty of other theatres.

The nearby *Volkstheater (☎ 524 72 63/4, e ticket@volkstheater.at; 07, Neustiftgasse 1)* is another popular venue for German theatre. Tickets range from €34.90 to €157.

The *Theater an der Wien (Map 7; ☎ 588 30 265; 06, Linke Wienzeile 6)* usually puts on musicals. Seated ticket prices range from €9.45 to €87.25, and can be booked at www.musicalvienna.at.

Buying Tickets

For information on buying tickets for performances at these venues, see the Buying Tickets section under Classical Music & Opera earlier.

BARS & PUBS

Despite its rather old-fashioned image, Vienna is a place where you can party all night. And unlike some other capital cities, you don't have to spend a lot of money in nightclubs to drink until late. Venues are by no means limited to the Innere Stadt – dozens of interesting small bars and cafes in all Vienna's districts stay busy until well after midnight, in particular inside the Gürtel. See the Getting Around chapter for information on getting home afterwards.

Keeping cool in the summer heat is a major consideration. In the Innere Stadt,

owing to noise and nuisance regulations most places with outside tables have to bring the punters inside after 11 pm. Exceptions are the cafes at the Secession and the Volksgarten.

Outside the Innere Stadt, the area around the U1 Donauinsel U-Bahn station (Map 4) on Danube Island comes alive with outdoor bars and clubs during summer. It's a popular haunt of both locals and tourists, especially on hot nights where the crowds party well into the early hours of the morning. The Alte AKH (old hospital; Map 3), now a university campus on the corner of Alser Strasse and Spitalgasse in the 9th district, is also worth heading to in the height of summer. Its tree-shaded courtyard hosts a number of bars, which are a welcome alternative to the hot and stuffy indoors.

Innere Stadt

All the following places can be found on Map 7 (the area code is 01).

The best-known area for a night out around Ruprechtsplatz, Seitenstettengasse, Rabensteig and Salzgries in the central zone near the Danube Canal. It's been dubbed the 'Bermuda Triangle' (Bermuda-Dreieck) as drinkers can disappear into the numerous bars and clubs and apparently be lost to the outside world. This area is very compact so it's easy just to walk around and dive into whatever place takes your fancy. But this doesn't mean it's the best area to go out, as it's usually teeming with teenagers and the bars' atmosphere can often be quite flat.

An exception to the rule is *First Floor (☎ 533 78 66)*, on the corner of Seitenstettengasse and Rabensteig. Choose from over 100 cocktails (from €6.55 upwards) and enjoy the 1930s interior, aquarium and eclectic crowd. It's open 7 pm to 4 am Monday to Saturday and to 3 am Sunday.

Krah Krah (☎ 533 81 93, Rabensteig 8) also in the Bermuda-Dreieck, has 55 different brands of beer (from €2.85 for a 500ml bottle), attracts a range of ages, and is open until 1 or 2 am daily. Winter Sundays there's jazz, blues or funk 11.30 am to 3 pm.

The *Palmenhaus (☎ 533 10 33)* on Burgring (entrance off Albertina), located in

A traditional red tram in front of the Staatsoper

You can find anything and everything at the Flohmarkt

Feeding time for the Schönbrunn seals

Loos Haus, right, with its 'eyebrowless' windows

Kunsthistorisches Museum – not to be missed

Votivkirche, celebration of failed assassination

beautifully renovated palmhouse, sits almost at the back door of the Hofburg. The main attraction is the building itself, but other bonuses include outside seating during summer and the occasional clubbing night. It's open 10 am to 2 am daily, and quality food is available until midnight.

The Volksgarten, at 01, Burgring 1, has three adjoining venues appealing to all tastes. The *Tanz Volksgarten* (☎ 532 42 41) is where serene and somewhat restrained couples waltz across the dance floor to 'evergreen' classics. There is dancing nightly in summer (it's closed in winter, as the venue is largely open-air); entry costs about €5.10 unless there's a live concert, when it costs about €10.20. It opens at around 7.30 pm.

The second Volksgarten venue is the 1950s-style *Volksgarten Pavillon* (☎ 532 09 07). Its large garden is incredibly popular on a warm evening, with views of the Hofburg and DJs providing a chilled-out atmosphere. It's open from 11 am to 2 am daily early May to September, with music from 10 pm and food available till midnight. Entry is free, except for occasional 'unplugged' concerts or garden barbecues.

See the Nightclubs section later for the third venue, Volksgarten Disco.

Bierhof (☎ 533 44 28, Naglergasse 13), with its entryway off Haarhof, has courtyard seating and four varieties of draught Ottakringer to try (€2.75 per Krügerl). It's open from 11.30 am (4 pm October to April) to 12.30 am, but is closed on Sunday.

Kolar (☎ 533 52 25, Kleeblattgasse, 5), a white bar with vaulted ceiling on a cobblestoned street, attracts a fairly young crowd. It has a good selection of beer on tap, and great *Fladenbrot* (bread similar to pizza, from €1.30) is available, cooked in the kiln oven in the centre of the bar. It's open 5 pm to 2 am daily.

As the name suggests, *Kleines Café* (*Franziskanerplatz 3*) is indeed small. But what it lacks in size it makes up for in bohemian atmosphere and its wonderful summer outdoor seating on Franziskanerplatz. It also featured in the movie *Before Sunrise*. Opening hours are 10 am to 2 am

Monday to Saturday and from 1 pm Sunday and holidays.

Irish bars have become trendy in Vienna and have popped up all over town. *Molly Darcy's Irish Pub* (☎ 533 23 11, Teinfaltstrasse 6) is probably the most authentic of them. It's open 11 am to 2 am Monday to Thursday, to 3 am Friday and Saturday and noon to 1 am Sunday. It's staffed by non-German-speaking Irish folk and serves Irish stew (€7.65), Guinness and Kilkenny (€4.70 per pint), and local beers (€2.75 for 500mL).

One of the original Irish bars is *Bockshorn* (☎ 532 94 38, Naglergasse 7), hidden away in an alley off Naglergasse. It fills up quickly as it's the size of a shoebox, and has a good selection of whiskies. For €7.30 you can get a pint of Guinness and a shot of the whiskey of the month. Bockshorn is open 4 pm to 2 am Monday to Friday, 1 pm to 2 am Saturday and 6 pm to midnight Sunday.

It's quite a surprise to walk into a bar and hear classical music, but that's what you get at *Santo Spirito* (☎ 512 99 98, Kumpfgasse 7). The music, which seems to increase in volume as the night progresses, helps to create a lively atmosphere and attracts a musical and artistic crowd, both straight and gay. In summer, customers spill out onto the cobblestoned street to take a break from the noise. The mainly Spanish and Italian dishes (mains from €6.40), available until 11.30 pm, are reputedly of a high standard. Opening hours are 11 am to 2 am Monday to Thursday, to 3 am Friday and Saturday and 10 am to 2 am Sunday.

Cocktail bars are currently popular in Vienna, and most have a distinctly American feel. The crowd is generally suited up and pretty stiff, and the drinks pricey.

The *American Bar* (☎ 512 32 83, Kärntner Strasse 10) was designed by Adolf Loos in 1908. It's basically a small box with enough room to fit about 20 people in comfortably, but the mirrored walls help to trick you into thinking it's much larger. Sip your cocktail (starting at €6.55) at the bar and listen to some chilled-out tunes from 6 pm to 4 am daily.

For the best cocktails in town head to *Dinos* (☎ 535 72 30, Salzgries 19), a bar right out of downtown Manhattan. Prices range from €5.80 to €8.35 and the music is decidedly jazz-oriented. It's open 6 pm to 3 am Sunday to Thursday and till 4 am Friday and Saturday.

Bigger and far less stylish is **Planter's Club** (☎ 533 33 93, Zelinkagasse 4), but the selection of rums and whiskies is unbelievable – its drinks card is more like a book! Resident DJs help dilute the self-important atmosphere with some 70s funk and Latin grooves. Opening hours are the same as Livingstone's, Planter's restaurant (see Top-End – Innere Stadt in the Places to Eat chapter).

Other Districts

Tunnel (Map 3; ☎ 405 34 65; 08, Florianigasse 39) is a student-type bar/cafe with low prices that does a great breakfast till 11 am (also see the Places to Eat chapter). There's a cellar bar with live music nightly from 9 pm; entry costs from €2.20, though on Sunday there's generally a free 'Jazzsession'.

Café Lange (Map 5; ☎ 408 51 41; 08, Lange Gasse 29) is not actually a cafe, but it is good for drinking beer and discussing the meaning of life. It attracts both a Viennese and English-speaking crowd and has Guinness on tap (€4); a Krügerl of fine Austrian beer costs from €2.40. It's open 6 pm to 2 am daily. It's easy to miss, as there is only a small sign on the doorway indicating the entrance.

Just off Alser Strasse is **Café Daun** (Map 3; ☎ 405 24 06; 08, Skodagasse 25), which becomes a bar in the evening, attracting a student crowd. It's quite relaxed during the day but the atmosphere picks up as the sun goes down. It's open 9 am to 1 am Monday to Saturday and from 3 pm Sunday. Food can be ordered until midnight.

Engel (Map 5; ☎ 523 14 74; 07, Neustiftgasse 82) is a bar and restaurant, often with live music or DJs spinning jazz and soul. It opens 6 pm to 4 am Monday to Saturday.

Competing with the Innere Stadt bars for the best cocktails is **Shultz** (Map 5; ☎ 522 91 20; 07, Siebensterngasse 31). The crowd is less stuffy and the decor more open and inviting, with glass walls through which you can watch fellow drinkers at the outdoor tables. It's open 9 am to 2 am Monday to Saturday and from 5 pm Sunday.

Andino (Map 5; ☎ 587 61 25; 06, Münzwardeingasse 2) is a Latin American bar and restaurant with lively murals and meals for under €7.30. It has been a popular place for years and opens from noon to 2 am daily, with food served till midnight. It has a venue for live music or 'theme' parties upstairs, usually on Friday and Saturday; entry costs €4.35 to €10.20 (cheaper if paid in advance).

Club Köö (Map 5; ☎ 526 63 03; 07, Kirchengasse 41) is a good place to play pool. Tables cost €5.70 per hour, or €3.65 on weekdays before 5 pm. It's open 10 am to 3 am Monday to Thursday, to 4 am Friday and Saturday and 1 pm to 2 am Sunday. Although it doesn't look it, this is different to the adjoining **Café Burg** (☎ 523 88 25; 07, Burggasse 28), which also has pool tables (€5.70 per hour). It opens 7.30 am to 2 am Monday to Friday, from 1 pm Saturday and 1 pm to midnight Sunday.

Don't let the smoke and the appearance of **Blue Box** (Map 5; ☎ 523 26 82; 07, Richtergasse 8) put you off. The music is great (regular DJs) and the atmosphere is lively. Superb breakfasts (between €3.80 and €7.85) are available 10 am to 5 pm. It's open 6 pm to 2 am Monday, 10 am to 2 am the rest of the week.

Slightly less grungy is another cool and popular bar around the corner from Blue Box, **Europa** (Map 5; ☎ 526 33 83; 07, Zollergasse 8). DJs are a common fixture in the evenings and it serves up a fine hangover breakfast 9 am to 2 pm (€8) on weekends. Opening hours are 9 am to 5 am daily.

If you're taken by the need to speak some English, join the expats at **Johnnys** (Map 5; ☎ 587 19 21; 04, Scheifmühlgasse, 11), an English-Irish pub. Most evenings it's lively, but especially so on Wednesday and Thursday, when the place is packed to the gunnels with people singing along to the live music. Johnnys is open 6 pm to 4 am Tuesday to Saturday and to 2 am Sunday and Monday.

With great views of the Votivkirche by Rooseveltplatz is **Café Stein** (Map 7; ☎ 310 95 15; 09, Kolingasse 1). During the day the three-floored cafe is frequented by students from the nearby university, who are joined in the evening by businesspeople with a lot more money to spend. DJs control the decks in the evenings and the food on offer all day is of a high standard. During the summer there is seating outside. The cafe opens 7 am to 1 am Monday to Saturday and from 9 am Sunday. (You can also surf the Internet here – see Post & Communications in the Facts for the Visitor chapter.)

The Gürtel has been making a recovery in recent years with a number of bars putting the *U-Bahnbogen* (Metro archways) to good use. Most look quite similar, with glass walls, original brickwork and outdoor seating. One exception is **Chelsea** *(Map 3; ☎ 507 93 09; 08, Lerchenfelder Gürtel 29–31)*, an old alternative haunt. There's a DJ spinning loud sounds (usually indie, sometimes techno) and live bands weekly, attracting a crowd usually dressed in black. On Sunday and one other time during the week (more if the Champions league is under way) you can sit and sip your Guinness or Kilkenny and watch TV coverage of English premier league football with expats and locals alike. It's open from 4 or 6 pm to 4 am daily.

If you go 100m north along the Gürtel you'll find another late-night drinking hole, **Rhiz** *(Map 3; ☎ 409 25 05; 08, Lerchenfelder Gürtel 37–38)*, a bar favouring invariably loud electronic music and guest DJs. Its outdoor seating is extremely popular in summer where you compete with the noise of Gürtel traffic and U-Bahn overhead. It's open 11 am to 4 am Wednesday to Monday and 6 pm to 4 am Tuesday, and doubles as an Internet cafe during the day. The Web site at www.rhiz.org provides a taste of the bar's political and musical slant.

Another 200m north is **B72** *(Map 3; ☎ 409 21 28; 08, Hernalser Gürtel 72)*, with a similar construction to Rhiz but featuring live bands and a wider spectrum of music. Expect an entrance fee when bands are playing, otherwise there's no charge to prop up the bar 6 pm to 4 am daily.

Q *(Map 3; Währinger Gürtel)* shows that the Gürtel scene is not limited to one area

and a mainly alternative crowd. It's about 2km north of B72 and attracts a more affluent audience who sip their cocktails (around €6.55) and tap their feet to the 70s to 90s dancefloor beats. It's open 6 pm to 4 am Monday to Saturday and is usually heaving by midnight.

Blaustern *(Map 3; ☎ 369 65 64; 19, Döblinger Gürtel 2)* caters for a similar crowd to Q but is a little more laid-back. It's a good place during the day for breakfast (€4.10), to sip the fine Blaustern Coffee or simply to watch the world go by through the cafe's large windows. At night it's much livelier and easily fills up in summer. Opening hours are 9 am to 2 am daily.

HEURIGEN

Heurigen (wine taverns) can be identified by a green wreath or branch (the *Busch'n*) hanging over the door. Many have outside tables in large gardens or courtyards. Inside they're fairly rustic but have an ambience all their own. Heurigen almost invariably have food, which you select yourself from hot and cold buffet counters; prices are generally reasonable. It was traditionally acceptable to bring your own food along instead, but it's unadvisable to try that nowadays.

Heurigen usually have a relaxed atmosphere that gets more and more lively as the customers get drunk. Many feature traditional live music, perhaps ranging from a solo accordion player to a fully fledged oompah band; these can be a bit touristy but great fun nonetheless. The Viennese tend to prefer a music-free environment.

Opening hours are usually about 3 or 4 pm (or before lunch on weekends) to 11 pm or midnight, though in the less touristy regions some may close for several weeks at a time before reopening. Similarly, some are only open in the summer, or maybe only from Thursday to Sunday.

The common measure for Heuriger wine is a *Viertel* (250mL) in a glass mug, costing around €1.85 to €2.20, though you can also drink by the *Achterl* (125mL). A *Viertel Gespritzer* (half wine, half soda water) costs €1.30 to €1.45. Beer is usually not available. Heurigen are particularly popular

ENTERTAINMENT

The Heurigen

The *Heurigen* (wine tavern) tradition in Vienna dates back to the Middle Ages, but it was Joseph II in 1784 who first officially granted producers the right to sell their wine directly from their own premises. It proved to be one of his more enduring reforms. These taverns are now one of Vienna's most popular institutions with visitors. The term *Heuriger* refers to the year's new vintage, which officially comes of age on St Martin's Day (11 November, a day of much drinking and consumption of goose). It continues to be Heuriger wine up to its first anniversary, at which time it is promoted (relegated?) to the status of *Alte* (old) wine.

A *Buschenschank* is a type of Heurigen that within the Vienna region may only open for 300 days a year. It can only sell its own wine, either new or old, and must close when supplies have dried up. The term is protected. Not so 'Heurigen': taverns can adopt the name even when they don't produce their own wine.

Austrian wine production is 80% white and 20% red. The most common variety (36%) is the dry white Grüner Veltliner; it also tends to be the cheapest on the wine list. Other common varieties are Riesling and Pinot Blanc. *Sekt* is a sparkling wine. Some of the young wines can be a little sharp, so it is common to mix them with 50% soda water, called a *Gespritzer* or *G'spritzer*. The correct salute when drinking a Heuriger is *'Prost'* (cheers). But the Viennese can't wait for 11 November to drink the new vintage, and are prepared to consume it early, as unfermented must *(Most)*, partially fermented *(Sturm)* or fully fermented but still cloudy *(Staubiger)*; they taste a little like cider. The correct salute when drinking these versions is *'Gesundheit'* (health), perhaps in recognition of the risk taken by the palate.

in September and October when *Sturm* and *Most* are available and consumed in vast quantities.

Heurigen are concentrated in the wine-growing suburbs to the north, west, north-west and south of the city. Once you pick a region to explore, the best approach is simply to go where the spirit moves you (or to whichever places happen to be open at the time); taverns are very close together and it is easy to visit several on the same evening.

Innere Stadt

Although there are a few Heurigen in the centre of Vienna, if you want a more authentic Heurigen experience you should make the trek to the surrounding districts.

Esterházykeller (Map 7; ☎ 533 34 82; 01, Haarhof 1), off Naglergasse, is a busy wine cellar which has cheap wine from €1.75 for 250mL. Meals and snacks are available and it's open 11 am (4 pm weekends) to 11 pm daily.

Zwölf Apostelkeller (Map 7; ☎ 512 67 77; 01, Sonnenfelsgasse 3) is a vast multi-level cellar, with the wine flowing 4.30 pm

to midnight daily creating a lively and rowdy atmosphere.

North-West

This is the best-known region. The area most favoured by tourists is Grinzing (Map 2) – count the tour buses lined up outside at closing time – and this is probably the best area to head for if you want to catch some live music and mix with a large crowd. However, bear in mind that this area is mostly eschewed as a tourist ghetto by the Viennese themselves. Most of the Heurigen are concentrated along Cobenzlgasse and Sandgasse, near the terminus of tram 38 (which starts at Schottentor on the Ring). The following Heurigen are all on Map 2.

One of the better tourist traps is *Reinprecht (☎ 320 14 71; 19, Cobenzlgasse 22)*, which is a very large place with a lively, sing-along environment.

To escape the busloads and enjoy supreme views over Vienna, make your way to *Weingut Am Reisenberg (☎ 320 93 93; 19, Oberer Reisenbergweg 15)*. It's a good 10-minute walk up a steep hill just north of

ENTERTAINMENT

Grinzing village, but the view makes exhausting yourself well worth the effort. Don't expect to find a rustic Heurigen though – the place and its patrons ooze money. For a nice walk to work off the wine and Schwiensbraten, continue on up Oberer Reisenbergweg for another 20 minutes to Cobenzl, where you'll find a cafe and even better views of Vienna.

From Grinzing, you can hop on the 38A bus to Heiligenstadt, where in 1817 Beethoven lived in the Beethovenhaus. It's now a Heurigen called *Mayer am Pfarrplatz* (☎ 370 12 87; 19, Pfarrplatz 2) with a large garden, and live music 7 pm to midnight.

From Heiligenstadt it's just a few stops on tram D north to Nussdorf, where a couple of Heurigen await right by the tram terminus. But far more rewarding Heurigen await you in the vineyards lining the hills north-west of Nussdorf.

Kahlenberger Strasse winds its way up to Kahlenberg, and about 20 minutes north of Nussdorf is *Sirbu* (☎ 320 59 28; 19, Kahlenberger Strasse 210), a small Heurigen surrounded by vineyards. The view makes the climb bearable.

One hill north of Sirbu is a fantastic little Heurigen, *Hirt* (☎ 318 96 41; 19, Eisernenhandgasse 165). Apart from the view north, the great food, wine and friendly service (English-speaking) are worth the trek. It's open Wednesday to Sunday April to October and Friday to Sunday November to March. Hirt is a 15-minute steep climb above Kahlenbergerdorf, which is one stop north of Nussdorf by train, or four stops north of Franz Josefs Bahnhof.

Farther west of Grinzing are the less touristy areas of Sievering (terminus of bus No 39A) and Neustift am Walde (bus No 35A). Both these buses link up with the No 38 tram route.

In Neustift is *Schreiberhaus* (☎ 440 38 44; 19, Rathstrasse 54), a large Heurigen with friendly staff and a fine garden.

Ottakring (Map 4) is a small but authentic Heurigen area a short walk west of the tram J terminus. Many Heurigen in this area are only frequented by locals and are quite basic affairs.

North

The Heurigen areas here in the 21st district are less visited by tourists and are therefore more typically Viennese, catering to a regular clientele. They are also cheaper: a Viertel costs around €1.60. Live music is not the norm. Stammersdorf (terminus of tram No 31) is Vienna's largest wine-growing district, producing about 30% of Vienna's wine. From the tram stop, get on to Stammersdorfer Strasse, the next street north and running east-west. There are many Heurigen on this street in the westward direction, including *Weinhof Wieninger* (☎ 292 41 06, Stammerdorfer Strasse 78), which stocks some reputable wine. *Klager* (☎ 292 41 07), at No 14, is also a popular Heurigen in the area.

Strebersdorf is at the terminus of tram No 32, or about a 30-minute walk west of Stammersdorf. The Heurigen are north of the tram terminus. *Weingut Schilling* (☎ 292 42 92, Langenzersdorferstrasse 54) has a good reputation for wine, but is only open every odd month. Another place to try is *Eckert* (☎ 292 25 96, Strebersdorfer Strasse 158), also open every odd month. Paintings by a different artist are featured every month and there's occasional live music (anything from jazz to rock & roll).

South

As in the north, tourists are less prevalent in these Heurigen. Mauer is in the south-west, on the edge of the Wienerwald. Take the U4 to Hietzing and then tram No 60 to Mauer Hauptplatz. Oberlaa is farther east. To get there, take the U1 to Reumannplatz, bus 66A or 67A to Wienerfeld, and then transfer to bus 17A. This runs along Oberlaaer Strasse, where there are several Heurigen.

NIGHTCLUBS

One of the most well-known clubs in Vienna is *U4* (Map 5; ☎ 815 83 07; 12, Schönbrunner Strasse 222). It's open nightly from (usually) 10 pm to 4 or 5 am. Drink prices aren't too bad, and there are two dancing rooms and a slide show. Each night has a different style of music and attracts a different clientele. Friday (80s and 90s music) is a popular night; Saturday is Boogie

ENTERTAINMENT

Night; Thursday is Heaven gay night; and if you can handle it, Monday is Deutsche Schlager. The cover charge is usually around €7.30. The entrance fee for the occasional live bands is more.

Down on the Danube Canal is one of Vienna's best clubs, *Flex (Map 4; ☎ 533 75 25; 01, Donaukanal, Augartenbrücke)*. The crowd is typically black-clad but everyone is up for a good time. Each night is a different theme, with Dub Club on Monday and London Calling (alternative and indie) on Wednesday among the most popular. It's quite common to find live bands or touring DJs performing on any given night. Flex is open 10 pm to 4 or 6 am daily; check the Web site at www.flex.at for upcoming events.

Volksgarten Disco (Map 7; ☎ 533 05 18; 01, Burgring 1) has different music each night; garage, hip-hop, house, rhythm and blues, or soul – check the weekly listings in newspapers. Entry cost ranges from €7.30 to €9.45 and it starts between 10 and 11 pm (5 pm on Sunday). There's a garden bar with beer from €4 and the dancefloor roof can be retracted to reveal the night sky.

P1 (Map 7; ☎ 535 99 95; 01, Rotgasse 9), a club attracting a very young crowd, plays mainstream dance anthems; admission costs €3.65 or €5.80, though Tuesday (hip-hop) is free. It's open till 4 or 6 am, and closed Monday.

Tenne (Map 7; ☎ 512 57 08; 01, Annagasse 3) aims for a slightly older audience, offering live music such as 'evergreen' classics, swing and big band. Entry usually costs only €2.20 (or €5.10 for the occasional variety acts), though drinks are around €3.65 or more. It's open from 8.30 pm to 2.30 am or later (closed Sunday).

Meierei (Map 7; ☎ 710 84 00; 03, Stadtpark 3, entrance Heumarkt) is quite the opposite of Tenne, and is at the leading edge of the Vienna DJ scene. The likes of Kruder & Dorfmeister and Goldie have featured on the turntables. On weekends the place is hot, steamy and heaving, but you can at least escape it all by taking a break outside. It's open 10 pm till sunrise Wednesday, Friday and Saturday, and entrance is around the €7.30 mark (with drinks on the expensive side).

Titanic (Map 7; ☎ 587 47 58; 06 Theobaldgasse 11) is generally packed o the weekends as it caters for a wide audi ence and creates a party atmosphere. Tw dancefloors compete for your attention, on pumping out Latin grooves and the othe mixing it up with funk and hip-hop from th 70s to present-day. It's open 10 pm to 3 ar daily, till 5 am Friday and Saturday.

Tanzcafé Jenseits (Map 4; ☎ 587 12 33 06, Nelkengasse 3) is supposedly a forme whorehouse, which is easy to believe con sidering the decor – lots of velvet and kitsch DJs perform every night except Monday an Wednesday and it fills up quickly, so don be surprised to find a queue. Jenseits is ope 9 pm to 2 am Monday to Saturday.

Roxy (Map 7; ☎ 597 26 75; 04, Opern gasse 24), on the corner of Faulmanngasse is another club that's in at the moment. It at tracts a good mixture of people, and the DJ mix it up as well – it can be a bit of a luck dip as to what you'll hear (ranging from garage to jazz and Brazilian sounds). It' open 11 pm to 4 am Monday to Saturday.

GAY & LESBIAN VENUES

If you don't manage to make it to Vienna t enjoy the summer festivities (see Gay an Lesbian Travellers in the Facts for the Vis itor chapter), there are a number of place around town to keep you entertained.

The popular *Café Berg (Map 3; ☎ 319 5 20; 09, Berggasse 8)* is modern and stylis hang-out and bookshop. It's open 10 am t 1 am daily.

Café Savoy (Map 5; ☎ 586 73 48; 06 Linke Wienzeile 36) has a more traditiona cafe feel to it, except for the feathers every where. Opening hours are 5 pm to 2 am Monday to Friday and from 9 am Saturday

Santo Spirito attracts both a gay and straight crowd; see Bars & Pubs – Inner Stadt for more details.

For clubbing, 'Heaven in U4' (see Night clubs earlier) is an extremely popular nigh for the gay and lesbian scene. *Why Not. (Map 7; ☎ 535 11 58; 01, Tiefer Graben 22* is a central club attracting mainly young guys; it only opens 10 pm to 4 am Thursday and to 5 am Friday and Saturday.

Other popular places in Vienna's gay and lesbian scene are the *Eagle Bar* *(Map 5; 06, Blümelgasse 1)*, a men's bar with a mostly leather-clad clientele, and the lesbian-owned *Orlando Restaurant (Map 5; ☎ 967 35 50; 06, Mollardgasse 3)*.

ROCK

Vienna manages to attract both big-name and new bands, mainly in the summer. Posters advertising future concerts can be found plastered all over the city, covering every available space, so it's easy to pick up on who's in town. Venues around town are invariably small and the crowds fairly subdued, making it easy to push your way to the front and not end up being crushed by the end of the night.

WUK (Map 3; ☎ 401 21 10; 09, Währinger Strasse 59) is an interesting venue offering a variety of events, including alternative bands, classical music, dance, theatre, children's events, political discussions and practical-skills workshops. It is governement subsidised but has freedom to pursue an independent course. Prices are not high; some events are even free. There's also a Beisl in the cobbled courtyard, open to 2 am daily.

Arena (Map 6; ☎ 798 85 95; 03, Baumgasse 80) is another good venue, centred in a former slaughterhouse. From May to September, headline rock, soul and reggae bands play on the outdoor stage (entry €18.20 to €25.45), but in August this space becomes an outdoor cinema. All year, smaller bands play in one of two indoor halls (entry from around €7.30), and there's sometimes theatre, dance and discussions. Keep an ear open for the once-a-month all-night parties (from €5.80), eg, 'Iceberg' (German/British 1970s new wave music) and various techno parties.

Stadthalle (Map 5; ☎ 98 10 0-0; 15, Vogelweidplatz 14) is the biggest hall for rock concerts and usually caters for large, mainstream rock bands and local heroes. Check the posters around town for upcoming shows.

Flex (see Nightclubs) and B72 (see Bars & Pubs) regularly host touring bands.

JAZZ

A good jazz club is *Porgy & Bess (Map 7; ☎ 503 70 09; 07, Museumplatz 1)*, in the Museumquartier. Opening times vary depending on the evening's entertainment, but the music usually kicks off around 9 pm. The entrance fee starts at €7.30.

Another good venue is *Jazzland (Map 7; ☎ 533 25 75; 01, Franz Josefs Kai 29)*, where the music usually kicks off at 9 pm; entry costs from €10.90.

Krah Krah (see Bars & Pubs) has occasional jazz on winter Sundays.

VIENNA BOYS' CHOIR

The Vienna Boys' Choir (Wiener Sängerknaben) is an institution of the city. It is actually four separate choirs; duties are rotated between singing in Vienna, touring the world, resting, and perhaps even occasionally going to school. The choir dates back to 1498 when it was instigated by Maximilian I and at one time numbered Haydn and Schubert in its ranks. The choir sings every Sunday (except during July and August) at 9.15 am in the Burgkapelle (Royal Chapel) in the Hofburg (see the Things to See & Do chapter).

Tickets for seats are €5.10 to €27.60 and must be booked weeks in advance (☎ 533 99 27, e hofmusikkapelle@asn-wien.ac.at), or you could try for a last-minute ticket at the Burgkapelle box office from 11 am to 1 pm and 3 to 5 pm Friday for the following Sunday. Standing room is free and you need to queue by 8.30 am to find a place inside the open doors, but you can get a flavour of what's going on from the TV in the foyer. Also interesting is the scrum afterwards when everybody struggles to photograph and be photographed with the serenely patient choir members.

The choir also sings a mixed program of music in the Musikverein (see the Classical Music & Opera section earlier) at 4 pm on Friday in May, June, September and October. Tickets cost €28.34 to €39.97, and you get them through Reisebüro Mondial (Map 7; ☎ 588 04 141, e ticket@mondial .at), 04, Faulmanngasse 4 and from hotels in Vienna.

ENTERTAINMENT

SPANISH RIDING SCHOOL

A Viennese institution with a difference are the Lipizzaner stallions, which strut their stuff in the Spanische Reitschule. The breed was first imported from Spain (hence 'Spanish') by Maximilian II in 1562, and in 1580 a stud was established at Lipizza (hence 'Lipizzaner'), now in Slovenia.

At the Spanish Riding School in the Hofburg (see the Things to See & Do chapter) the stallions perform an equine ballet to a program of classical music while the audience cranes to see from pillared balconies, and chandeliers shimmer above. The mature stallions are all snow-white (though they are born dark) and the riders wear traditional garb, from their leather boots up to their bicorn hats. It's a long-established Viennese institution, truly reminiscent of the old Habsburg era.

Reservations to see them perform are booked up weeks in advance: write to the Spanische Reitschule, Michaelerplatz 1, A-1010 Wien; fax 535 01 86, [e] office@srs.at. (Buy direct – travel agents charge at least 22% commission.) Otherwise, ask in the office about cancellations; unclaimed tickets are sold around two hours before performances. You need to be pretty keen on horses to be happy about paying €18.20 to €65.40 for seats or €14.55 for standing room, although a few of the tricks, such as seeing a stallion bounding along on only its hind legs like a demented kangaroo, do tend to stick in the mind.

Tickets to watch them train can be bought the same day (€7.30, children €2.20) at gate No 2, Josefsplatz in the Hofburg. Training is from 10 am to noon, Tuesday to Friday and some Saturdays. The stallions go on their summer holidays (seriously!) to Lainzer Tiergarten, west of the city, during July and August. They can be seen training for much of the rest of the year (except Christmas to mid-February), though they are sometimes away on tour. Queues are very long early in the day, but if you try at around 11 am most people have gone and you can get in fairly quickly – indicative of the fact that training is relatively dull except for a few isolated high points. If you only

MICK WELDON

A Prancing Horse

want to grab a few photos, you can try waiting to see them cross between the school and the *Stallburg* (stables), which usually happens on the half-hour.

CINEMAS

Entry prices start at €5.10 for the cheap seats; Monday is known as *Kinomontag*, when all cinema seats are €5.10. Sometimes films are in English: look out for *OF (Original Fassung)* or *OV (Original Version)*, meaning the film is shown in the original language; *OmU (Original mit Untertiteln)* means it's shown in the original language with subtitles. Cinemas that show original-language films include:

Artis International (Map 7; ☎ 535 65 70; 01, Schultergasse 5)
Audimax der TU (Map 7; ☎ 588 01-41930; 06, Getreidemarkt 9) – actually a lecture theatre in the Technical University; prices lower than conventional cinemas.
Burg Kino (Map 7; ☎ 587 84 06; 01, Opernring 19) – *The Third Man* is shown regularly here.

English Cinema Haydn (Map 5; ☎ 587 22 62; 06, Mariahilfer Strasse 57)
Filmcasino (Map 5; ☎ 587 90 62; 05, Margaretenstrasse 78)
Filmhaus am Spittelberg (Map 7; ☎ 522 48 16; 07, Spittelberggasse 3)
Filmhaus Stöbergasse (Map 5; ☎ 546 66 0; 05, Stöbergasse 11–15)
Flotten Center (Map 5; ☎ 586 51 52; 06, Mariahilfer Strasse 85–87)
IMAX Filmtheater (Map 5; ☎ 894 01 01; 14, Mariahilfer Strasse 212) – giant screen, prices from €8.35, or €7.30 for students.
Österreichische Filmmuseum (Hofburg map; ☎ 533 70 54; 01, Augustinerstrasse 1) – closed 1 July to 30 September; annual membership required (€7.30), then €4.35 entry; monthly retrospectives covering a group of directors or a certain theme are common (several films shown daily, check www.filmmuseum.at for listings).
Top Center (Map 7; ☎ 587 55 57; 06, Rahlgasse 1)
Votivkino (Map 3; ☎ 317 35 71; 09, Währinger Strasse 12)

In mid-October Vienna is home to the *Viennale*, an international film festival. By no means as prestigious at Cannes, it still attracts top-quality films from all over the world and is geared to the viewer rather than the filmmakers. For two weeks a number of cinemas continuously play screenings which could broadly be described as fringe, ranging from documentaries to short and feature films, and tickets for the more popular ones can be hard to come by. The Viennale Zelt, a tent set up in Stadtpark while the festival is on, is a good place to mix with other film buffs over a drink and is open from 6 pm to 2 am. Tickets can be bought two weeks before the first films are screened from a number of stands around town. Call ☎ 713 20 00 or check the Web site at www.viennale.at for more information.

CASINO
Vienna's casino (Map 7; ☎ 512 48 36; 01, Kärntner Strasse 41) is near the Staatsoper. Ascend the stairs to play blackjack, roulette and other games; stakes are from €3.65 (€7.30 after 9 pm) up to much more than you can probably afford. There's no entry fee as such. Show identification to get in, whereupon you'll be given a voucher for €21.80 worth of chips; to use the voucher you'll have to pay €18.90. Smart dress is required, ie, no trainers or jeans, a shirt with collar, a tie (in winter) and jacket (a jacket and tie can be hired for a refundable deposit if required). Casino opening hours are 3 pm to 3 am. Downstairs, slot machines are open from 11 am to 1 am (no dress code).

SPECTATOR SPORTS
As in any large city, there are plenty of sports to choose from. International and domestic football (soccer) is played at the Ernst-Happel-Stadion (Map 6; ☎ 72 71 80), 02, Meiereistrasse 7, in the Prater. The Stadthalle (Map 5; ☎ 98 100), 15, Vogelweidplatz 15, hosts a national football tournament at the end of December, and other events as diverse as a tennis tournament (mid-October) and a horse show (early November). The swimming pool here is a major venue for aquatic events like races, water polo and synchronised swimming. Another important pool is the Stadionbad (Map 6; ☎ 720 21 02), which has swimming and diving competitions from time to time (check with the venue for dates).

Other popular sports that can be played and watched include golf, handball and baseball. Horse racing is at Freudenau (Map 2), 02, Rennbahnnstrasse 65. Call ☎ 728 95 31 for information. In the Prater, there are trotting races at Krieau (Map 4).

Vienna's Spring Marathon is run (jogged, walked, abandoned – depending upon the fitness of the participants) in April or May. The route takes in Schönbrunn, the Ringstrasse and the Prater.

At 2 pm on New Year's Eve the Ringstrasse empties of cars and fills with runners, all mad enough to brave the winter cold for a bit of fun. The run, which anyone can enter, consists of one lap of the Ring (about 5km), and many participants dress up for the occasion, some even in their birthday suits.

Shopping

Vienna is not a place for cheap shopping, but it does offer numerous elegant shops and quality products. Local specialities include porcelain, ceramics, handmade dolls, wrought-iron work and leather goods. As you wander around you'll also see many shops selling stamps *(Briefmarken)*, coins *(Münze)*, and second-hand odds and ends *(Altwaren)*. Many of the more expensive hotels have a free guide called *Shopping in Vienna*, listing products and outlets, mostly in the Innere Stadt and Mariahilfer Strasse. Falter's *Best of Vienna* has a large and typically idiosyncratic section on shopping (in German).

Shops are generally open from 8 or 9 am to about 6 pm on weekdays and 8 am to noon or 1 pm on Saturday. Since the late 1990s shops have been allowed to open till 7.30 pm on weekdays and 5 pm on Saturdays, but only some supermarkets and larger stores exercise this option. Some shops cling to the old habit of opening to 5 pm on the first Saturday of the month (called *Langersamstag* or *Einkaufsamstag*).

Bargaining is not the norm in shops, though you can certainly haggle when buying second-hand. For special reductions, look out for signs saying 'Aktion'. The Viennese advertise their second-hand goods in *Bazar* (€1.85), a thrice-weekly magazine available from pavement newsstands.

Major credit cards are often accepted. See Taxes & Refunds in the Facts for the Visitor chapter for information on reclaiming the VAT on large purchases (for non-EU residents only).

WHAT TO BUY
Souvenirs & Crafts
There are various souvenir shops in the arcade connecting the old and new Hofburgs (Map 7), selling typical artefacts like mugs, steins, dolls, petit-point embroidery, porcelain Lipizzaner stallions and so on. Kärntner Strasse (Map 7) has numerous souvenir shops; Pawlata, at No 14, seems to have

lower prices than most, and also stocks lot of distinctive tableware from Gmunden.

The Augarten Porcelain Factory (Map 7 ☎ 512 14 94), 01, Stock im Eisen Platz and (Map 5) 06, Mariahilfer Strasse 99, produces a variety of gifts and ornaments, including Lipizzaners; see the Web site a www.augarten.at.

A specialist outlet for porcelain and crystal is Albin Denk, 01, Graben 13. Next door Kober, 01, Graben 14–15, sells toys, souvenirs and tin soldiers. Spielzeug OASE on the corner of Seilerstätte and Weih burggasse in the Innere Stadt, has man dolls and toys at discount prices. (These three are all on Map 7.)

Österreichische Werkstätten (Map 7 ☎ 512 24 18), 01, Kärntner Strasse 6, is cooperative with jewellery, handicrafts an ornaments, in eye-catching and colourfu designs. J & L Lobmeyr (Map 7), 01 Kärntner Strasse 26, is well known fo glassware, and has a small museum up stairs (open 9 am to 6 pm weekdays an 10 am to 5 pm Saturday; free).

Jewellery & Watches
Haban (Map 7), 01, Graben 12 and 01 Kärntner Strasse 2, has the largest range c clocks in Vienna, and a king's ransom c quality jewellery. CF Rothe & Neffe (Ma 7), 01, Kohlmarkt 7, sells traditional garne jewellery. Orth-Blau (Map 7; ☎ 512 89 13 01, Krugerstrasse 17, has ornaments an jewellery ranging from modern to antiqu styles. Other top outlets are: AE Köchert, 01 Neuer Markt 15; Rudolf Hübner, 01, Grabe 28; and Wagner, 01, Kärntner Strasse 32.

Art & Antiques
Selling works of art is big business; chec the auctions at the Dorotheum (Map 7; ☎ 51 60-0), 01, Dorotheergasse 17; Web site a www.dorotheum.com. Founded in 1707 b Joseph I, this state-owned institution is no in the process of being privatised. It's inter esting to watch the proceedings even if yo

don't intend to buy anything. Lots can be inspected in advance with the opening prices marked. If you don't have the confidence to bid yourself you can commission an agent to do it for you.

A range of objects ends up for sale, not only expensive antiques but also affordable household ornaments. The hammer price usually excludes VAT; you'll have to pay this but you may be able to claim it back later. On the 2nd floor is the *'Freier Verkauf'* section, where you can buy on the spot at marked prices. There are some great items here (jewellery, ornaments, oil paintings etc) and it's fun just to wander around, and look, and dream...

There are many antique shops and art galleries nearby along Dorotheergasse and the surrounding streets. Farther afield, Dreimäderlhaus (Map 6; ☎ 505 85 28), 04, Wiedner Hauptstrasse 69, is a second-hand shop that buys and sells art and antiques. Much of it is good-quality stuff, though there are some junk-shop odds and ends like books, records and old postcards.

Furniture & Fittings

Szaal (Map 3; ☎ 406 63 30), 08, Josefstädter Strasse 74, is a specialist in Biedermeier and baroque furniture. The store can arrange shipment back to your home country.

Wiener Messing Manufaktur (Map 5), 08, Lerchenfelder Strasse 27, sells lights and lampshades in interesting designs (90% are made in its own workshop), and brass fittings. Styles include Art Nouveau and Art Deco. Opposite is Beranek, with imported contemporary lamps. Design Rampf (Map 3; ☎ 402 17 01), 09, Kinderspitalgasse 3, covers the same ground, but even more creatively.

Fashion

High fashion commands high prices. Renowned stores in the Innere Stadt (Map 7) include: Eduard Kettner, Seilergasse 12; Fürnkranz-Couture, Kärntner Strasse 39; Jonak, Trattnerhof 1; and Silhouette, Kärntner Strasse 35. For men's fashion try Adonis, Kohlmarkt 11; Linnerth, Am Lugeck 1–2; and E Braun & Co, Graben 8.

Loden-Plankl, Michaelerplatz 6, is a specialist in traditional Austrian wear (eg, the green collarless loden jackets, made of pressed felt). Aigner, in the Ringstrassen Galerien, offers clothes and all sorts of leather accessories, such as handbags and belts. Rag, Sterngasse 4, is the spot for youth fashions.

For expensive and fashionable shoes go to Denkstein, 01, Bauernmarkt 8, or Dominici, 01, Singerstrasse 2. For something more affordable, look to the Humanic chain, with branches on all the main shopping streets (eg, 01, Kärntner Strasse 51; 06, Mariahilfer Strasse 94; or 08, Alser Strasse 35). Markenschuh-Diskont (Map 6), 04, Rilkeplatz 3, stocks footwear ranging from the functional to the fashionable, but at discounts of up to 50%.

Music

The biggest outlet is the Virgin Megastore at 06, Mariahilfer Strasse 37–39; there are two floors crammed with CDs, DVDs, records, tapes and videos. Another place with a wide selection is EMI Austria at 01, Kärntner Strasse 30. To pursue operatic interests, try Arcadia, 01, Kärntner Strasse 40. (All on Map 7.)

Teuchtler (Map 7; ☎ 586 21 33), 08, Windmühlgasse 10, is a second-hand shop that buys, sells and exchanges records and CDs, including rare and deleted titles. It has classical, jazz and rock sections, and it's open 1 to 6 pm weekdays and 10 am to 1 pm Saturday.

Other specialist record shops include Red Octopus (Map 3; ☎ 408 14 22), 08, Josefstädter Strasse 99, for jazz, and Black Market (Map 7; ☎ 533 76 17-0), 01, Gonzagagasse 9, for soul, funk, hip-hop and other genres (and some clothing).

Books & CD ROMs

Look for branches of the Libro chain for cheap books, stationery and CD ROMs (eg, in the Ringstrassen Galerien). Wollzeile, near Stephansdom, is a street with many different bookshops; Morawa (Map 7; ☎ 515 62) at No 11 is the biggest. There are also bookshops on Graben. The British Bookshop (Map 7; ☎ 512 19 45), 01, Weihburggasse 24, has the largest selection of English-language books. Shakespeare & Co Booksellers (Map 7; ☎ 535 50 53), 01, Sterngasse 2, is a smaller place and has some second-hand books. Big Ben (Map 3; ☎ 409 35 67-11) 09, Alser Strasse 4, is another English bookshop.

Freytag & Berndt (Map 7; ☎ 533 20 94), 01, Kohlmarkt 9, stocks a vast selection of maps, and has travel guides in English. Reisebuchladen (Map 7; ☎ 317 33 84), 09, Kolingasse 6, is a travel bookshop with many Lonely Planet guides.

Amadeus is a chain of large bookshops with English-language books, CD ROMs and (usually) free Internet access. There are branches at 06, Mariahilfer Strasse 99 and 37, at 03, Landstrasser Hauptstrasse 2a (Map 7; by Wien Mitte), and in Steffl at 01, Kärntner Strasse 19.

Food & Drink

The best place to buy wine is Wein & Co (☎ 08000-8020 8020): prices are low and the selection is wide. Branches include: 01, Habsburgergasse 3 (Map 7); 07, Mariahilfer Strasse 32–34, and in Lugner City. If you have a craving for brands from the UK or USA, drop by Bobby's Food Store (Map 6) at 04, Schleifmühlgasse 8.

Hotel Sacher has a shop on Kärntner Strasse, by the tourist office, selling its famous Sacher Torte. Close by on Kohlmarkt, Demel has a section selling its cakes to take away. Or look into Anzinger (Map 7), 01, Tegetthoffstrasse 7, for a wide range of chocolatey concoctions.

WHERE TO SHOP

The main shopping streets in the Innere Stadt are the pedestrian-only thoroughfares of Kärntner Strasse, Graben and Kohlmarkt. Mainly upmarket and specialist shops are to be found along here. Haas Haus on Stephansplatz also houses plush shops. Generally speaking, outside the Ring is where you'll find shops catering for those with shallower pockets. Mariahilfer Strasse is regarded as the best shopping street, particularly the stretch between the Ring and Westbahnhof, and has large department stores like Gerngross, which are mostly

missing from the central zone (though Kärntner Strasse does have the Steffl department store at No 19). Other prime shopping streets are Landstrasser Hauptstrasse, Favoritenstrasse and Alser Strasse.

For major shopping expeditions, the Viennese head south of the city to Shopping City Süd, marketed simply as SCS. It's said to be the biggest shopping centre in Europe. Parking places are difficult to find here after about 10 am on Saturday, so a good alternative is to take the IKEA bus departing from opposite the Staatsoper (near the tram No 2 stop) to the IKEA furniture shop. The bus there is free, but coming back you pay €1.50. The bus runs from the city every 90 minutes, 10 am to 5.30 pm weekdays and 8.30 am to 4 pm Saturday; it returns 45 minutes later. The Lokalbahn tram service to Baden, departing opposite the Hotel Bristol every 15 minutes, stops at SCS; the fare is €2.80, or €1.40 supplement if you already have a city travel card (buy tickets from the booth in advance, or make sure you have the correct change for the on-board ticket machine). SCS is just south of

International Shoppers

Ever since Hungary's borders opened in 1989, the Viennese have flocked to the town of Sopron to do their shopping. (Appropriately, the name is pronounced 'Shop-ron'.) Just 8km from the Austrian border, Sopron was Eastern Europe's first free trade shopping zone, and has spawned numerous supermarkets, fashion boutiques, dentists, money-changers and much else. Prices are much lower than they are in Vienna's plush boulevards, for everything from alcohol and cigarettes to salami and household goods to dental fillings and beauty treatments. Foie gras is highly prized. Sopron is also an attractive town in its own right, boasting cobbled streets and plentiful medieval buildings.

Sopron is about an hour's drive south-east of Vienna, or it's accessible by Austrian trains (travelling first via Wiener Neustadt or Neusiedl am See). The Viennese also head into Bratislava in Slovakia to snap up cheap goods and foodstuffs – see the Excursions chapter.

the city precincts at Vösendorf, near the junction of the A21 and A2.

The Ringstrassen Galerien is a pleasant shopping centre beside the Hotel Bristol (Map 7) on Kärntner Ring, in two adjoining buildings split by Akademiestrasse. Another good shopping centre is Lugner City (Map 5), in the 15th district on Gablenzgasse not far from the Gürtel ring road. This large shopping mall is cool in summer, with an atrium and a glass roof. Branches of most of the main chain stores are here, plus there are restaurants, cafes and supermarkets. Opening hours are 9 am to 7 pm weekdays and to 5 pm Saturday; it has its own parking garage (first hour free, thereafter €0.60 per 30 minutes). The even larger Donauzentrum shopping centre (Map 4) is farther afield, but conveniently next to the Kagran U1 station.

Around the church on Mexikoplatz is an interesting place for a wander. There are many shops selling cheap electrical goods, watches and clothing.

Niedermeyer has stores all round the city, and they're good places to buy a hi-fi, radios, TVs, video and audio tapes, photography equipment, computer hardware and software and other goods. Hartlauer is similar, and also sells eye glasses. Cosmos (in Lugner City and elsewhere) has great prices for photography film, tapes, CDs, CD ROMs and so on.

Markets

The biggest and best-known market is the Naschmarkt (Maps 5 & 7), extending for over 500m along Linke Wienzeile. It's a 'farmer's market', mainly consisting of stalls selling meats, fruit and vegetables, but there are some stalls selling clothes and curios. Prices are said to get lower the farther from the Ring end you go. Opening times are 6 am to 6 pm weekdays, and 6 am to 5 pm Saturday. The Naschmarkt is also a good place to eat cheaply in snack bars – doner kebabs are a real favourite (€2.55).

On Saturday a flea market (Flohmarkt; Map 5) is tacked onto the south-western end of the Naschmarkt, extending for several blocks. It's very atmospheric and shouldn't be missed, with goods piled up in apparent chaos on the walkway. You can find anything you want (and everything you don't want): books, clothes, records, ancient electrical goods, old postcards, ornaments, carpets ... you name it. We even saw a blow-up doll (second-hand, of course). Bargain for prices here. If you can't make it on Saturday, there are plenty of junk shops to explore in nearby streets, particularly on Kettenbrückengasse.

Another atmospheric food market is at 16, Brunnengasse, between Thaliastrasse and Gaullachergasse.

Other markets are:

Antiques crafts, books and ornaments 01, Am Hof (Map 7); 10 am to 6 pm Friday and Saturday, March to mid-December

Arts & crafts 01, Schönlaterngasse (Map 7); first weekend of the month from April to November and each weekend in December

Arts & crafts 07, Spittelberg (Map 7); daily from mid-November to Christmas, and on occasional weekends in summer

Children's flea market Along the south bank of the Danube Canal, north of Salztorbrücke (Map 7); noon to 5 pm every second Saturday, May to September

Excursions

There are some excellent day trips near Vienna. Perhaps the best excursions are to the small towns and villages along the Danube, and the best part of the Danube is the wine-growing stretch known as the Wachau. This lies in the province of Lower Austria (Niederösterreich), which completely surrounds Vienna. Other major attractions close to Vienna are the Wienerwald (Vienna Woods), also in Lower Austria, and the nearby province of Burgenland. If you stay overnight in one of these places, inquire at the tourist office or your hotel if there's a 'guest card', as these bring useful discounts, especially in the Wachau. Cards are funded by a resort tax of about € 0.80 per adult per night, which is usually included in quoted accommodation prices.

If you're interested in taking a two- or three-day trip farther afield the possibilities are many. Graz, Salzburg, Prague and Budapest are all within easy reach and well worth a visit. For reasons of space these destinations aren't covered here, though the nearby Slovak capital of Bratislava is described briefly.

The Danube Valley

The historical importance of the Danube (Donau) Valley as a corridor between east and west ensured that control of this area was hotly contested. As a result there are some 550 castles and fortresses in Lower Austria alone, including many monasteries and abbeys that have defences to match conventional castles. The Wachau section of the Danube, between Krems and Melk, is the most scenic, with wine-growing villages, forested slopes, vineyards and imposing fortresses at nearly every bend.

St Pölten is the state capital of Lower Austria, though its tourist office (☎ 02742-353 354) only has information about St Pölten and its immediate vicinity. You'd be better off contacting the local tourist offices

direct, or there's the Niederösterreich Information head office (☎ 536 10-6200, fax -6060, ⓔ noe.tourist-info@ping.at) in Vienna; see the Web site at www.noe.co.at.

Attractions along the Danube Valley are covered below in order from west to east.

GETTING THERE & AROUND
It's very easy to take a day trip from Vienna to the Wachau and include a boat trip along the river.

Bus
Four weekday Bundesbuses (two or three on weekends) go between Melk and Krems. It takes 65 minutes and the fare is €5.40. There are also two or three buses daily except Sunday from Krems to Spitz (€3.20, 40 minutes), which call at Dürnstein and Weissenkirchen.

Train
To Melk, direct trains depart from Vienna's Westbahnhof and take an hour (€11.35). Some trains involve changing at St Pölten, but that only adds a few minutes to the trip.

Trains to Krems go from Franz Josefs Bahnhof (€9.70); they leave hourly, calling at Tulln en route, and also take about an hour. From Krems a slowish train runs along the northern bank to St Valentin, stopping at all Wachau villages on that side. Another line links Krems to St Pölten.

Car & Motorcycle
The road route alongside the river is scenic. Highway 3 links Vienna and Linz and stays close to the northern bank of the Danube for much of the way. Along the Wachau stretch another road hugs the southern bank.

Bicycle
Cycling is extremely popular in summer. There is a bicycle track along the southern bank from Vienna to Krems, and along both sides of the river from Krems to Linz. Heading east from Vienna, a bicycle track also

uns north of the river to Hainburg. Many
hotels along the Danube have facilities for
the numerous guests on cycling trips.

Boat

The main operator is DDSG Blue Danube
(☎ 588 80-0, fax -440, **e** info@ddsg-blue-
danube.at), 01, Friedrichstrasse 7, Vienna,
with a Web site at www.ddsg-blue-danube.at.
G Glaser (☎ 726 08 201, **e** g.glaser@
xpoint.at), 02, Handelskai 265, Vienna, is a
helpful sales agent that sells tickets for all
boat services. Check the Web site at www
.user.xpoint.at/g.glaser/shipping.htm.

There's only one boat linking Vienna and
the Wachau: DDSG has a Sunday service
from mid-May to 1 October; Vienna to
Dürnstein costs €14.55 and takes 5¾ hours.
The Vienna–Krems stretch of the Danube
has few highlights, which explains why the
service is so sparse.

However, taking a boat trip is a popular
way of exploring the Wachau between
Krems and Melk. DDSG operates steamers
between Melk and Krems from 1 April to
late October, with three departures daily
(only one in the first and last few weeks of
the season). The full trip takes 100 minutes
going downstream and an hour longer going
upstream (ie, Krems to Melk). The cost is
€14.55, or €19.65 return. From either town
to Spitz costs €8, or €10.90 return. Boats
also stop at Dürnstein. Commentary en route
(in English) highlights points of interest. If
you have certain rail passes (eg, Inter-Rail,
Eurail or Austrian Domino) you get a discount of 20% on DDSG's Wachau fares.
Bikes can be taken on board free of charge.
Brandner (☎ 07433-25 90-0, **e** schiff
fahrt@ brandner.at) has two boats daily on
the Krems–Melk stretch, sailing from late
April to mid-October. Prices are the same as
with DDSG, but it costs AS20 extra to take
a bicycle. Buying through G Glaser, you
can do Krems–Melk for €13.85/18.90 one
way/return. G Glaser also sells tickets on a
paddle steamer going from Tulln to Melk on
weekends from May to September (€10.95/
17.45 one way/return).
Ardagger (☎ 07479-64 64-0) connects
Linz (west of Melk) and Krems three times

a week in each direction from 1 May to
early October. Boats go from Linz to Krems
during the day on Sunday, Tuesday and
Thursday (7¾ hours), returning overnight
on Monday, Wednesday and Friday (9¾
hours). Each sector of the trip costs €5.85
or €7.30, with the full trip adding up to
€37.80 each way.

MELK
☎ 2752 • pop 6500
Lying in the lee of its imposing monastery-
fortress, Melk is an essential stop on the
Danube trail.

Orientation & Information
The train station is 300m from the town centre. Walk straight ahead for 50m down
Bahnhofstrasse to get to the post office
(Postamt 3390), where money exchange is
available to 5 pm on weekdays and 10 am on
Saturday. Turn right for the youth hostel or
continue straight on, taking the Bahngasse
path, for the central Rathausplatz. Turn right
at Rathausplatz to get to the tourist office
(☎ 23 07-32, fax -490, **e** melk@smaragd
.at) at Babenbergerstrasse 1. It's closed from
November to March; otherwise it's open
from 9 am to noon and 2 to 6 pm weekdays,
10 am to 2 pm Saturday. In summer, hours
are 9 am to 7 pm Monday to Saturday, 10 am
to 2 pm Sunday.

If you stay anywhere in the Wachau, your
guest card entitles you to free entry to Melk's
open-air swimming pool in the summer.

Things to See & Do
The **Stift Melk** dominates the town from the
hill and provides an excellent view. Guided
tours (often in English, but phone ahead to
be sure) of this Benedictine abbey explain
its historical importance and are well worth
the extra money.

The huge monastery church is baroque
gone mad, with endless prancing angels and
gold twirls, but it's very impressive nonetheless. The fine library and the mirror room
both have an extra tier painted on the ceiling (by Paul Troger) to give the illusion of
greater height. The ceilings are slightly
curved to aid the effect. Imperial rooms,

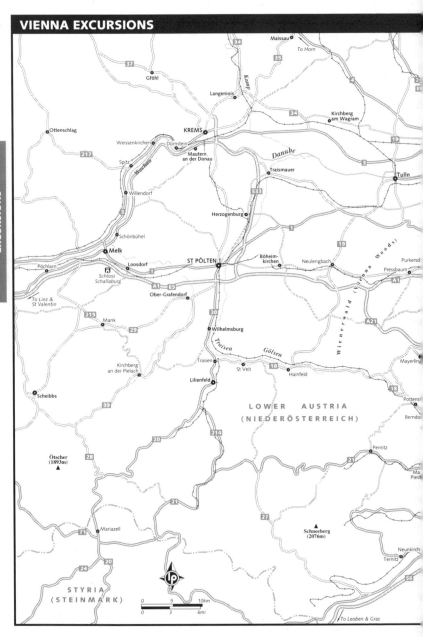

VIENNA EXCURSIONS

senstadt's Hausptstrasse – Josef Haydn's High Street

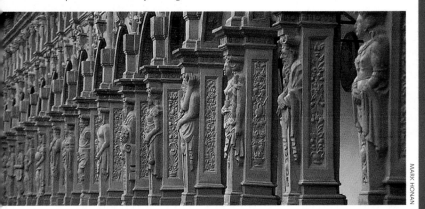

erracotta arches at Schallaburg Castle, outside Melk

he picturesque medieval village of Dürnstein

The Benedictine abbey dominates Melk

A Rust *Buschenschank* (wine tavern)

Schloss Esterházy, Eisenstadt

Labouring for the good of the grape, Dürnstein

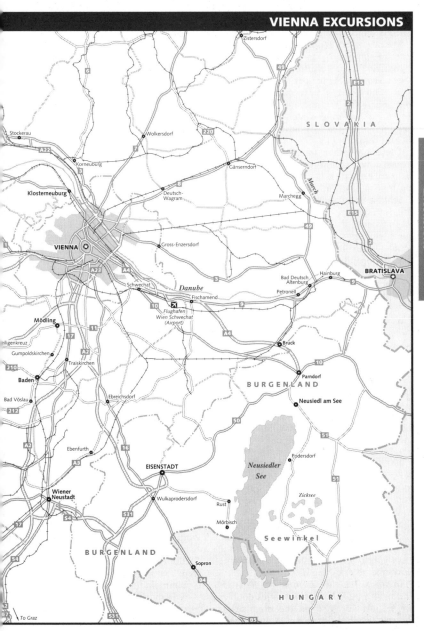

EXCURSIONS

where various dignitaries (including Napoleon) stayed, contain museum exhibits.

The monastery is open from the Saturday before Palm Sunday to All Saints' Day (1 November) from 9 am to 5 pm, except between May and September when it closes at 6 pm. Entry costs €5.10 (students aged up to 27 years €2.55), and the guided tour is €1.45 extra. During winter, the monastery can only be visited by guided tour (☎ 555-232 for information).

There are other interesting buildings around town, dating mostly from the 16th and 17th centuries. Try following the **walking tour** outlined in the tourist office map.

Schloss Schallaburg, 5km south of Melk, is a 16th-century Renaissance palace with magnificent terracotta arches and prestigious temporary exhibitions. There's also a permanent exhibition of toys through history. It's open from late April to late October and entry costs €6.55, or €2.95 for students. A reduced combination ticket with Stift Melk monastery is available.

Places to Stay & Eat

Camping Melk is on the west of the canal where it joins the Danube, and is open from March to October. Charges, excluding resort tax (€0.80), are €3.30 per adult, €2.55 per tent and €1.85 for a car. Reception is in the restaurant *Melker Fährhaus* (☎ 532 91, Kolomaniau 3), which is open 8 am to midnight Wednesday to Sunday (daily in summer). When it's closed, just camp and pay later. The restaurant has decent lunchtime fare from €5.50.

The HI *Jugendherberge* (☎ 526 81, fax 542 57, Abt Karl Strasse 42) has good showers and four-bed dorms, as well as sports and games facilities and parking spaces. Beds are €10.65 (€8.65 for those aged under 19), plus a €1.85 surcharge for single-night stays. The reception is closed from 10 am to 5 pm, but during the day you can reserve a bed and leave your bags. The hostel is closed from 1 November to mid-March.

Gasthof Weisses Lamm (☎ 540 85, Linzer Strasse 7) has a few singles/doubles for €25.45/40. Also on the premises is *Pizzeria Venezia* (open daily), with many

tasty pizzas starting at €4.75, and some Greek dishes.

Gasthof Goldener Stern (☎ 522 14, fax -4, Sterngasse 17) provides slightly cheaper accommodation, charging €23.30/40 or less, depending on the length of stay. It's closed Friday and Saturday in winter, or Tuesday evening and Wednesday in summer. There's a restaurant serving affordable Austrian food.

Gasthof zum Goldenen Hirschen (☎/fax 522 57, Rathausplatz 13) is a 16th-century house; pleasant, compact singles/doubles from €30/46 have private shower and (usually) WC. Its *Rathauskeller* restaurant has daily menus with soup for about €7, and other dishes from €6.

Stadt Melk (☎ 525 47, fax 524 75-19, Hauptplatz 1) has three-star rooms from €48/55.30, as well as a gourmet restaurant with a huge wine list.

A *supermarket* is at Rathausplatz 9.

Getting There & Around

For information on getting to Melk from Vienna see Getting There & Away under The Danube Valley earlier in this chapter. Boats leave from the canal by Pionierstrasse, 400m to the rear of the monastery. Bicycle rental is available in Melk at the train station. Bicycle is perhaps the best way to reach Schloss Schallaburg, as the bus (€2.20) is very infrequent.

MELK TO DÜRNSTEIN

In addition to the grape vines, peaches and apricots are grown along this 30km stretch of the river. Shortly after departing Melk you pass **Schloss Schönbühel** on the southern bank, which marks the beginning of the Wachau. Also here is a 17th-century Servite monastery (the Servites were a mendicant order of friars), and the ruins of the 12th-century Burg Aggstein. On the opposite bank **Willendorf** soon appears, where a 25,000-year-old sandstone statuette of Venus was discovered; another made from a mammoth tusk was also found.

A farther 5km brings **Spitz** into view, a village with attractive houses and a peaceful aura. The parish church at Kirchenplatz is unusual for its chancel, which is out of line with the main body of the church. Another noteworthy feature is the 15th-century statues of the 12 apostles lining the organ loft. Most wear an enigmatic expression, as if being tempted by an unseen spirit to overindulge in the Communion wine. It's a Gothic church with crisscross ceiling vaulting, yet has baroque altars. The fountain in front of the church and the vine-covered hills rising behind make a pretty picture.

Six kilometres farther along the northern bank is **Weissenkirchen**. Its centrepiece is a fortified parish church rising from a hill. This Gothic church was built in the 15th century and has a baroque altar. The garden terrace, if open, provides good views of the river. Below the church is the charming Teisenhoferhof arcaded courtyard, with a covered gallery and lashings of flowers and dried corn. The **Wachau Museum** (☎ 02715-2268) is here and has work by artists of the Danube School. It's open 10 am to 5 pm from 1 April to 31 October (closed Monday) and entry costs €2.20 (students €1.10).

After Weissenkirchen the river sweeps around to the right, and soon yields a fine perspective of Dürnstein.

DÜRNSTEIN
☎ 02711 • pop 1000
Dürnstein achieved 12th-century notoriety by its imprisonment of King Richard the Lion-Heart of England. Today, this picturesque village is one of the prime destinations in the Wachau.

Orientation & Information
From the train station, walk ahead and then right for the village walls (five minutes). En route you pass the tourist office (☎ 200), in a little hut in the corner of the east car park. It's only open from April to October: 1 to 7 pm Monday, Thursday and Friday, 11 am to 7 pm Saturday and Sunday. All year during office hours you can get information from the Rathaus (☎ 219, fax 442, e duernstein@ netway.at) in Hauptstrasse, the main street. The boat landing stage is below the dominating feature of the village centre, the blue and white parish church.

Things to See & Do
High on the hill, commanding a marvellous view of the curve of the Danube, stand the ruins of **Kuenringerburg**, where Richard was incarcerated from 1192 to 1193. His crime was to have insulted Leopold V; his misfortune was to be recognised despite his disguise when journeying through Austria on his way home from the crusades; his liberty was achieved only upon the payment of a huge ransom. The hike up from the village takes 15 to 20 minutes.

In the village, Hauptstrasse is a cobbled street with some picturesque 16th-century houses, wrought-iron signs and floral displays. The **parish church**, formerly the abbey church (Chorherrenstift), has been meticulously restored. The baroque interior effectively combines white stucco and dark wood balconies. Entry costs €2.20, which includes access to the porch overlooking the blue Danube (where photo opportunities abound) and an exhibition on the Augustinian monks who once ruled the roost here (up until the monastery was dissolved by Joseph II in 1788). It's open 9 am to 6 pm daily from 1 April to 31 October.

Places to Stay & Eat
Pension Alte Rathaus (☎/fax 252, Hauptstrasse 26), behind the Rathaus, is reached through an attractive courtyard. Singles/doubles with private shower and WC are €36.35/50.90.

Pension Böhmer (☎ 239, Hauptstrasse 22) doubles as a wine shop and has slightly smaller doubles with shower and WC for around €40.

Private rooms are cheaper: *Hermine Wagner* (☎ 265, Hauptstrasse 29) has four beds from € 14.55 per person.

Gasthof Sänger Blondel (☎ 253, fax -7, Klosterplatz), named after the faithful minstrel who discovered where King Richard was incarcerated, has rooms from €54.50/77 with private shower, WC and TV. Its restaurant has a shady garden and food above €7. It's closed Sunday evening and Monday.

Another good option for food is *Goldener Strauss* (Hauptstrasse 18), which has

EXCURSIONS

a curved cellar-like ceiling and a small garden. Meals start at €6.20 (closed Tuesday).

Alter Klosterkeller is an attractive Buschenschank tavern on Anzuggasse, just outside the village walls (on the east side) and overlooking the vineyards. Wine is €1.60 a Viertel and a selection of cold snacks and cold meals are served (€1.90 to €4.75). It opens at 3 pm (2 pm on weekends and holidays) and is closed on Tuesday.

Restaurant Loibnerhof (☎ 02732-828 90, Unterloiben 7), about 1.5km east of Dürnstein, is highly regarded and reasonably priced (closed Monday and Tuesday).

Getting There & Away
By train, the fare is €1.90 to either Krems or Weissenkirchen. Dürnstein's train station is called Dürnstein-Oberloiben.

KREMS
☎ 2732 • pop 23,000
Krems reclines on the northern bank of the Danube, surrounded by terraced vineyards, and has been a centre of the wine trade for most of its history.

Orientation & Information
Krems comprises three linked parts: Krems to the east, the smaller settlement of Stein 2km to the west, and the connecting suburb of Und – an unusual name which inspires an example of Austrian humour: 'Krems and *(und* in German) Stein are three towns'. Krems' town centre is 300m in front of the train station, stretching along a pedestrian-only street, Obere and Untere Landstrasser. The main post office is to the left of the station on Brandströmstrasse 4–6 (Postamt 3500).

The tourist office (☎ 826 76, fax 700 11, e austropa.krems@netway.at), halfway between Krems and Stein, is part of the Austropa travel agency at Undstrasse 6, in the Kloster Und. It's open 9 am to 7 pm weekdays and 10 am to noon and 1 to 7 pm weekends. From 1 November to 30 April hours are 9 am to 6 pm weekdays only. Upstairs is the Tourismusregion Wachau office (☎ 856 20, fax 874 71, e wachau@netway.at); see the Web site at www.tiscover.com/wachau.

Things to See & Do
The best thing to do in Krems is to relax and enjoy the peaceful ambience. The street plan from the tourist office details various points of interest. Take your time and wander around the cobbled streets, quiet courtyards and ancient city walls. The most interesting streets are Obere and Untere Landstrasse in Krems and Steiner Landstrasse in Stein.

Krems has several churches worth peeking inside. The **Pfarrkirche St Veit** on the hill at Pfarrplatz is baroque in style, with frescoes by Martin Johann Schmidt, an 18th-century local artist. The **Piaristenkirche**, up behind St Veit's on Frauenbergplatz, has Gothic vaulting, huge windows and baroque altars. The **Dominikanerkirche**, Dominikanerplatz, contains collections of religious and modern art and the Weinstadt museum with wine-making artefacts. It's open 1 to 6 pm (9 am to 6 pm Tuesday; closed Monday) from 1 March to 30 November. Entry costs €3.65 (€2.55 concession).

Krems is a wine-growing centre and there's **wine-tasting** in the Kloster Und, 1 to 7 pm from Wednesday to Sunday – for €13.10 you can taste up to 100 different wines. For more modest experimentation, visit the municipal winery, Weingut der Stadt Krems, Stadtgraben, where you can try up to five wines for €0.75.

By the Kremsertor (gate) is a new arts centre, the **Kunsthalle** (☎ 826 69). Some of its exhibitions are held in the **Minoritenkirche** in Stein.

Places to Stay & Eat
ÖAMTC Donau Camping (☎ 844 55, Wiedengasse 7), near the boat station, is open Easter to mid-October and costs €3.65 per adult, from €2.20 for a tent and €2.95 for a car.

The HI *Jugendherberge* (☎ 834 52, Ringstrasse 77) has excellent facilities for cyclists, such as a garage and an on-site repair service. Beds in four- or six-bed dorms are €11.65, plus €1.45 surcharge for stays of only one or two nights. It's open from April to October.

Many hotels also have a surcharge for short stays. The cheapest choice is private ooms, which are listed on the tourist of-ice's accommodation leaflet. *Haus Hietz-ern (☎ 761 84, Untere Landstrasse 53)* is deally central and has two doubles and two riples for around €21.50 per person, with rivate shower and WC. They're available rom 1 June to 31 August.

In Stein, *Gästehaus Einzinger (☎ 823 16, teiner Landstrasse 82)* offers attractive ooms around a courtyard: singles/doubles re €25.45/50.90 with shower, WC and TV.

Gasthof Alte Poste (☎ 822 76, fax 843 6, Obere Landstrasse 32) is a historic 500-ear-old house with an enchanting court-ard. It has good singles/doubles for €24.75/46.55, or €35.65/53.80 with pri-ate shower, and doubles for €61.05 with hower and WC. It's a fine place to eat too, vith daily menus from €6.50 and local vine from €2 per Viertel (closed Tuesday vening and Wednesday).

Hotel Klinglhuber (☎ 821 43, Wiener-rrasse 12) is newly built in modern style. 'our-star rooms have all facilities, and plenty f light from big windows. Singles/doubles tart at €62.50/98.85. Along the road at No 2, by the bridge, is its Gasthof. Rooms here ave shower, toilet, TV, telephone and pol-shed wooden floors; prices start from €43.65/69.80. The restaurant is also here, nd has a terrace overlooking the river. Most neals are above €8.75 and it's open daily rom 7 am to at least 11 pm.

To find other places to eat, ask the tourist ffice for the Heurigen list. Alternatively, ust wander along Obere and Untere Land-trasser – there's plenty of choice, including heap takeaway stands. *Schwarze Kuchl Untere Landstrasse 8)* has meals from €4.75, served until 6.30 pm on weekdays nd 1 pm on Saturday. *China-Restaurant 'ai Yang (Obere Landstrasse 5)* is back rom the street and has courtyard seating nd lunch menus (from €4.40).

Supermarkets include a *Spar (Obere andstrasse 15)* and a *Zielpunkt* in the hopping centre by the Steinertor.

Getting There & Away

'he boat station is a 20-minute walk from the ain station, towards Stein on Donaulände.

Bikes can be rented at the train station and camp site.

TULLN
☎ 02272 • pop 12,300

Formerly a Roman camp called Comagena, and named as a town settlement in 791, Tulln trumpets itself as the 'Birthplace of Austria', and was in effect the nation's first capital.

Orientation & Information

Tulln is 29km west of Vienna, on the south bank of the Danube River. The centre of town is the pedestrian-only Hauptplatz. The tourist office (☎ 658 36, fax 658 38) is one block north at Minoritenplatz 2. It's open 9 am to 6 pm Monday to Friday, and 1 to 6 pm weekends and holidays (9 am to noon weekdays only from 1 October to 30 April).

Things to See & Do

Next to the tourist office, in the Minoriten-kloster, is a complex of museums called the **Tullner Museen**. Collections cover the city's history, both ancient and modern (in-cluding geology and Roman finds); one sec-tion deals with fire-fighting. It's open 3 to 6 pm Wednesday to Friday, 2 to 6 pm Satur-day, and 10 am to 6 pm Sunday (closed early January to early February). Admission to all parts costs €2.20 (€1.45 concession).

On the riverside is the **Egon Schiele Mu-seum**, open 9 am to noon and 2 to 6 pm Tuesday to Sunday; admission €2.95 (€2.20 concession). It vividly tells the life story of the Tulln-born artist – ask for the extensive English notes. Schiele is famous for his provocative nudes and he was briefly imprisoned following the seizure of 125 erotic drawings (some were of pubescent girls, and Schiele was also in trouble for al-lowing children to see his explicit works). Appropriately, the premises are a former jail and contain a mock-up of his cell, though Schiele was actually jailed in Neulengbach. There are 100 of his works on display (plus copies), mostly sketches and early paintings.

Churches of interest include the newly restored **Minoritenkirche** (18th century) and the **Pfarrkirche St Stephan** (12th-century Romanesque, with alterations in Gothic and baroque style). Behind the latter is a polygonal funerary chapel dating from the 13th century, with frescoes depicting some not very evil-looking devils. The crypt below has stacks of exhumed bones – if you want a look, ask for the key in the Paulussaal at the other end of the church.

Places to Stay & Eat

Donaupark Camping Ground (☎ 652 00, fax 652 01) is open from mid-May to early October; it's east of the centre, near the river on Hafenstrasse.

Beside the river and 500m west of the Egon Schiele Museum you'll find *Alpenvereins Herberge (☎ 626 92)*, with dorm beds for €11.85 and (if you have your own sleeping bag) a mattress on the floor for €9.65. There's also an inexpensive restaurant. It's reached by a pedestrian/cycling path and only open 1 May to 31 October.

Private rooms are also a good option. Central choices are *Haus Elisabeth (☎ 642 27, Nussallee 5)*, with a garden and doubles for €40.70 with shower and toilet or €28.35 without; and *Elisabeth Keindl (☎ 633 37, Wilhelmstrasse 16)*, charging €36.35 for doubles with shower, WC and TV.

Hotel-Restaurant Zur Rossmühle (☎ 624 11-0, fax -33, e rossmuehle@tulln.com, Hauptplatz 12) is a four-star place with a veritable jungle of plants in the lobby, complete with tweeting birds, and there's also a pleasant garden. Singles/doubles have high ceilings and shower, WC and TV, and start from €50.90/66.15. The restaurant is good quality, with interesting presentations of national dishes for around €11 to €18.

China Restaurant Pagode (Brudergasse 5), off Hauptplatz, has good weekday lunch menus from €4.30, or a lunch buffet for €4.95. There's also a sushi bar. For Austrian cooking, go to *Albrechtsstuben (Albrechtsgasse 24)*. It has a garden and two-course lunch menus for €4.75 (closed Sunday after 3 pm and Monday).

Getting There & Away

Tulln is reached by train or S-Bahn (S40) from Franz Josefs Bahnhof (€4.15). The train is quicker (25 minutes), but only stops

at the main Tulln station. Save yourself 10-minute walk by getting the S40 to Tul Stadt (50 minutes), which is more centra Tulln to Krems takes 40 minutes (€5.55).

KLOSTERNEUBURG
☎ 02243

Overlooking the river, only a little north west of Vienna's provincial territory ar within hiking distance of Kahlenberg (at th end of bus No 38A from Vienna), Kloste neuburg is known for its large Augustinia abbey, **Stift Klosterneuburg**, founded i 1114. The abbey buildings are mostl baroque and can be visited daily by an hou long guided tour (€5.10), but only fro May to October. The tour can be in Englis with advance notice (☎ 411-212). Th abbey church is also baroque, despite i neogothic spires. An annexe to the church St Leopold's Chapel, which has the *Verdu Altar*, covered in 51 enamelled pane showing biblical scenes. It was made i 1181 by Nicholas of Verdun and is an u surpassed example of medieval enam work. Check the Web site at www.stif klosterneuburg.at.

Getting There & Away

Klosterneuburg is on the S-Bahn route fro Vienna to Tulln: Klosterneuburg-Kierling the station closest to the abbey (€1.40 fro Franz Josefs Bahnhof).

PETRONELL
☎ 02163 • pop 1250

The village of Petronell lies close to th Danube, 38km east of Vienna. In Roma times it was the site of Carnuntum, a re gional capital believed to have had 50,00 inhabitants. The ruins extend towards Ba Deutsch-Altenburg, 4km to the east.

Orientation & Information

Petronell train station is 1km south of th main street, Hauptstrasse. At the entrance t the archaeological park, Hauptstrasse 296, i an office containing the March-Donaulan tourist office (☎ 335 55-10, fax -12, e m online@netway.at), and the archaeologica park information office (☎ 3377-0, fax -5

info@carnuntum.co.at). It's open 8 am to
pm daily.

hings to See & Do

elics of former glories are not particularly
tunning, but together they make a reason-
bly diverting day. They include an amphitheatre that formerly seated 15,000 (€1.90)
nd the archaeological park on the site of
the old civilian town (€3.60). This park in-
ludes ruins of the public baths, a recon-
tructed temple, and tours and activities for
hildren. Like the amphitheatre, it is open
am to 5 pm (to 6 pm on weekends and
olidays) from 1 April to 2 November. The
leidentor (Heathen Gate) was once the
outh-west entrance to the city and now
tands as an isolated anachronism amid
ields of corn – it's undergoing restoration
vork until November 2001 (free entry).

Bad Deutsch-Altenburg has a museum
evoted to the Carnuntum era at Badgasse
0–46; it's open 10 am to 5 pm Tuesday to
unday (closed mid-December to mid-
anuary). Admission is €4.40, or €7.30 for
combination ticket with the amphitheatre
nd archaeological park. Bad Deutsch-
Altenburg is also a health spa, with iodine
ulphur springs (28°C).

Hainburg, farther east, is a possible addi-
ional excursion. It has further ancient
elics, in the form of sturdy city gates and
illtop ruins.

Places to Stay & Eat

*Gasthof Zum Heidentor (☎/fax 2201,
Hauptstrasse 129)* has renovated singles/
oubles for €21.80/36.35 with shower, WC
nd satellite TV. The restaurant offers a
unch menu for €4.40 with soup, and has a
eer garden and children's play area. It's
losed Monday and after 2 pm on Sunday.

*Hotel Marc Aurel (☎ 2285, fax -60,
Hauptstrasse 173)* is only a small step up in
uality, but charges from €40/50.20. The
new owner will probably make some
changes after 2001. The restaurant has Aus-
rian dishes for €7 or more (open daily).

Bad Deutsch-Altenburg has a wider
ange of places to stay and eat – a good
street to explore is the central Badgasse. Try

*Früstückspension Mittermayer (☎ 02165-
628 74, Badgasse 20)* with simple, pleasant
rooms for €18.90/34.90 using hall shower.
*Pension Riedmüller (☎ 02165-624 73, fax
-32, e riedmueller@netway.at, Badgasse
28)* charges €21.85 per person for rooms
with private shower and WC, and has a cafe.

Getting There & Away

Take the hourly S7 from Wien Nord or
Wien Mitte (direction: Wolfsthal); the one-
hour journey costs €5.55, or €4.15 if you
have a city travel pass. To get to Bad
Deutsch-Altenburg or Hainburg costs an
extra €1.40.

NATIONALPARK DONAU-AUEN

This national park, established in 1996, runs
in a thin strip on both sides of the Danube,
extending from the edge of Vienna to the
Slovakian border. It was created to try to
protect an environment that was threatened
by the building of a hydroelectric power
station in Hainburg. You'll find plentiful
flora and fauna, including 700 species of
fern and flowering plants, and a high density of kingfishers (feeding off the 50
species of fish). There are guided tours by
foot or boat. For more information contact
Nationalpark Donau-Aeun (☎ 02212-3450,
fax -17, e nationalpark@donauauen.at).

BRATISLAVA

☎ (421) 07 • pop 452,000

The capital of Slovakia is 65km east of Vienna and a popular day trip. People come
here to shop and eat, not because the quality and range is particularly good but because prices are about half those in Vienna.
Slovak *koruna* (crowns) are easily changed
at the boat station or banks.

Orientation & Information

The boat station is on the northern bank of
the Danube. You can get information,
maps and help with accommodation from
the Bratislava Information Service (BIS;
☎ 54 43 37 15, e bis@bratislava.sk),
Klobučnícka 2, open 8 am to 7 pm weekdays (to 4.30 pm from October to May) and
8.30 am to 1 pm Saturday.

EXCURSIONS

Things to See & Do

Bratislava hasn't quite the charm of Prague or Budapest, though many beautiful monuments survive in the old town to tell of its history under Hungarian rule. There are also some bleak communist-era edifices, and the sea of standardised apartment blocks to the south is a depressing sight.

Bratislava Castle, rebuilt several times since the 9th century, stands on the hill but the building itself has little to excite the visitor. However, there's a decent view from the top, and the castle holds a couple of interesting museums (both closed Monday) – the Historical Museum and the Museum of Folk Music.

There are many other museums, the best being the **Municipal Museum** in the old town hall (1421) on Hlavné nám, featuring historical artefacts, decorated rooms and torture chambers (closed Monday).

Historical resonances are best experienced in the **cathedral**, near the foot of the castle, where 11 Habsburg kings were crowned, and at the **Primatial Palace**, next to the Historical Museum, where Napoleon signed a peace treaty with Austria's Franz I in 1805.

The **Nový Bridge** is a modernist lopsided structure (1972) with a restaurant at the top. A lift will whisk you up there, after which you can enjoy a beer, the view, and the unnerving quivering of the floor as the traffic rumbles below and the wind buffets the windows.

The main shopping district (and hub for trams) is Kamenné námestie (square).

Places to Eat

You'll have no problem finding somewhere suitable – the centre of town offers plenty of cheap cafeteria-style buffets, as well as some reasonably priced restaurants.

Divesta (Laurinská 8), open 11 am to 3 pm weekdays, provides low-calorie food and a vegetarian menu. Pizza and pasta are excellent at **Spaghetti & Co**, on the corner of Hviezdoslavovo nám and Rybárska brána, open daily to 1 am. Two good, inexpensive pubs serving typical Slovak food for lunch and dinner are **Prašná bašta** (Zámočnická 11) and **Piváreň u Eda** on Biela.

If you have more crowns to burn, try the wine restaurant **Vináreň Veľký františán** (Františánske nám 10) in the old monastery beside the Mirbach Palace.

The master chef at **Slovenská reštaurácia** (Hviezdoslavovo nám 20) prepares excellent Slovak national dishes, some of which he modifies to his taste. This does not come cheap but it's worth a splurge, especially compared to what you'd have to pay for equivalent quality in Vienna.

Getting There & Away

See the Getting There & Away chapter for information on boats, buses and trains to Bratislava. Boat tickets back to Vienna cost 745 Sk one way.

Bratislava's main train station is 1.5km north of the centre (take tram No 1). There are four local trains a day to Vienna Südbahnhof (220 Sk, 1¼ hours). The bus station is to the east on Mlynské nivy, within walking distance of the city centre. Seven buses a day connect Bratislava to Vienna (285 Sk, 1½ hours) – buy your ticket at the ticket window inside the bus station.

If you want to walk back to Austria, the border is about 4km beyond Nový most (bridge) along Viedenská cesta. Take bus No 81 from Hodžovo nám southbound across the bridge and get off at the next stop after high-rise Hotel Incheba. Walk 2km to the border and clear customs. From the Austrian border town of Wolfsthal, the S Bahn train S40 will take you back to Vienna (€6.95, or €5.55 with a Vienna city travel pass; 100 minutes).

Wienerwald

The Wienerwald (Vienna Woods), west of Vienna, is a place to get off the beaten track and enjoy nature. Attractive settlements speckle the area, such as the wine-growing centres of Perchtoldsdorf, Mödling and Gumpoldskirchen. **Mayerling** has little to see now, but the bloody event that occurred there still brings people to the site; the Carmelite convent can be visited (see the boxed text 'Mystery at Mayerling').

Mystery at Mayerling

It's the stuff of lurid pulp fiction: the heir to the throne found dead in a hunting lodge with his teenage mistress. It became fact in Mayerling on 30 January 1889, yet for years the details of the case were shrouded in secrecy and denial.

The heir was Archduke Rudolf, 30-year-old son of Emperor Franz Josef, husband of Stephanie of Coburg, and something of a liberal who was fond of drinking and womanising. Rudolf's marriage was little more than a public facade by the time he met 17-year-old Baroness Marie Vetsera in the autumn of 1888. The attraction was immediate, but it wasn't until 13 January of the following year that the affair was consummated, an event commemorated by an inscribed cigarette case, a gift from Marie to Rudolf.

On 28 January Rudolf secretly took Marie with him on a shooting trip to his hunting lodge in Mayerling. His other guests arrived a day later; Marie's presence, however, remained unknown to them. On the night of the 29th, the valet, Loschek, heard the couple talking until the early hours, and at about 5.30 am a fully dressed Rudolf appeared and instructed him to get a horse and carriage ready. As Loschek was doing his master's bidding, two gunshots resounded through the still air. He raced back to discover Rudolf lifeless on his bed, with a revolver by his side. Marie was on her bed, also fully clothed, also dead. Just two days earlier Rudolf had discussed a suicide pact with a former mistress. Apparently he hadn't been joking.

Almost immediately the cover-up began. Count Hoyos, a guest at the lodge, told Marie's mother that it was Marie who killed both herself and the archduke with the aid of poison. The official line was proffered by Empress Elisabeth, who claimed Rudolf died of heart failure. There was no hint of suicide or a mistress. The newspapers swallowed the heart-failure story, though a few speculated about a hunting accident. It was only much later that Rudolf's suicide letter to his wife was published in her memoirs, in which he talked of going calmly to his death. Even now a definitive picture has yet to be established. As late as 1989 – the 100th anniversary of the tragedy – Empress Zita claimed publicly that the heir had actually been murdered.

Throughout the lies and misinformation, the real victim remains Marie. How much of a willing party she was to the suicide will never be known. What has become clear is that Marie, after her death, represented not a tragically curtailed young life but an embarrassing scandal that had to be discreetly disposed of. Her body was left untouched for 38 hours, after which it was loaded into a carriage in such a manner as to imply that it was a living person being aided rather than a corpse beyond help. Her subsequent burial was a rude, secretive affair, during which she was consigned to the ground in an unmarked grave (her body was later moved to Heiligenkreuz). Today the hunting lodge is no more – a Carmelite nunnery stands in its place.

EXCURSIONS

About 6km to the north-east is **Heili-genkreuz**, where Marie's grave can be seen. The 12th-century Cistercian abbey here is the final resting place of most of the Babenberg dynasty that ruled Austria until 1246. The church and cloister combine Romanesque and Gothic styles. The abbey museum contains models by Giovanni Giuliani, who also created the trinity column in the courtyard. Tours (☎ 02258-8703-0) are conducted daily and cost €4.75 (students €2.20).

Between Mödling and Heiligenkreuz, boat tours (☎/fax 02236-263 64) can be taken of **Seegrotte Hinterbrühl**, Europe's largest underground lake. The site was used by the Nazis in WWII to build aircraft. The tours (in English with advance notification) last 45 minutes and cost €4 (children €2.20). Hinterbrühl is open daily, with tours from 10 am to 4 pm.

Getting There & Away

To explore this region, it's best if you have your own transport. Trains skirt either side of the woods and the bus service is patchy. The Baden–Alland Bundesbus stops at

Heiligenkreuz and alternately at Mayerling Altes Jagdschloss or Mayerling Höhe, but it's fairly infrequent, especially on Sunday. From Mödling (reached on the Vienna Süd-bahnhof–Baden train route), there are frequent buses (Nos 364 and 365) going to Hinterbrühl (17 minutes) that sometimes continue to Heiligenkreuz and Mayerling.

BADEN
☎ 02252 • pop 23,500

On the eastern edge of the Wienerwald, the spa town of Baden (full name: Baden bei Wien) has a long history. The Romans were prone to wallow in its medicinal springs. Beethoven heard about its healing properties and came here many times in hope of a cure for his deafness. The town flourished in the early 19th century after being adopted by the Habsburgs as their favourite summer retreat. Baden mostly closes down in winter.

Orientation & Information

The centre is a 10-minute walk north-west of the train station: cut across the small park, continue along Bahngasse and then bear right on Wassergasse. This will bring you to Hauptplatz and the centre of town. Follow the signs to the left for the tourist office (☎ 220 00, fax 807 33, e touristinfo .baden@ netway.at) at Brusattiplatz 3, open 9 am to 6 pm Monday to Saturday and 9 am to noon Sunday and holidays (9 am to 5 pm weekdays only November to Easter).

Things to See & Do

Baden exudes health and 19th-century affluence, an impression endorsed by the many Biedermeier-style houses. The **Dreifaltigkeitssäule** (trinity column) on Hauptplatz dates from 1714.

The town attracts plenty of promenading Viennese on the weekends. All and sundry make for the **Kurpark**, a magnificent setting for a stroll. Rows of white benches are neatly positioned under manicured trees in front of the bandstand, and elaborate flowerbeds complement monuments to famous artists (Mozart, Beethoven, Strauss, Grillparzer etc). The **Undine Brunnen** (fountain) is a fine amalgam of human and fish images. Free

spa concerts *(Kurkonzerte)* are performed i the bandstand from May to September, us ally at 4.30 pm daily except Monday.

The **Emperor Franz Josef Museum** Hochstrasse 51, north of the centre, displa local folklore (open 2 to 6 pm, closed Mo day and during winter; €2.20, studen €0.75). The **Rollett Museum**, Weikersdo fer Platz 1, south-west of the centre, cove aspects of the town's history (eg, bom damage in WWII). The most unusual ex hibit is the collection of skulls, busts an death masks amassed by the founder (phrenology, Josef Gall (1752–1828). Th museum is open 3 to 6 pm except Tuesda (€2.20, seniors €0.75). Beethoven's forme house at Rathausgasse 10 has Beethove esque exhibits. It's open 9 to 11 am and 4 t 6 pm weekends and holidays, 4 to 6 p Tuesday to Friday (€2.20, seniors €1.10).

Baden's reputation as a health spa res on its 14 **hot springs**, which are enriche with sulphur, chlorine and sulphates. Th town has various indoor and outdoor po complexes suitable for medicinal or frivo lous purposes. Predominantly in the latte category is the Thermalstrandbad, to th west at Helenenstrasse 19–21 (open May t September; entry from €4).

Places to Stay

The few private rooms are the only optio for those on a tight budget; get a list fror the tourist office. *Lakies* (☎ 229 38, Vös lauerstrasse 11), just south of Josefsplatz has singles with shower for €13.10, an one double. Phone ahead.

Pension Garni Margit (☎ 897 18, fa 226 27, Mühlgasse 15–17) is an eight minute walk east of Hauptplatz. It has homy ambience and a garden but the few singles/doubles for €26/45 have no acces to a shower. Pay €31/49 or more for privat facilities. There are also a few apartments

The three-star *Pension Maria* (☎ 430 33 fax -32, Elisabethstrasse 11) has rooms fo €32.75/53.45 with shower and WC. There' a swimming pool (summer only) and off street parking.

Hotel Rauch (☎ 445 61, Pelzgasse 3) west of Hauptplatz, is next to the Doblhoff

ark in a typical Baden building with high
eilings. Rooms (with WC and mini-baths)
ost up to €35.65/58.90, depending on the
ze and season.

Places to Eat

here is a *Billa* supermarket at Wassergasse
4, but the best places for compiling hot or
old snacks are the market stalls you'll find
n Brusattiplatz.

Goldener Löwe (Braitnerstrasse 1) has
any Chinese lunch menus (Monday to
aturday) for about €4.30, and outside tales overlooking the Schwechat River.

Euro Café (Beethovengasse 10) has
izza and pasta from €5.05 in a modern,
oungish environment. It's open 10 am to
am Monday to Saturday.

*Gasthaus Zum Reichsapfel (Spiegel-
asse 2)* is like a small beer hall, with sev-
ral varieties of ale on tap. It also serves
eals from €5.80, including a decent range
f vegetarian choices. It's open 5 to 11.30
m Tuesday to Friday and 11 am to 2 pm
nd 5 to 11 pm Saturday and Sunday.

*Ackerl's Badner Stüberl (Gutenbrunner-
rasse 19)* is a typically Austrian place with
id-price food (closed Tuesday).

Getting There & Away

egional and S-Bahn trains run to and from
aden up to four times an hour from Süd-
ahnhof (€4.20, or €2.80 if you have a
ienna city pass), with services till around
1 pm. The trip takes 20 to 30 minutes. For
e same price, you could instead take the
mall 'Lokalbahn' tram from opposite the
otel Bristol on Kärntner Ring, which ter-
inates at Josefsplatz in Baden and goes
very 15 minutes (62 minutes; correct
hange needed for the on-board ticket ma-
hine, or buy in advance from the kiosk).
here's also an hourly bus that goes between
e Vienna Staatsoper and Josefsplatz (40
inutes; €4.75, or €3.35 with city pass).

Burgenland

Vhen Austria lost control of Hungary after
VWI, it was ceded the German-speaking
part of that country in 1921 following a
favourable plebiscite. Renamed Burgenland, this agricultural province is known for
its wines, and wine-tasting tours are popular with visitors. One-fifth of present-day
Burgenland is owned by the Esterházys,
erstwhile employers of Josef Haydn and
one of the richest families in Austria.

EISENSTADT

☎ 02682 • pop 12,500

Tourism in Eisenstadt is primarily centred
on one factor – the town's association with
Josef Haydn. It has been the provincial capital of Burgenland since 1925.

Orientation & Information

Eisenstadt lies 50km south of Vienna. From
the train station, walk straight ahead down
Bahnstrasse until you get to the pedestrian-
only Hauptstrasse, a street with cafes, shops
and restaurants (10 minutes). Turn left for
Schloss Esterházy, which houses the tourist
office, Eisenstadt Tourismus (☎ 673 90, fax
673 91, e tve.info@bnet.at). It's open daily
from 9 am to 5 pm (1 pm on Sunday; closed
weekends from 1 November to early May).
Free maps are available, and a brochure listing hotels, private rooms and museum
opening times and prices.

The provincial office (☎ 02682-633 84-
23, fax -32, e info@burgenland-tourism
.co.at) is also here but they don't accept in-
person visits.

Things to See & Do

Josef Haydn revealed that Eisenstadt was
'where I wish to live and to die'. He
achieved the former, being a resident for 31
years, but it was in Vienna that he finally tin-
kled his last tune. He also rather carelessly
omitted any directive about his preferred
residency after death. His skull was stolen
from a temporary grave shortly after he died
in 1809, and later became a museum exhibit
in Vienna. The headless cadaver was subsequently returned to Eisenstadt (in 1932), but
it wasn't until 1954 that the skull joined it.

Haydn's white marble tomb can now be
seen in the **Bergkirche**. The church itself is
remarkable for the Kalvarienberg, a unique

EXCURSIONS

Calvary display; access is via a separate entrance to the rear of the church. Life-sized figures depict the Stations of the Cross in a series of suitably austere, dungeon-like rooms. It's open 9 am to noon and 2 to 5 pm daily between 1 April and 31 October; the admission price of €2.20 (seniors €1.45, students €1.10) includes Haydn's tomb, or you can pay €1.45 to see the tomb alone.

The baroque, 14th-century **Schloss Esterházy** is open for guided tours from 9 am to 5 pm (to 6 pm from Easter to October). The highlight is the frescoed Haydn Hall, which has the second-best acoustics of any concert hall in Austria (after Vienna's Musikverein). Entry costs €4.40, or €2.95 for students and seniors, and the 40-minute guided tour is in German (phone ahead and you might be able to get one of the occasional English tours; otherwise ask for the English notes). A festival of Josef Haydn's music is staged here in September.

Behind the palace is a large, relaxing park, the **Schlosspark**, the setting for the Fest der 1000 Weine (Festival of 1000 Wines) in late August. There are several museums in the town, most of which are shut on Monday.

Places to Stay & Eat

Eisenstadt has only a few hotels, though the tourist office can help find accommodation. There are even fewer private rooms: *Toth Ewald* (☎ 642 22, Vicedom 5), off Domplatz, has singles/doubles with shower and WC for €21.80/37.80, with cooking facilities and a TV area. Rooms are only offered from July to September.

Gasthof Zum Haydnhaus (☎/fax 646 36, Josef Haydn Gasse 24) is conveniently central, and has nondescript but sizable rooms with a private shower and toilet for €29.10/43.60. *Hotel Mayr* (☎ 627 51, fax -4, Kalvarienbergplatz 1) is of a similar standard to the Gasthof, though rooms have TV (€29.10/50.90).

For lunch, you can do worse than think Chinese: *Asia* (Hauptstrasse 32), entrance on Matthias Markhl Gasse, and *Mandarin* (Wiener Strasse 2), by the Bergkirche, both have weekday lunches for about €4.30

(both open daily). Or there are branches of the fast-food *Schnitzelhaus* chain at Esterházystrasse 16 and Domplatz 17. Also on Domplatz is *Emma* supermarket. Gasthof Zum Haydnhaus, mentioned above, has regional and Austrian dishes from €4.75 (open daily).

Getting There & Away

Regular trains depart from Vienna's Südbahnhof, calling at Wien Meidling. One train a day is direct, otherwise you will have to change at Neusiedl am See (€5.55, 80 minutes) or Wulkaprodersdorf (€6.95, 70 minutes). If you have a Vienna city card, it will cost €5.55 by either route. Direct buses take 70 minutes and depart from Südtiroler Platz (€6.95).

LAKE NEUSIEDL

Bird-watchers flock to Neusiedler See, the only steppe lake in Central Europe. It's ringed by a wetland area of reed beds, providing an ideal breeding ground for nearly 300 bird species. The lake only averages 1m to 2m in depth and there is no natural outlet, giving the water a slightly saline quality. Naturalists are particularly attracted to **Seewinkel** on the east shore, a national park of grassland interspersed with myriad smaller lakes. A cycle track winds all the way around the reed beds, making it possible to complete a circuit of the lake, but remember to take your passport as the southern section is in Hungary.

Though birdlife is important, this is very much a summer holiday region too. Water sports are popular, with boats and windsurfing boards for hire at various resorts around the lake. The main town on the shores is **Neusiedl am See**, 50 minutes by train from Vienna's Südbahnhof. It has a tourist office (☎ 02167-2229, fax 2637) in the Rathaus at Hauptplatz 1, and a HI *Jugendherberge* (☎/fax 02167-2252) at Herbergsgasse 1 (open March to October).

A bus ride south-east of Neusiedl is **Podersdorf**, a holiday resort on the shore of the lake. You can get more details from its tourist office (☎ 02177-2227, fax 2170, e podersdorf-tourism@bnet.co.at). Plenty of places in the resort rent out bikes for excursions to Seewinkel.

RUST
☎ 02685 • pop 1700

Rust, 14km east of Eisenstadt, is famous for storks and wine, though its name derives from *Rüster*, the German word for elm tree. The town's prosperity has been based on wine for centuries. In 1524 the emperor granted local vintners the exclusive right to display the letter 'R' on their wine barrels; corks today bear the same insignia.

Storks descend on Rust from the end of March, rear their young, then fly off in late August. Many homes in the centre have a metal platform on the roof to try to entice storks to build a nest there. A good vantage point is attained from the tower of the **Katholische Kirche** at the southern end of Rathausplatz (€0.75, accessible summer only). The **Fischerkirche** at the other end of Rathausplatz is the oldest church in Rust (12th to 16th century).

Access to the **lake** is 1km down the reed-fringed Seepromenade. Here you'll find a swimming pool (€2.95 per day) as well as motorboats, pedal boats and sailing boats for hire, and schools for windsurfing and sailing.

For more information, contact the tourist office (☎ 502, fax -10, ⓔ info@rust.or.at) in the Rathaus, Conradplatz 1. Opening hours vary with demand, ranging from closing at 4 pm weekdays in winter, up to opening weekend mornings in summer.

Places to Stay & Eat

Rust's *camping ground (☎ 595)* is near the swimming pool/boating complex, and open from April to October. Also nearby is *Jugendgästehaus Rust (☎ 591, fax -4, Ruster Bucht 2)*, built in 1998. It costs €13.85 per person in double rooms or €11.65 in four-bed dorms, and also offers half and full board.

In the centre, private rooms are the best budget option. *Gästehaus Ruth (☎ 277, Dr Ratz Gasse 1)*, off Weinberggasse, has rooms with shower for €20.40/33.45 a single/double. *Pension Halwax (☎ 520, Oggauer Strasse 21)* has six rooms for €21.10 per person, each with shower and WC.

Enjoy three-star comfort and an outdoor swimming pool at *Pension Magdalenenhof (☎ 373, fax -4, Feldgasse 40)*, which charges €32/54.

To eat, look no further than the many *Buschenschenken* (wine taverns) around town. A place with good food and wine is *Schandl (Hauptstrasse 20)*, open daily from 4 pm (11 am on weekends and holidays) to midnight. Nearby is *Haydn-Keller (Haydngasse 4)* where the eel *(Aal)* is recommended; it's open 8 am to 10 pm daily. Another option is to compile a picnic at the *ADEG supermarket (Oggauer Strasse 3)* to eat by the lake.

Getting There & Away

Buses run approximately hourly to and from Eisenstadt (€2.80, 30 minutes). Services stop in the early evening. Several places in the centre rent out bikes.

MÖRBISCH
☎ 02685 • pop 2400

Six kilometres around the lake from Rust, Mörbisch is just a couple of kilometres short of the Hungarian border. It's worth spending an hour or so here, enjoying the relaxed atmosphere and the quaint white-washed houses with hanging corn and flower-strewn balconies. There is a tourist office here (☎ 02685-8856, ⓔ tourismus@ moerbisch.com), Hauptstrasse 23, which can fill you in on Seefestspiele, a summer operetta festival (mid-July to late August).

Getting There & Away

By bus, the fare to Rust is €1.40 (10 minutes); though note that it costs the same to go from Mörbisch to Eisenstadt (€2.80) as it does only going from Rust to Eisenstadt. South of Mörbisch, cyclists may cross into Hungary but there's no road for cars.

EXCURSIONS

Language

The Viennese speak German, with an accent similar to that found in Bavaria. Though the grammar is the same as standard German, there are also many words and expressions that are used only by the Viennese. Many Viennese speak some English, and young people are usually quite fluent. Tourist office and train information staff almost invariably speak English; hotel receptionists and restaurant servers usually do too, especially in higher class places. Nevertheless, some knowledge of German would be an asset and any attempt to use it, no matter how clumsy, will be appreciated. One characteristic of German is that all nouns are written with a capital letter.

Pronunciation

Unlike English or French, German has no real silent letters: you pronounce the **k** at the start of the word *Knie* (knee), the **p** at the start of *Psychologie* (psychology), and the **e** at the end of *ich habe* (I have).

Vowels

As in English, vowels can be pronounced long (as in 'pope'), or short (as in 'pop'). As a rule, German vowels are long before single consonants and short before double consonants: the **o** is long in the word *Dom* (cathedral), but short in the word *doch* (after all).

a	short, as the 'u' in 'cut'; long, as in 'father'
au	as the 'o' in 'vow'
ä	short, as the 'a' in 'act'; long, as the 'e' in 'there'
äu	as the 'oi' in 'boy'
e	short, as in 'bet'; long, as in 'they'
ei	as the 'i' in 'pile'
eu	as the 'oi' in 'boy'
i	short, as in 'sit'; long, as in 'marine'
ie	as in 'believe'
o	short, as in 'not'; long, as in 'note'
ö	as the 'er' in 'fern'
u	as in 'pull'
ü	similar to the 'u' in 'pull' but with stretched lips

Consonants

Most German consonants sound similar to their English counterparts. One important difference is that **b**, **d** and **g** sound like 'p', 't' and 'k', respectively, at the end of a word.

b	normally as the English 'b', but as 'p' when at the end of a word
ch	similar to the 'ch' in Scottish *loch*
d	normally as the English 'd', but as 't' when at the end of a word
g	normally like the English 'g'; at the end of a word, either as 'k', or as the 'ch' in Scottish *loch* if preceded by **i**
j	as the 'y' in 'yet'
qu	as 'k' plus 'v'
r	can be trilled or guttural, depending on the region
s	normally as in 'sun', but as the 'z' in 'zoo' when followed by a vowel
sch	as the 'sh' in 'ship'
sp/st	the **s** is as the 'sh' in 'ship' when at the start of a word
-tion	the **t** is as the 'ts' in 'hits'
v	as the 'f' in 'fan'
w	as the 'v' in 'van'
z	as the 'ts' in 'hits'

Greetings & Civilities

Good day.	*Guten Tag.*
Hello.	*Grüss Gott.*
Goodbye.	*Auf Wiedersehen.*
Bye.	*Tschüss.*
Yes.	*Ja.*
No.	*Nein.*
Please.	*Bitte.*
Thank you.	*Danke.*
That's fine, you're welcome.	*Bitte sehr.*
Sorry. (excuse me, forgive me)	*Entschuldigung.*

Say it Vienna-Style

See the Places to Eat chapter for more vocabulary on Viennese food and drink. Most of the following Viennese dialect and slang words would not be understood by High German speakers. On the other hand, the 'normal' German equivalent would be understood by the Viennese.

Baba!	Bye!
Beisl	small tavern
Bim	tram
Blunzn	black pudding
Faschiertes	minced meat
Gerstl	money
Gefüllte Paprika	stuffed green pepper
Guglhupf	Viennese cake
Haberer	friend
Hasse	sausage
I'hob an dulliö.	I'm drunk.
Kohle	money
Obers	cream
Maroni	(roasted) chestnut
Maut	motorway toll charge
Müch	milk
Paradeiser	tomatoes
Scherzl	crust of bread
Servus.	Hello.
Stamperl	glass (for Schnapps)
Stiftl	glass (for wine)
verdrahn	to sell
Weimberl	raisin

Language Difficulties

Do you speak English?	*Sprechen Sie Englisch?*
Does anyone here speak English?	*Spricht hier jemand Englisch?*
I understand.	*Ich verstehe.*
I don't understand.	*Ich verstehe nicht.*
How much is it?	*Wieviel kostet es?*
Just a minute.	*Ein Moment.*
Please write that down.	*Können Sie es bitte aufschreiben.*

Getting Around

What time does ... leave?	*Wann fährt ... ab?*
What time does ... arrive?	*Wann kommt ... an?*

What time is the next boat?	*Wann fährt das nächste Boot?*
next	*nächste*
first	*erste*
last	*letzte*
the boat	*das Boot*
the bus (city)	*der Bus*
the bus (intercity)	*der (Überland) Bus*
the tram	*die Strassenbahn*
the train	*der Zug*
I'd like ...	*Ich möchte ...*
a one-way ticket	*eine Einzelkarte*
a return ticket	*eine Rückfahrkarte*
1st class	*erste Klasse*
2nd class	*zweite Klasse*
Where is the bus stop?	*Wo ist die Bushalte-stelle?*
Where is the tram stop?	*Wo ist die Strassen--bahnhaltestelle?*
Can you show me (on the map)?	*Können Sie mir (auf der Karte) zeigen?*
Go straight ahead.	*Gehen Sie geradeaus.*
Turn left.	*Biegen Sie links ab.*
Turn right.	*Biegen Sie rechts ab.*
near	*nahe*
far	*weit*

Around Town

I'm looking for ...	*Ich suche ...*
a bank	*eine Bank*
the city centre	*die Innenstadt*
the ... embassy	*die ... Botschaft*
my hotel	*mein Hotel*
the market	*den Markt*
the police	*die Polizei*
the post office	*das Postamt*
a public toilet	*eine öffentliche Toilette*
the telephone centre	*die Telefonzentrale*
the tourist office	*die Touristen-information*

beach	*Strand*
bridge	*Brücke*
castle	*Schloss/Burg*
cathedral	*Dom*
church	*Kirche*

Signs

Campingplatz	**Camping Ground**
Pension/	**Guesthouse**
Gästehaus	
Jugendherberge	**Youth Hostel**
Zimmer Frei	**Rooms Available**
Voll/Besetzt	**Full/No Vacancies**
Eingang	**Entrance**
Ausgang	**Exit**
Auskunft	**Information**
Offen/Geöffnet	**Open**
Geschlossen	**Closed**
Bahnhof (Bf)	**Train Station**
Polizei	**Police**
Polizeiwache	**Police Station**
Toiletten (WC)	**Toilets**
Herren	**Men**
Damen	**Women**

hospital	*Krankenhaus*
island	*Insel*
main square	*Hauptplatz*
market	*Markt*
monastery/convent	*Kloster*
mosque	*Moschee*
old city	*Altstadt*
palace	*Palast*
ruins	*Ruinen*
square	*Platz*
tower	*Turm*

Accommodation

Where is a cheap hotel?	*Wo ist ein billiges Hotel?*
What is the address?	*Was ist die Adresse?*
Could you please write the address?	*Könnten Sie bitte die Adresse aufschreiben?*
Do you have any rooms available?	*Haben Sie noch freie Zimmer?*

I'd like ...	*Ich möchte ...*
a single room	*ein Einzelzimmer*
a double room	*ein Doppelzimmer*
a room with bath	*ein Zimmer mit Bad*
to share a dorm	*einen Schlafsaalteilen*
a bed	*ein Bett*

How much is it ...?	*Wieviel kostet es ...?*
per night	*pro Nacht*
per person?	*pro Person*

May I see it?	*Kann ich es sehen?*
Where is the bath/ shower?	*Wo ist das Bad/ die Dusche?*

Food

bakery	*Bäckerei*
grocery	*Lebensmittelgeschäft*
delicatessen	*Delikatessengeschäft*
restaurant	*Restaurant/Gaststätte*
breakfast	*Frühstück*
lunch	*Mittagessen*
dinner	*Abendessen*

I'd like the set lunch, please.	*Ich hätte gern das Tagesmenü, bitte.*
Is service included in the bill?	*Ist die Bedienung inbegriffen?*
I'm a vegetarian.	*Ich bin Vegetarier/ Vegetarierin.* (m/f)

Time & Dates

today	*heute*
tomorrow	*morgen*
in the morning	*morgens*
in the afternoon	*nachmittags*
in the evening	*abends*

Monday	*Montag*
Tuesday	*Dienstag*
Wednesday	*Mittwoch*
Thursday	*Donnerstag*
Friday	*Freitag*
Saturday	*Samstag/Sonnabend*
Sunday	*Sonntag*

January	*Jänner*
February	*Februar*
March	*März*
April	*April*
May	*Mai*
June	*Juni*
July	*Juli*
August	*August*
September	*September*
October	*Oktober*
November	*November*
December	*Dezember*

40	*vierzig*
50	*fünfzig*
60	*sechzig*
70	*siebzig*
80	*achtzig*
90	*neunzig*
100	*hundert*
1000	*tausend*

Emergencies

Help!	*Hilfe!*
Call a doctor!	*Holen Sie einen Arzt!*
Call the police!	*Rufen Sie die Polizei!*
I'm lost.	*Ich habe mich verirrt.*
Go away!	*Gehen Sie weg!*

one million	*eine Million*

Numbers

0	*null*
1	*eins*
2	*zwei* (*zwo* on phone or public anouncements)
3	*drei*
4	*vier*
5	*fünf*
6	*sechs*
7	*sieben*
8	*acht*
9	*neun*
0	*zehn*
1	*elf*
2	*zwölf*
3	*dreizehn*
4	*vierzehn*
5	*fünfzehn*
6	*sechzehn*
7	*siebzehn*
8	*achtzehn*
9	*neunzehn*
0	*zwanzig*
1	*einundzwanzig*
2	*zweiundzwanzig*
0	*dreissig*

Health

I'm ...	*Ich bin ...*
diabetic	*Diabetiker/ Diabetikerin* (m/f)
epileptic	*Epileptiker/ Epileptikerin* (m/f)
asthmatic	*Asthmatiker/ Asthmatikerin* (m/f)

I'm allergic to ...	*Ich bin gegen ... allergisch.*
antibiotics	*Antibiotika*
penicillin	*Penizillin*

antiseptic	*Antiseptikum*
aspirin	*Aspirin*
condoms	*Kondome*
constipation	*Verstopfung*
contraceptive	*Verhütungsmittel*
diarrhoea	*Durchfall*
medicine	*Medizin*
nausea	*Übelkeit*
sunblock cream	*Sunblockcreme*
tampons	*Tampons*

Glossary

Abfahrt – departure (trains)
Achterl – 125mL glass (drinks)
Ankunft – arrival (trains)
Altwaren – junk shops
ANTO – Austrian National Tourist Office
Apotheke – pharmacy
Ausgang – exit
Autobahn – motorway
Autoreisezug – motorail train

Bad – bath (spa resort)
Bahnhof – train station
Bahnsteig – train station platform
Bankomat – automated teller machine
Bauernhof – farmhouse
Besetzt – occupied, full (ie, no vacancy) in a hotel/pension
Beisl – Viennese term for a down-to-earth inn or restaurant
Bezirk – (town or city) district
Biedermeier period – 19th century art movement in Germany and Austria; applies particularly to a decorative style of furniture from this period
Bierkeller – beer cellar
Boot – boat
Brauerei – brewery
Bundesbus – state bus, run by either the federal railway (Bahnhbus) or the post office (Postbus)
Bundesländer – federal province (government)
Bundesrat – Federal Council (upper house – government)
Buschenschank – wine tavern

Denkmal – memorial
Dirndl – traditional skirt

EEA – European Economic Area, comprising European Union states plus Iceland, Liechtenstein and Norway
Einbahnstrasse – one-way street
Eingang, Eintritt – entry
Einkaufsamstag – 'long' Saturday, when shops have extended opening hours (usually on the first Saturday of the month)

EU – European Union

Fahrplan – timetable
Fahrrad – bicycle
Feiertag – public holiday
Ferienwohnungen – self-catering holiday apartments
Flohmarkt – flea market
Flugpost – air mail
Föhn – hot, dry wind that sweeps down from the mountains, mainly in early spring and autumn
FPÖ – Freedom Party (political party)

Gästehaus – guesthouse, perhaps with a restaurant
Gasthaus – inn or restaurant, without accommodation
Gasthof – inn or restaurant, usually with accommodation
Gästekarte – guest card
Gemütlichkeit – 'cosiness'; a quality much revered by Austrians
Gendarmerie – police (in Vienna they're usually 'Polizei')
Glockenspiel – carillon
Glockenturm – clock tower

Haltstelle – bus or tram stop
Hauptbahnhof – main train station
Hauptpost – main post office
Heurigen – wine tavern

Imbiss – snack bar

Jugendherberge/Jugendgästehaus – a youth hostel
Jugendstil – Art Nouveau

Kaffeehaus/Café Konditorei – coffee house
Kino – cinema
Konsulat – consulate
Krügerl – 500mL glass (drinks)
Kurzparkzone – short-term parking zone

Landesmuseum – provincial museum

Landtag – provincial assembly government)

Langersamstag – another name for Einkaufsamstag

LIF – Liberal Forum (political party)

Maut – toll (or indicating a toll booth); also Viennese dialect for a tip (gratuity)

Mehrwertsteuer (MWST) – value-added tax

Mensa – university restaurant

Menü – meal of the day. The menu (ie, food list) is called Speisekarte

Mitfahrzentrale – hitching (ride-sharing) organisation

Nationalrat – National Council (lower house – government)

Not(ruf) – Emergency (call)

ÖAMTC – national motoring organisation

ÖBB – Austrian federal railway

ÖVP – Austrian People's Party (political party)

Parkschein – parking voucher

Pedalos – paddle boats

Pension – B&B guesthouse

Pfarrkirche – parish church

Polizei – police

Postamt – post office

Postlagernde Briefe – poste restante

Radverleih – bicycle rental

Rathaus – town hall

Red Vienna – describes the period of socialist reforms instigated by the city government from 1919 to 1934

Ruhetag – 'rest day', on which a restaurant is closed

Saal – hall or large room

Sammlung – collection

Säule – column, pillar

Schiff – ship

Schloss – palace or stately home

Schrammelmusik – popular Viennese music for violins, guitar and accordion

Secession – early 20th century movement in Vienna seeking to establish a more functional style in architecture; led by Otto Wagner (1841–1918)

Selbstbedienung (SB) – self-service (restaurants, laundries etc)

SPÖ – Social Democrats (political party)

Stadtmuseum – city museum

Studentenheime – student residences

Szene – scene (ie, where the action is)

Tabak – tobacconist

Tagesteller/Tagesmenü – the set meal or menu of the day in a restaurant

Telefon-Wertkarte – phonecard

Tierpark or Tiergarten – animal park or zoo

Trettboot – paddle boats

Tor – gate

Urlaub – holiday

U-Bahn – underground rail network (metro)

Vienna Circle – group of philosophers centred on Vienna University in the 1920s and 30s

Vienna Group (Wienergruppe) – literary/art movement formed in the 1950s, whose members incorporated surrealism and Dadaism in sound compositions, textual montages and actionist happenings

Viertel – 250mL glass (drinks); also a geographical district

Wäscherei – laundry

Wien – Vienna

Wiener Werkstätte – workshop established in 1903 by Secession artists

Würstel Stand – sausage stand

Zimmer frei/Privat Zimmer – private rooms (accommodation)

Zeitung – newspaper

LONELY PLANET

ON THE ROAD

Travel Guides explore cities, regions and countries, and supply information on transport, restaurants and accommodation, covering all budgets. They come with reliable, easy-to-use maps, practical advice, cultural and historical facts and a rundown on attractions both on and off the beaten track. There are over 200 titles in this classic series, covering nearly every country in the world.

 Lonely Planet Upgrades extend the shelf life of existing travel guides by detailing any changes that may affect travel in a region since a book has been published. Upgrades can be downloaded for free from **www.lonelyplanet.com/upgrades**

For travellers with more time than money, **Shoestring** guides offer dependable, first-hand information with hundreds of detailed maps, plus insider tips for stretching money as far as possible. Covering entire continents in most cases, the six-volume shoestring guides are known around the world as 'backpackers bibles'.

For the discerning short-term visitor, **Condensed** guides highlight the best a destination has to offer in a full-colour, pocket-sized format designed for quick access. They include everything from top sights and walking tours to opinionated reviews of where to eat, stay, shop and have fun.

CitySync lets travellers use their Palm™ or Visor™ hand-held computers to guide them through a city with handy tips on transport, history, cultural life, major sights, and shopping and entertainment options. It can also quickly search and sort hundreds of reviews of hotels, restaurants and attractions, and pinpoint their location on scrollable street maps. CitySync can be downloaded from **www.citysync.com**

MAPS & ATLASES

Lonely Planet's **City Maps** feature downtown and metropolitan maps, as well as transit routes and walking tours. The maps come complete with an index of streets, a listing of sights and a plastic coat for extra durability.

Road Atlases are an essential navigation tool for serious travellers. Cross-referenced with the guidebooks, they also feature distance and climate charts and a complete site index.

ESSENTIALS

Read This First books help new travellers to hit the road with confidence. These invaluable predeparture guides give step-by-step advice on preparing for a trip, budgeting, arranging a visa, planning an itinerary and staying safe while still getting off the beaten track.

Healthy Travel pocket guides offer a regional rundown on disease hot spots and practical advice on predeparture health measures, staying well on the road and what to do in emergencies. The guides come with a user-friendly design and helpful diagrams and tables.

Lonely Planet's **Phrasebooks** cover the essential words and phrases travellers need when they're strangers in a strange land. They come in a pocket-sized format with colour tabs for quick reference, extensive vocabulary lists, easy-to-follow pronunciation keys and two-way dictionaries.

Miffed by blurry photos of the Taj Mahal? Tired of the classic 'top of the head cut off' shot? **Travel Photography: A Guide to Taking Better Pictures** will help you turn ordinary holiday snaps into striking images and give you the know-how to capture every scene, from frenetic festivals to peaceful beach sunrises.

Lonely Planet's **Travel Journal** is a lightweight but sturdy travel diary for jotting down all those on-the-road observations and significant travel moments. It comes with a handy time-zone wheel, world maps and useful travel information.

Lonely Planet's eKno is an all-in-one communication service developed especially for travellers. It offers low-cost international calls and free email and voicemail so that you can keep in touch while on the road. Check it out on **www.ekno.lonelyplanet.com**

FOOD & RESTAURANT GUIDES

Lonely Planet's **Out to Eat** guides recommend the brightest and best places to eat and drink in top international cities. These gourmet companions are arranged by neighbourhood, packed with dependable maps, garnished with scene-setting photos and served with quirky features.

For people who live to eat, drink and travel, **World Food** guides explore the culinary culture of each country. Entertaining and adventurous, each guide is packed with detail on staples and specialities, regional cuisine and local markets, as well as sumptuous recipes, comprehensive culinary dictionaries and lavish photos good enough to eat.

LONELY PLANET

OUTDOOR GUIDES

For those who believe the best way to see the world is on foot, Lonely Planet's **Walking Guides** detail everything from family strolls to difficult treks, with 'when to go and how to do it' advice supplemented by reliable maps and essential travel information.

Cycling Guides map a destination's best bike tours, long and short, in day-by-day detail. They contain all the information a cyclist needs, including advice on bike maintenance, places to eat and stay, innovative maps with detailed cues to the rides, and elevation charts.

The **Watching Wildlife** series is perfect for travellers who want authoritative information but don't want to tote a heavy field guide. Packed with advice on where, when and how to view a region's wildlife, each title features photos of over 300 species and contains engaging comments on the local flora and fauna.

With underwater colour photos throughout, **Pisces Books** explore the world's best diving and snorkelling areas. Each book contains listings of diving services and dive resorts, detailed information on depth, visibility and difficulty of dives, and a roundup of the marine life you're likely to see through your mask.

OFF THE ROAD

Journeys, the travel literature series written by renowned travel authors, capture the spirit of a place or illuminate a culture with a journalist's attention to detail and a novelist's flair for words. These are tales to soak up while you're actually on the road or dip into as an at-home armchair indulgence.

The new range of lavishly illustrated **Pictorial** books is just the ticket for both travellers and dreamers. Off-beat tales and vivid photographs bring the adventure of travel to your doorstep long before the journey begins and long after it is over.

Lonely Planet **Videos** encourage the same independent, tough-minded approach as the guidebooks. Currently airing throughout the world, this award-winning series features innovative footage and an original soundtrack.

Yes, we know, work is tough, so do a little bit of deskside dreaming with the spiral-bound Lonely Planet **Diary**, the tearaway page-a-day **Day-to-Day Calendar** or a Lonely Planet **Wall Calendar**, filled with great photos from around the world.

TRAVELLERS NETWORK

Lonely Planet Online. Lonely Planet's award-winning Web site has insider information on hundreds of destinations, from Amsterdam to Zimbabwe, complete with interactive maps and relevant links. The site also offers the latest travel news, recent reports from travellers on the road, guidebook upgrades, a travel links site, an online book-buying option and a lively traveller's bulletin board. It can be viewed at **www.lonelyplanet.com** or AOL keyword: lp.

Planet Talk is a quarterly print newsletter, full of gossip, advice, anecdotes and author articles. It provides an antidote to the being-at-home blues and lets you plan and dream for the next trip. Contact the nearest Lonely Planet office for your free copy.

Comet, the free Lonely Planet newsletter, comes via email once a month. It's loaded with travel news, advice, dispatches from authors, travel competitions and letters from readers. To subscribe, click on the Comet subscription link on the front page of the Web site.

LONELY PLANET

Guides by Region

Lonely Planet is known worldwide for publishing practical, reliable and no-nonsense travel information in our guides and on our Web site. The Lonely Planet list covers just about every accessible part of the world. Currently there are 16 series: Travel guides, Shoestring guides, Condensed guides, Phrasebooks, Read This First, Healthy Travel, Walking guides, Cycling guides, Watching Wildlife guides, Pisces Diving & Snorkeling guides, City Maps, Road Atlases, Out to Eat, World Food, Journeys travel literature and Pictorials.

AFRICA Africa on a shoestring • Cairo • Cairo City Map • Cape Town • Cape Town City Map • East Africa • Egypt • Egyptian Arabic phrasebook • Ethiopia, Eritrea & Djibouti • Ethiopian (Amharic) phrasebook • The Gambia & Senegal • Healthy Travel Africa • Kenya • Malawi • Morocco • Moroccan Arabic phrasebook • Mozambique • Read This First: Africa • South Africa, Lesotho & Swaziland • Southern Africa • Southern Africa Road Atlas • Swahili phrasebook • Tanzania, Zanzibar & Pemba • Trekking in East Africa • Tunisia • Watching Wildlife East Africa • Watching Wildlife Southern Africa • West Africa • World Food Morocco • Zimbabwe, Botswana & Namibia
Travel Literature: Mali Blues: Traveling to an African Beat • The Rainbird: A Central African Journey • Songs to an African Sunset: A Zimbabwean Story

AUSTRALIA & THE PACIFIC Auckland • Australia • Australian phrasebook • Australia Road Atlas • Cycling Australia • Cycling New Zealand • Fiji • Fijian phrasebook • Healthy Travel Australia, NZ and the Pacific • Islands of Australia's Great Barrier Reef • Melbourne • Melbourne City Map • Micronesia • New Caledonia • New South Wales • New Zealand • Northern Territory • Outback Australia • Out to Eat – Melbourne • Out to Eat – Sydney • Papua New Guinea • Pidgin phrasebook • Queensland • Rarotonga & the Cook Islands • Samoa • Solomon Islands • South Australia • South Pacific • South Pacific phrasebook • Sydney • Sydney City Map • Sydney Condensed • Tahiti & French Polynesia • Tasmania • Tonga • Tramping in New Zealand • Vanuatu • Victoria • Walking in Australia • Watching Wildlife Australia • Western Australia
Travel Literature: Islands in the Clouds: Travels in the Highlands of New Guinea • Kiwi Tracks: A New Zealand Journey • Sean & David's Long Drive

CENTRAL AMERICA & THE CARIBBEAN Bahamas, Turks & Caicos • Baja California • Bermuda • Central America on a shoestring • Costa Rica • Costa Rica Spanish phrasebook • Cuba • Dominican Republic & Haiti • Eastern Caribbean • Guatemala • Guatemala, Belize & Yucatán: La Ruta Maya • Healthy Travel Central & South America • Jamaica • Mexico • Mexico City • Panama • Puerto Rico • Read This First: Central & South America • World Food Mexico • Yucatán
Travel Literature: Green Dreams: Travels in Central America

EUROPE Amsterdam • Amsterdam City Map • Amsterdam Condensed • Andalucía • Austria • Baltic States phrasebook • Barcelona • Barcelona City Map • Berlin • Berlin City Map • Britain • British phrasebook • Brussels, Bruges & Antwerp • Brussels City Map • Budapest • Budapest City Map • Canary Islands • Central Europe • Central Europe phrasebook • Corfu & the Ionians • Corsica • Crete • Crete Condensed • Croatia • Cycling Britain • Cycling France • Cyprus • Czech & Slovak Republics • Denmark • Dublin • Dublin City Map • Eastern Europe • Eastern Europe phrasebook • Edinburgh • Estonia, Latvia & Lithuania • Europe on a shoestring • Europe phrasebook • Finland • Florence • France • Frankfurt Condensed • French phrasebook • Georgia, Armenia & Azerbaijan • Germany • German phrasebook • Greece • Greek Islands • Greek phrasebook • Hungary • Iceland, Greenland & the Faroe Islands • Ireland • Italian phrasebook • Italy • Krakow • Lisbon • The Loire • London • London City Map • London Condensed • Madrid • Malta • Mediterranean Europe • Mediterranean Europe phrasebook • Moscow • Mozambique • Munich • Netherlands • Norway • Out to Eat – London • Out to Eat – Paris • Paris • Paris City Map • Paris Condensed • Poland • Portugal • Portuguese phrasebook • Prague • Prague City Map • Provence & the Côte d'Azur • Read This First: Europe • Romania & Moldova • Rome • Rome City Map • Russia, Ukraine & Belarus • Russian phrasebook • Scandinavian & Baltic Europe • Scandinavian phrasebook • Scotland • Sicily • Slovenia • South-West France • Spain • Spanish phrasebook • St Petersburg • St Petersburg City Map • Sweden • Switzerland • Tuscany • Ukrainian phrasebook • Venice • Vienna • Walking in Britain • Walking in France • Walking in Ireland • Walking in Italy • Walking in Spain • Walking in Switzerland • Western Europe • World Food France • World Food Ireland • World Food Italy • World Food Spain
Travel Literature: Love and War in the Apennines • The Olive Grove: Travels in Greece • On the Shores of the Mediterranean • Round Ireland in Low Gear • A Small Place in Italy • After Yugoslavia

LONELY PLANET

Mail Order

Lonely Planet products are distributed worldwide.They are also available by mail order from Lonely Planet, so if you have difficulty finding a title please write to us. North and South American residents should write to 150 Linden St, Oakland, CA 94607, USA; European and African residents should write to 10a Spring Place, London NW5 3BH, UK; and residents of other countries to Locked Bag 1, Footscray, Victoria 3011, Australia.

INDIAN SUBCONTINENT Bangladesh • Bengali phrasebook • Bhutan • Delhi • Goa • Healthy Travel Asia & India • Hindi & Urdu phrasebook • India • Indian Himalaya • Karakoram Highway • Kerala • Mumbai (Bombay) • Nepal • Nepali phrasebook • Pakistan • Rajasthan • Read This First: Asia & India • South India • Sri Lanka • Sri Lanka phrasebook • Tibet • Tibetan phrasebook • Trekking in the Indian Himalaya • Trekking in the Karakoram & Hindukush • Trekking in the Nepal Himalaya
Travel Literature: The Age of Kali: Indian Travels and Encounters • Hello Goodnight: A Life of Goa • In Rajasthan • A Season in Heaven: True Tales from the Road to Kathmandu • Shopping for Buddhas • A Short Walk in the Hindu Kush • Slowly Down the Ganges

ISLANDS OF THE INDIAN OCEAN Madagascar & Comoros • Maldives • Mauritius, Réunion & Seychelles

MIDDLE EAST & CENTRAL ASIA Bahrain, Kuwait & Qatar • Central Asia • Central Asia phrasebook • Dubai • Farsi (Persian) phrasebook • Hebrew phrasebook • Iran • Israel & the Palestinian Territories • Istanbul • Istanbul City Map • Istanbul to Cairo on a shoestring • Jerusalem • Jerusalem City Map • Jordan • Lebanon • Middle East • Oman & the United Arab Emirates • Syria • Turkey • Turkish phrasebook • World Food Turkey • Yemen
Travel Literature: Black on Black: Iran Revisited • The Gates of Damascus • Kingdom of the Film Stars: Journey into Jordan

NORTH AMERICA Alaska • Boston • Boston City Map • California & Nevada • California Condensed • Canada • Chicago • Chicago City Map • Deep South • Florida • Great Lakes • Hawaii • Hiking in Alaska • Hiking in the USA • Las Vegas • Los Angeles • Los Angeles City Map • Miami • Miami City Map • New England • New Orleans • New York City • New York City City Map • New York City Condensed • New York, New Jersey & Pennsylvania • Oahu • Out to Eat – San Francisco • Pacific Northwest • Rocky Mountains • San Francisco • San Francisco City Map • Seattle • Southwest • Texas • USA • USA phrasebook • Vancouver • Virginia & the Capital Region • Washington, DC • Washington, DC City Map • World Food Deep South, USA
Travel Literature: Caught Inside: A Surfer's Year on the California Coast • Drive Thru America

NORTH-EAST ASIA Beijing • Beijing City Map • Cantonese phrasebook • China • Hiking in Japan • Hong Kong • Hong Kong City Map • Hong Kong Condensed • Hong Kong, Macau & Guangzhou • Japan • Japanese phrasebook • Korea • Korean phrasebook • Kyoto • Mandarin phrasebook • Mongolia • Mongolian phrasebook • Seoul • Shanghai • South-West China • Taiwan • Tokyo
Travel Literature: In Xanadu: A Quest • Lost Japan

SOUTH AMERICA Argentina, Uruguay & Paraguay • Bolivia • Brazil • Brazilian phrasebook • Buenos Aires • Chile & Easter Island • Colombia • Ecuador & the Galapagos Islands • Healthy Travel Central & South America • Latin American Spanish phrasebook • Peru • Quechua phrasebook • Read This First: Central & South America • Rio de Janeiro • Rio de Janeiro City Map • South America on a shoestring • Trekking in the Patagonian Andes • Venezuela
Travel Literature: Full Circle: A South American Journey

SOUTH-EAST ASIA Bali & Lombok • Bangkok • Bangkok City Map • Burmese phrasebook • Cambodia • Hanoi • Healthy Travel Asia & India • Hill Tribes phrasebook • Ho Chi Minh City • Indonesia • Indonesian phrasebook • Indonesia's Eastern Islands • Java • Lao phrasebook • Laos • Malay phrasebook • Malaysia, Singapore & Brunei • Myanmar (Burma) • Philippines • Pilipino (Tagalog) phrasebook • Read This First: Asia & India • Singapore • Singapore City Map • South-East Asia on a shoestring • South-East Asia phrasebook • Thailand • Thailand's Islands & Beaches • Thailand, Vietnam, Laos & Cambodia Road Atlas • Thai phrasebook • Vietnam • Vietnamese phrasebook • World Food Thailand • World Food Vietnam

ALSO AVAILABLE: Antarctica • The Arctic • The Blue Man: Tales of Travel, Love and Coffee • Brief Encounters: Stories of Love, Sex & Travel • Chasing Rickshaws • The Last Grain Race • Lonely Planet Unpacked • Not the Only Planet: Science Fiction Travel Stories • On the Edge: Extreme Travel • Sacred India • Travel with Children • Travel Photography: A Guide to Taking Better Pictures

LONELY PLANET

You already know that Lonely Planet produces more than this one guidebook, but you might not be aware of the other products we have on this region. Here is a selection of titles that you may want to check out as well:

Austria
ISBN 0 86442 577 5
US$16.95 • UK£10.99

German phrasebook
ISBN 0 86442 451 5
US$5.95 • UK£3.99

Western Europe
ISBN 1 86450 163 4
US$27.99 • UK£15.99

Central Europe
ISBN 1 86450 204 5
US$24.99 • UK£14.99

Central Europe phrasebook
ISBN 1 86450 226 6
US$7.99 • UK£4.50 FF

Europe on a shoestring
ISBN 1 86450 150 2
US$24.99 • UK£14.99

Read This First: Europe
ISBN 1 86450 136 7
US$14.99 • UK£8.99

Europe phrasebook
ISBN 1 86450 224 X
US$8.99 • UK£4.99

Available wherever books are sold

Index

Bold indicates maps.

Boxed Text

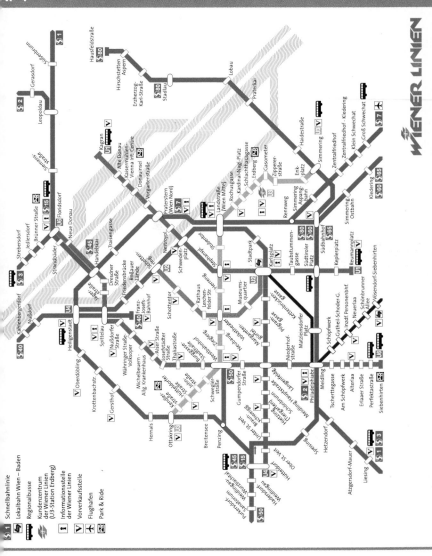

WIENER LINIEN

Schnellbahnlinie
Lokalbahn Wien – Baden
Regionalbusse
Kundenzentrum der Wiener Linien (U3-Station Erdberg)
Informationsstelle der Wiener Linien
Vorverkaufsstelle
Flughafen
Park & Ride

MAP 2 - GREATER VIENNA

PLACES TO STAY
1 Sophienalpe
2 Celtes
12 Schloss Wilhelminenberg & Schlossherberge am Wilhelminenberg
15 Camping Wien West
18 Jugendgästehaus Hütteldorf-Hacking
20 Camping Neue Donau
22 Pension Weber
26 Camping Rodaun

PLACES TO EAT
16 Hawei
19 Prilisauer

OTHER
3 Schreiberhaus (Heurigen)
4 Weingut Am Reisenberg (Heurigen)
5 Krapfenwaldbad (Swimming Pool)
6 Reinprecht (Heurigen)
7 Sirbu (Heurigen)
8 Hirt (Heurigen)
9 Mayer am Ofarrplatz (Heurigen); Beethovenhaus
10 Floridsdorfer Brücke Tourist Office
11 Angelibad
13 Kirche am Steinhof
14 Wagner Villas
17 Auhof Tourist Office
21 Freudenau Horse Racing
23 Zentralfriedhof
24 Unfallkrankenhaus Meidling (Hospital)
25 A2 Tourist Office
27 Kirche zur Heiligsten Dreifaltigkeit
28 Hermesvilla

MAP 3

MAP 5

MAP 2 - GREATER VIENNA

MAP 3 - NORTH WEST VIENNA

Pötzleinsdorf

Pötzleinsdorfer Str

Krottenbachstrasse

Glanzinggasse

Felix-Dahn-Str

Hartäckerstr

Peter-Jordan

Pötzleinsdorfer Schlosspark

Ladenburghöhe

Schafberggasse

Geyergasse

Währing
18

Buchleitengasse

Hockegasse

Gersthof

Gersthofer Str

Finzigasse

Ferrogasse

Wallrissstrasse

Herbeckstrasse

Thimiggasse

Schindlergasse

Czartoryskigasse

Czartoryskigasse

Schöffelgasse

PLACES TO STAY
- 3 Blue House Hostel
- 8 Hotel Arkadenhof
- 9 Auge Gottes
- 14 Albatros
- 22 Jugendgästehaus Hernals
- 25 Porzellaneum
- 26 Hotel Boltzmann
- 28 Hotel Atlanta
- 30 Pension Falstaff
- 38 Auer
- 39 Thüringer Hof
- 41 Hotel Maté Dependance
- 42 Hotel Maté
- 43 Hotel Donauwalzer
- 46 Pension Ani
- 49 Hostel Zöhrer
- 56 Theater-Hotel

PLACES TO EAT
- 1 Saletti
- 2 Restaurant Sailer
- 4 Schnitzelhaus
- 16 Feuervogel
- 21 Vegi Rant
- 36 Afro-Asiatisches Institut Mensa
- 40 Avocado American Diner
- 45 Cafe Benno
- 51 Kräuterdrogerie
- 54 Tunnel Bar & Café
- 57 Ruffinio
- 58 Die Fromme Helene
- 60 Café Hummel

OTHER
- 5 Eroica House
- 6 Spittelau Incinerator
- 7 Blaustern

- 10 Schnell & Sauber Waschcenter (Laundrette)
- 11 Post Office
- 12 Q
- 13 Schubert's Birth House
- 15 Train Ticket Office
- 17 Niedermeyer Store
- 18 Hofer Supermarket
- 19 Volksoper
- 20 WUK; Frauenzentrum
- 23 US Embassy
- 24 Palais Liechtenstein
- 27 Allgemeines Krankenhaus (Hospital)
- 29 Josephinum (Museum of Medical History)
- 31 International Theatre
- 32 Sigmund Freud Museum
- 33 Polizeifundamt (Lost Property Office)
- 34 Café Berg
- 35 Ökista (Travel Agency)
- 37 Votivkino
- 44 B72
- 47 Niedermeyer
- 48 Städtische Hauptbücherei (Library)
- 50 Café Daun
- 52 Big Ben Bookshop; Ökista (Travel Agency)
- 53 Odyssee Mitwohnzentrale (Accommodation Agency)
- 55 American Reference Center
- 59 Miele Selbstbedienung (Laundrette)
- 61 Szaal
- 62 Red Octopus
- 63 Rhiz
- 64 Chelsea
- 65 Ottakringer Bad (Swimming Pool)

Alszeile

Richthausen

Kalmusgasse

Lidlgasse

Zeillergasse

Hernalser

Lascygasse

Hegelgasse

Sautergasse

Hauptstrasse

Hernals

Rötzergasse

Wattgasse

Baumeistergasse

Kongresspark

Lobmeyrgasse

22

Albrechtskreithgasse

Wieland gasse

Mariengasse

Effingergasse

Lobenhauergasse

Seeböckgasse

Seeböckgasse

Wilhelminenstrasse

Wilhelminenstrasse

Geblergasse

Kulmgasse

Wilhelminenstrasse

Rosensteingasse

Degengasse

Erdbrustgasse

Amethgasse

Gallitzinstrasse

Sandleitengasse

Amethgasse

Ottakringer Str

Ottakring
16

65

Johann-Staud-Str

Rankgasse

Ottakring

Thallastrasse

Thallastrasse

Montleartstrasse

Enenkelstrasse

Hüttelbergstrasse

Kandlgasse

Hasnerstrasse

MAP 5

Flötzersteig

Maroltingergasse

Wernhardtstr

Hettenkofergasse

Pfenninggeldgasse

221

Possingergasse

Köppstrasse

0 250 500m
0 250 500yd

LP

MAP 3 - NORTH WEST VIENNA

MAP 4

Arbesbachgasse
Ruthgasse
Barawitzkagasse
Weinberggasse
Oberdöbling
Billrothstrasse
Silbergasse
Hofzeile
Wertheimsteinpark
Pyrkergasse
Pokornygasse
Krottenbachstrasse
Osterleitengasse
Krottenbachstrasse
Gatterburggasse
Hartäckerstrasse
Peter-Jordan-Str
Cottagegasse
Lannerstrasse
Türkenschanzpark
Hasenauerstrasse
Sternwartestrasse
Währinger Park
Nussdorfer Strasse

Oberdöbling

Währing 18

Gentzgasse
Michaelerstrasse
Gentzgasse
Sechsschimmelgasse
Währinger Strasse Volksoper
Severingasse
Schumanng
Michelbeuern
Alser Strasse
Jörgerstrasse
Lazarettegasse
Marianneng

Alsergrund 9

Währing 18

Spittelau
Brigittenau 20
Franz Josefs Bahnhof
Friedensbrücke
Liechtenstein park
Rossauer Lände

Josefstadt 8

Innere Stadt

Rathaus (City Hall)
Universität
Schottentor
MAP 7

MAP 4 - NORTH EAST VIENNA

An der oberen Alten Donau

Obere Alte Donau

Kagran

Donauturmstrasse

Arbeiterstrandbadstrasse

Anton-Sadtler-Gasse

Wagramer Str

Donaustadtstrasse

Bernoullistrasse

Donaupark

Kagraner-brücke

Alte Donau

Donaustadt
22

Leonard-Bernstein-Str

Leonard-Bernstein-Str

UNO City

Erzherzog-Karl-Str

Kaisermühlen Vienna International Centre

Wagramer Str

An der unteren Alten Donau

Florian-Berndl-Gasse

Rehlackenweg

Ammelmenstrasse

Industriestrasse

Fitzweg

Lagerwiesenweg

Schüttaustrasse

Schiffmühlen

Libenberg

Eipeldauerstrasse

Am Kaisermühlendamm

Bellegardegasse

Mengergasse

Mendelgasse

Meissaugasse

Schrittenweg

Reichbridgasse

Strandbad Gänsehäufel

Grosses Gänsehäufel

Untere Alte Donau

Lange Allee

Schwimsteg-brücke

Donauinsel

Reichbrücke

Koplatz

Handelskai

Engerthstrasse

Kaisermühlen-brücke

Neue Donau

Donau

Kleines Gänsehäufel

LP

Messegelände

Südportalstrasse

Vorgartenstrasse

Trabrennstrasse

Engerthstrasse

Handelskai

Krieau Trotting Races

Hauptallee

MAP 6

PLACES TO STAY
1 Jugendgästehaus Brigittenau
8 Strandhotel Alte Donau

PLACES TO EAT
24 Gasthaus Hansy
26 Zum Inder
31 Schweizerhaus
32 Estancia Santa Cruz
33 Café-Restaurant Luftberg

OTHER
2 Lorenz Böhler Unfallkrankenhaus (Hospital)
3 Donauturm
4 Arbeiterstrandbad
5 Strandbad Alte Donau
6 Hofbauer Boat Rentals
7 Donauzentrum
9 Gänsehäufel (Swimming Pool)
10 Kukis Boat Rentals
11 Hofbauer Kiosk
12 Austria Center Vienna
13 Hofbauer Boat Rentals
14 Departure point for Hydrofoils and DDSG Blue Danube Tours; Mahart Tours; G Glaser
15 Gustinus Ambrosi Museum
16 Flak Tower
17 Stadt Kinderfreibad
18 Flak Tower
19 Vienna Tourist Board Head Office
20 Flex
21 Innere Stadt Police Headquarters
22 ÖJHV (Youth Hostel Head Office)
23 Wiener Kriminalmuseum
25 HOSI
27 KunstHausWien
28 Planetarium; Pratermuseum
29 Riesenrad
30 Pedal Power
34 Bowling Alley

0   250   500m
0   250   500yd

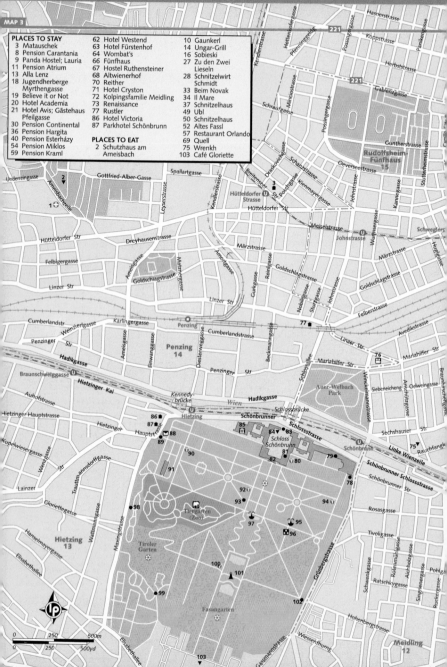

MAP 5 - SOUTH WEST VIENNA

MAP 3

PLACES TO STAY
3 Matauschek
8 Pension Carantania
9 Panda Hostel; Lauria
11 Pension Atrium
13 Alla Lenz
18 Jugendherberge
   Myrthengasse
19 Believe it or Not
20 Hotel Academia
21 Hotel Avis; Gästehaus
   Pfeilgasse
30 Pension Continental
36 Pension Hargita
40 Pension Esterházy
54 Pension Miklos
59 Pension Kraml

62 Hotel Westend
63 Hotel Fürstenhof
64 Wombat's
66 Fünfhaus
67 Hostel Ruthensteiner
68 Altwienerhof
70 Reither
71 Hotel Cryston
72 Kolpingsfamilie Meidling
73 Renaissance
77 Rustler
86 Hotel Victoria
87 Parkhotel Schönbrunn

PLACES TO EAT
2 Schutzhaus am
   Ameisbach

10 Gaunkerl
14 Ungar-Grill
16 Sobieski
27 Zu den Zwei
   Lieseln
28 Schnitzelwirt
   Schmidt
33 Beim Novak
34 Il Mare
37 Schnitzelhaus
49 Ubl
50 Schnitzelhaus
52 Altes Fassl
57 Restaurant Orlando
69 Quell
75 Wrenkh
103 Café Gloriette

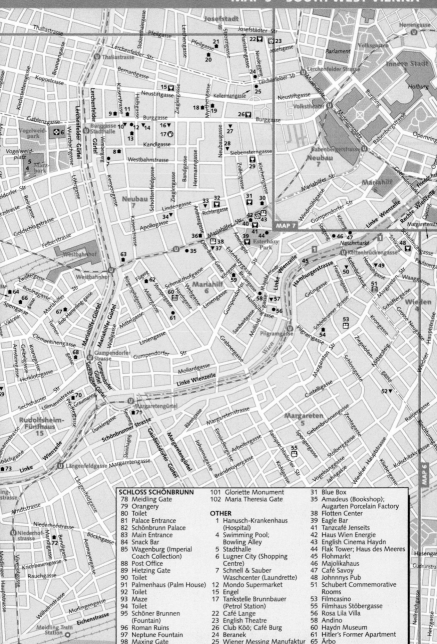

MAP 5 - SOUTH WEST VIENNA

SCHLOSS SCHÖNBRUNN
78 Meidling Gate
79 Orangery
80 Toilet
81 Palace Entrance
82 Schönbrunn Palace
83 Main Entrance
84 Snack Bar
85 Wagenburg (Imperial Coach Collection)
88 Post Office
89 Hietzing Gate
92 Toilet
93 Maze
94 Toilet
95 Schöner Brunnen (Fountain)
96 Roman Ruins
97 Neptune Fountain
98 Maxing Gate
99 Meierei Gate
100 Toilet
101 Gloriette Monument
102 Maria Theresia Gate

OTHER
1 Hanusch-Krankenhaus (Hospital)
4 Swimming Pool; Bowling Alley
5 Stadthalle
6 Lugner City (Shopping Centre)
7 Schnell & Sauber Waschcenter (Laundrette)
12 Mondo Supermarket
15 Engel
17 Tankstelle Brunnbauer (Petrol Station)
22 Café Lange
23 English Theatre
24 Beranek
25 Wiener Messing Manufaktur
29 Shultz
30 Europa
31 Blue Box
35 Amadeus (Bookshop); Augarten Porcelain Factory
38 Flotten Center
39 Eagle Bar
41 Tanzcafé Jenseits
42 Haus Wien Energie
43 English Cinema Haydn
44 Flak Tower; Haus des Meeres
45 Flohmarkt
46 Majolikahaus
47 Café Savoy
48 Johnnys Pub
51 Schubert Commemorative Rooms
53 Filmcasino
55 Filmhaus Stöbergasse
56 Rosa Lila Villa
58 Andino
59 Haydn Museum
61 Hitler's Former Apartment
65 Ärbo
74 U4
76 IMAX Filmtheater

MAP 6 - SOUTH EAST VIENNA

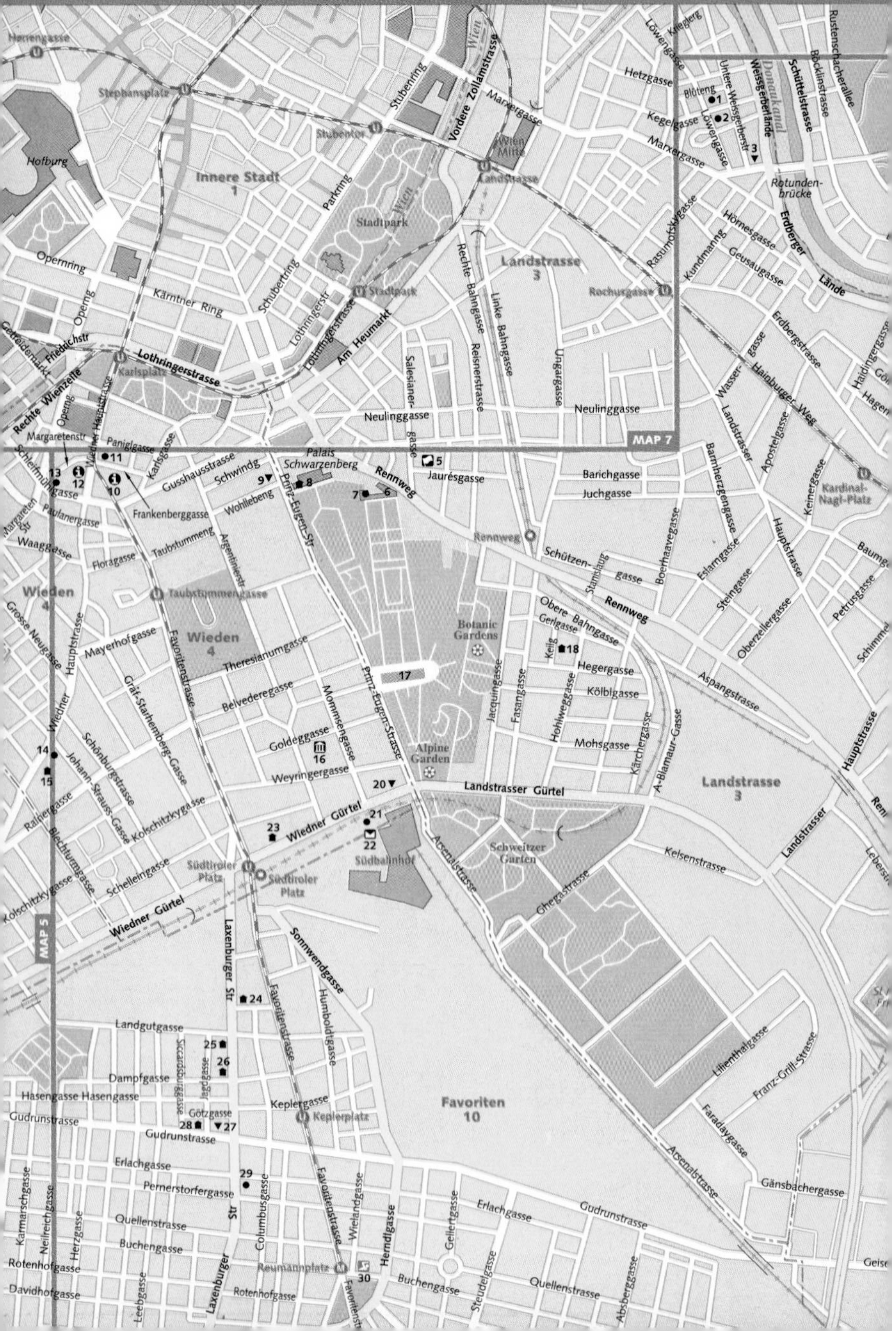

Herrengasse

Weyrburg

Stephansplatz

Stubenring

Vordere Zollamtsstrasse

Wien

Hetzgasse

Plößeng

Marxergasse

Unter Weissgerberstr

Kegelgasse

Löwengasse

Stubentor

Wien Mitte

Landstrasse

Marxergasse

Schüttelstrasse

Böcklinstrasse

Rustenschacherallee

Rotunden-
brücke

Hofburg

Innere Stadt
1

Stadtpark

Landstrasse
3

Rasumofskygasse

Hörnesgasse

Kundmanng

Geusaugasse

Lände

Opernring

Kärntner Ring

Schubertring

Stadtpark

Rochusgasse

Erdbergstrasse

Hainburger-West

Hagelg

Operng

Lothringerstrasse

Am Heumarkt

Rechte Bahngasse

Linke Bahngasse

Reisnerstrasse

Salesianerg

Ungargasse

Wassergasse

Landstrasse

Apostelgasse

Kardinal-
Nagl-Platz

Karlsplatz

Rechte Wienzeile

Neulinggasse

Neulinggasse

MAP 7

Margaretenstr

Panigl gasse

Palais
Schwarzenberg

Rennweg

Jauresgasse

5

Barichgasse

Juchgasse

Herzgasse

Baumg

Kardinal

13
12
10
11

Gushausstrasse

Schwindg

Wohlleben

9

8

7

6

Rennweg

Schützen-
gasse

Borhanngasse

Eslarngasse

Petrusgasse

Waaggasse

Paulanergasse

Frankenberggasse

Taubstummeng

Argentinierstr

Prinz-Eugen-Str

Rennweg

Stanngasse

Obere Bahngasse

Obere Bahngasse

Steingasse

Oberzellergasse

Schimm

Wieden
4

Floragasse

Taubstummengasse

Mayerhofgasse

Graf Starhembergg-Gasse

Favoritenstrasse

Theresianumgasse

Wieden
4

Belvederegasse

Botanic
Gardens

Gerlgasse

18

Hegergasse

Kölblgasse

Jacquingasse

Fasangasse

Hohlweggasse

Aspangstrasse

Kärntnergasse

A-Blumauer-Gasse

Landstrasse
3

Hauptstrasse

Rennw

14
15

Johann Strauss-Gasse

Schönburgstrasse

Kolschitzkygasse

Goldeggasse

16

Mommsengasse

Weyringergasse

Alpine
Garden

Mohsgasse

17

Landstrasser Gürtel

Landstrasse
3

Radetz

Blechturmgasse

20

Schweizer
Garten

Kelsenstrasse

MAP 5

23

Wiedner Gürtel

21
22

Arsenalstrasse

Südtiroler
Platz

Südbahnhof

Ghegastrasse

Südtiroler
Platz

Wiedner Gürtel

Laxenburger Str

Sonnwendgasse

Favoritenstrasse

Humboldtgasse

24

Landgutgasse

25
26

Dampfgasse

Keplergasse

Favoriten
10

Hasengasse Hasengasse

Gudrunstrasse

Götzgasse

28

27

Keplergasse

Keplerplatz

Gudrunstrasse

Ackerstr

Erlachgasse

29

Pernerstorfergasse

Columbusgasse

A23

Wielandgasse

Herndlgasse

Erlachgasse

Gudrunstrasse

Kärntnerg

Neilreichg

Quellengasse

Buchengasse

Laxenburger

Rotenhofgasse

Reumannplatz

30

Buchengasse

Steudelgasse

Quellenstrasse

Davidgasse

Rotenhofgasse

MAP 6 - SOUTH EAST VIENNA

Krieau
Trotting
Races

Kaiserallee

Hauptallee

Wehlistrasse

Handelskai

Praterbrücke

Stadionallee

Meiereistrasse

Ichmaningasse

Praterbrücke

Leopoldstadt
2

Ernst-
Happel-
Stadion

Donau

Rustenschacherallee

Stadionbad

Handelskai

Schüttelstrasse

Hauptallee

Wehlistrasse

Erdberger
Lände

Heustadelwasser

Praterkai

ichgasse

Stadionallee

Meiereistrasse

Südosttangente Wien

Biberhaufenwasser

Praterkai

4

Lechnerstrasse

A23

Leopoldstadt
2

rdbergstrasse

Lusthausstrasse

Hauptallee

Stemmerallee

burger Weg

Stadion-
brücke

Unterer Prater

Aspernallee

Schlachthausgasse

Schlachthausgasse

Erdberger
Brücke

Fasangarten

Erdbergstrasse

Baumgasse

Markhof

Belvedereallee

Landstrasse
3

U Erdberg

Erdberger Lände

Donaukanal

Baumgasse

19

Franzosengraben

Erdbergstrasse

Litfassstrasse

Gusgasse

Döblerhofstrasse

Gasometer

Haidequerstrasse

Simmeringer Hauptstrasse

Simmering
11

Hallergasse

Rinnböckstrasse

Am Kanal

U Zippererstrasse

Einfeldstrasse

Kopalgasse

Simmering
Aspangbahn

Leberstrasse

Kopalgasse

Haidestrasse

Hutterergasse

Leberstrasse

Rappachgasse

Sedlitzkygasse

Lautenschlägergasse

gasse

Enkplatz

Geiselberg Str

LP

0   250   500m
0   250   500yd

MAP 7 - CENTRAL VIENNA

Schwarzspstr.
Alsergrund 9
Währinger Strasse
Hörlgasse
Kolingasse
Schottenring
19
Zelinkagasse
Gonzagagasse
Schwarzspur
Garnisongasse
Waaggasse
Maria-Theresien-Strasse
20
Neutorgasse
Franz-Josefs-K

Alser Strasse
Universitätsstrasse
Schottengasse
Schottenring
Börse Palais
Werdertorgasse
26
Rudolfs-platz

Wickenburggasse
Roosevelt-platz
Schottentor
Börseplatz
Heinrichsgasse
27
Salztgries
28

Liebiggasse
Ebendorferstrasse
8
Mölker Bastei
11
Helferstorferstrasse
Rockhgasse
18
25
24
Salvatorgasse
Galldorgasse
29

Florianigasse
Grillparzerstrasse
Reichsratstrasse
Universität
9
Schreyvogelgasse
Schottenstift
17
16
Renngasse
Tiefer Graben
23
21
22
Wipplingerstrasse
Juden-platz
30

Tulpengasse
Felderstrasse
Rathaus Park
99
Opoltzergasse
Teinfaltstrasse
14
Freyung
15
Strauchgasse
93
Am Hof
87
86
Kurrentg.
85
84

Lenau
100
Rathaus (City Hall)
101
Lichtenfelsgasse
97
96
Bankgasse
94
92
88
82
83
76

Josefstadt 8
102
Rathausplatz
Dr. Karl Lueger Ring
Burgtheater (National Theatre)
98
95
Leopold Figl Gasse
Minoritenplatz
90
89
80
81
79
126

städter Strasse
Stadiongasse
Parlament
109
Innere Stadt 2
Herrengasse
110 111
112
113
116
125
127
135

103
Doblhoffgasse
Volksgarten
108
Ballhaus-platz
Schaufflergasse
Michaeler-platz
117
118
119
124
Dorotheergasse
133
134
132
139

104
Josefsgasse
Schmerling-platz
107
106
105
Justizpalast (Palace of Justice)
Hofburg
Josefs-platz
123
128
131
142
143

Trautsongasse
Lerchen-felder Strasse
Naturhistorisches Museum
Heldenplatz
120
121
122
130
185
186
184

Neustiftgasse
Volks-theater
Volkstheater
Maria Theresien Platz
Burggarten
Johannesgasse
Führichgasse
18

Burggasse
205
Gutenberggasse
Schottenfeldgasse
206
207
208
209
Siebensterngasse
Museumsquartier
204
Babenbergerstrasse
Künstlerhaus Museum
202
201
Opernring
198
Staatsoper (State Opera)
190
189 183 182
179
178

Neubau 7
Schottenfeldgasse
Breite Gasse
Kirchberggasse
Karl Schweighofer Gasse
Kunsthistorisches Museum
203
Elisabethstrasse
200
199
196 195
194
192
193
191
Kärntner Ring
Ringstrassen Galerian

217
220
Schillerplatz
Akademie der bildenden Künste (Academy of Fine Art)
230
Bösendorferstrasse
Karlsplatz
Karlski

211
218
216
Königsklostergasse
Theobaldgasse
223
225
Secession Building
229
233
Künstler-haus

215
214
Theobaldgasse
219
221
Lehárgasse
226
Rechte Wienzeile
232
Karlsplatz

212
213
Gumpendorfer Strasse
Mariahilf 6
222
224
Naschmarkt
Linke Wienzeile
227
228
231
Wieden 4
Karlskir

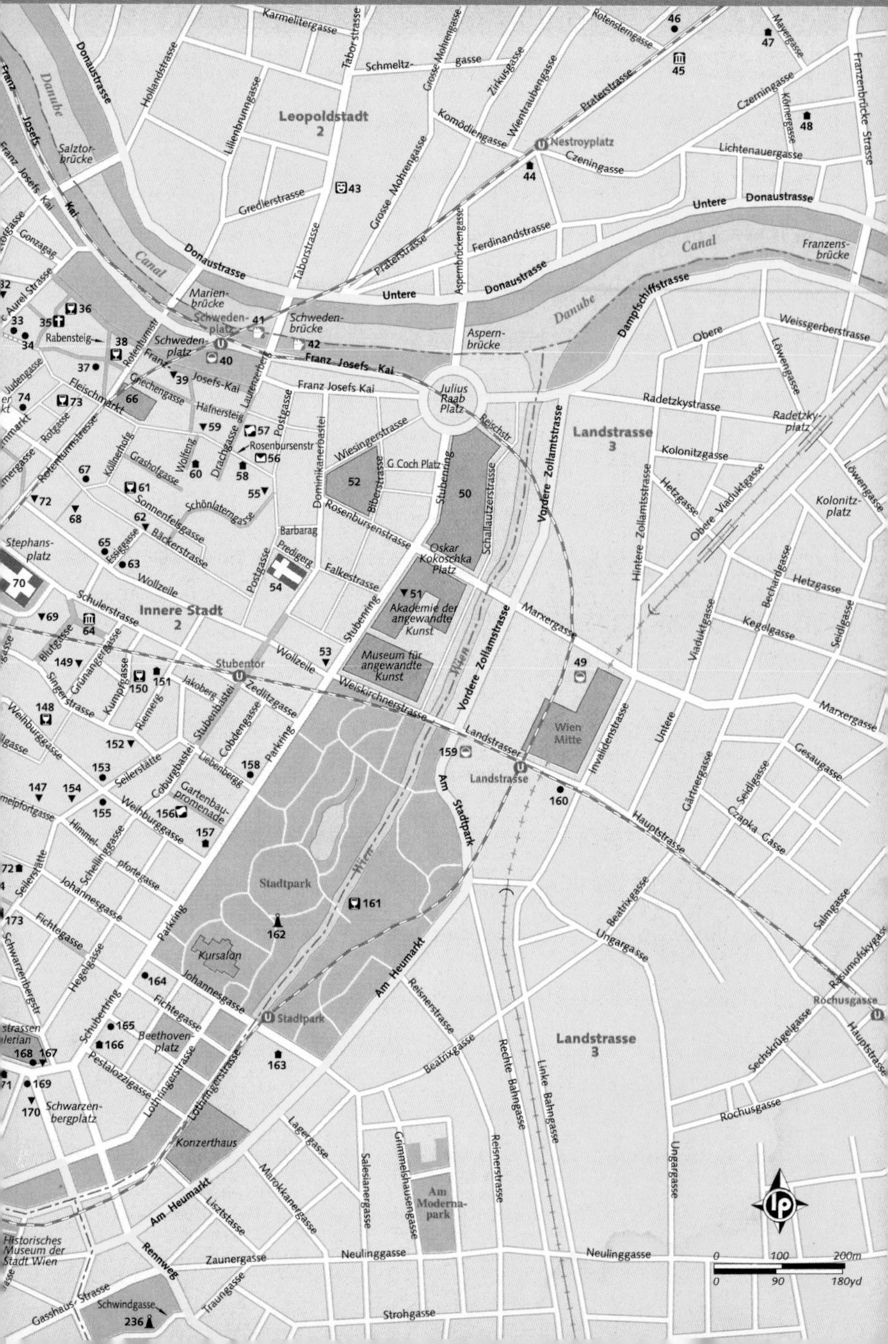

MAP 7 - CENTRAL VIENNA

Karmelitergasse
Rolenslemgasse
46
47
Mayergasse

Schmeltz-gasse
Grosse Mohrengasse
Zirkusgasse
45
Praterstrasse
Franzensbrücke

Leopoldstadt
2
Komödlengasse
Wienztraubengasse
Nestroyplatz
Czerningasse
48

Hollandstrasse
Lilienbrunngasse
Taborstrasse
Grosse Mohrengasse
Czeningasse
Lichtenauergasse

Donaustrasse
43
Ferdinandstrasse
44
Untere
Donaustrasse

Gredlerstrasse
Taborstrasse
Praterstrasse
Aspernbrückengasse
Untere
Danube
Canal
Franzens-brücke

Salztor-brücke
Canal
Donaustrasse
Untere
Donaustrasse
Dampfschiffstrasse
Obere
Weissgerberstrasse

Marien-brücke
Schweden-platz
41
Schweden-brücke
Aspern-brücke
Julius
Raab
Platz
Radetzkystrasse
Löwengasse
Radetzky-platz

Franz Josefs Kai
Salzt
36
35
33
34
Rabensteig
38
Schweden-platz
40
42
Franz Josefs Kai
Landstrasse
3
Kolonitzgasse

37
Franz
Josefs-Kai
Reichr.
Vordere Zollamtsstrasse
Hetzgasse
Kolonitz-platz

74
73
Fleischmarkt
66
Chreohergasse
Hafnersteig
Wiesingerstrasse
G Coch Platz
50
Obere Viaduktgasse
Hintere Zollamtsstrasse

67
Grashofgasse
Bäbenstrasse
Stubenring
52
Rosenbursenstrasse
Oskar
Kokoschka
Platz
Bechardgasse

72
68
Sonnenfelsgasse
62
Bäckerstrasse
58
55
Dominikanerbastei
Postgasse
Schallautzerstrasse
Marxergasse
Viaduktgasse
Kegelgasse

Stephans-platz
70
65
63
Wollzeile
Barbarag
Predigerg.
Falkestrasse
51
Akademie der
angewandte
Kunst
49
Seidlgasse

69
64
Schulerstrasse
Innere Stadt
2
Stubentor
Wollzeile
53
Museum für
angewandte
Kunst
Wien
Mitte
Marxergasse

149
151
150
Jakoberg.
Zedlitzgasse
Weiskirchnerstrasse
Vordere Zollamtsstrasse
159
Landstrasse
160
Hauptstrasse

148
152
153
Seilerstätte
Liebenberg.
158
Parkring
Landstrasse
Invalidenstrasse
Gärtnergasse
Marxergasse

147
154
155
156
Gartenbau-
promenade
157
Am
Stadtpark
Untere
Seidlgasse
Czapla Gasse
Gesaugasse

72
4
173
Johannesgasse
Stadtpark
161
162
Beatrixgasse
Ungargasse
Salmgasse

164
Johannesgasse
Stadtpark
163
Landstrasse
3
Rochusgasse

165
166
167
168
169
170
Beethoven-platz
Pestalozzigasse
Lisztstrasse
Sechskrügelgasse
Rochusgasse

71
Schwarzen-bergplatz
236
Konzerthaus
Am Heumarkt
Rennweg
Lagergasse
Salesianergasse
Grimmelshausengasse
Reisnerstrasse
Rechte Bahngasse
Linke Bahngasse
Am
Moderna-park

Historisches
Museum der
Stadt Wien
Gasshaus-Strasse
Schwindgasse
Zaunergasse
Traungasse
Strohgasse
Neulinggasse
Neulinggasse

0   100   200m
0   90   180yd

MAP 7 CENTRAL VIENNA

PLACES TO STAY
24 Hotel Orient
27 Schweizer Pension Solderer
44 Aphrodite
47 Praterstern
48 Hotel Adlon
58 Hotel Post
60 Hotel Austria
77 Hotel am Stephansplatz
83 Hotel Wandl
89 Pension Nossek
103 Auersperg
104 Pension Wild
131 Hotel Ambassador
138 Hotel Kaiserin Elisabeth
151 Appartement Pension Riemergasse
157 Hotel Marriott
163 Hotel Inter-Continental
166 Hotel am Schubertring
171 Hotel Imperial
172 Music Academy Hotel & Mensa
177 Ana Grand
180 Hotel zur Wiener Staatsoper
187 Hotel Sacher & Café
189 Pension am Operneck
192 Hotel Bristol
213 Kolping-Gästehaus
216 Quisisana
218 Hotel Tyrol
225 Hotel-Pension Schneider

PLACES TO EAT
5 University Mensa
6 Katholisches Studenthaus Mensa
7 Café Bierkeller Zwillings Gewölb
20 Livingstone; Planter's Club
22 Brezel Gwölb
31 Würstelstand am Hoher Markt
32 China Restaurant Turandot
39 Pizza Bizi (Takeaway)
51 Academy of Applied Art Cafeteria
53 Café Prückel
55 Beim Czaak
59 Griechenbeisl
62 Alt Wien
68 Figlmüller
69 Haas & Haas
72 Pizza Bizi
76 Wrenkh
78 DO & CO Restaurant; Haas Haus
81 Yohm
93 Akakiko

94 Café Central
99 Café Restaurant Landtmann
100 Wiener Rathauskeller; Grinzinger Keller
110 Café Griensteidl
112 Demel
122 Yugetsu Saryo
124 Café Bräunerhof
126 Café Hawelka
127 Trzesniewski
136 McDonald's
137 Akakiko
140 Drei Husaren
143 Nordsee
144 Zur Fischerin Capua
145 Zum Weissen Rauchfangkehrer
147 Zum Kuckuck
149 La Crêperie
152 Zu den 3 Hacken
154 East to West
167 Café Schwarzenberg
170 Naschmarkt Restaurant
175 DO & CO Restaurant
179 Restaurant Marché Movenpick
182 Coffeeshop Company
183 Restaurant Siam
191 Korso
200 Restaurant Smutny
203 Grotta Azzurra
205 La Gondola
207 Amerlingbeisl
208 Plutzer Bräu
209 Centimetre II
212 K&K Bierkanzlei
217 Pizza Bizi (Takeaway)
221 Café Sperl
222 Café Drechsler
224 Toko Ri
226 Indian Pavillon
230 Café Museum
231 Technical University Mensa

BARS & NIGHTCLUBS
12 Molly Darcy's Irish Pub
23 Why Not?
28 Dinos
36 Jazzland
37 First Floor
38 Krah Krah
61 Zwölf Apostelkeller (Heurigen)
73 P1
85 Kolar
90 Bockshorn
91 Esterházykeller (Heurigen)
92 Bierhof
105 Volksgarten Disco
106 Tanz Volksgarten

107 Volksgarten Pavillon
120 Palmenhaus
133 American Bar
148 Kleines Café
150 Santo Spirito
161 Meierei
181 Tenne
204 Porgy & Bess
219 Titanic
228 Roxy

OTHER
1 Ökista (Travel Agency)
2 Café Stein
3 Reisebuchladen (Bookshop & Bus Tours)
4 Votivkirche
8 University Library
9 Austrobus Buses
10 Columbus Reisen
11 Pasqualati House
13 Vienna Police Headquarters
14 Palais Kinsky
15 Palais Ferstal
16 Schottenkirche
17 Schottenkirche Museum Entrance
18 ÖJHW (Youth Hostel Head Office)
19 Behindertenberatungsstelle
21 Former Civic Armoury
25 Cityrama Bus Tours
26 Black Market
29 Altes Rathaus
30 Böhmische Hofkanzlei
33 Rag
34 Shakespeare & Co Booksellers
35 Ruprechtskirche
37 Stadttempel
40 Night Bus Departures
41 DDSG Blue Danube Canal Tour Departures
42 Donau Schiffahrt Canal Tour Departures
43 Serapionstheater im Odeon
45 Johann Strauss Residence
46 2 Rad-Börse
49 Busbahnhof Wien Mitte
50 Former Kriegsministerium
52 Postsparkasse
54 Dominikanerkirche
56 Main Post Office
57 Canadian Embassy
63 Libro (Bookshop)
64 Mozart's Apartment (Figaro House)
65 Morawa
66 Spar Supermarket
67 Linnerth

MAP 7 CENTRAL VIENNA

The fascinating interior of Stephansdom (St Stephen Cathedral).

MAP LEGEND

CITY ROUTES

Freeway	Freeway		Unsealed Road
Highway	Primary Road		One Way Street
Road	Secondary Road		Pedestrian Street
Street	Street		Stepped Street
Lane	Lane		Tunnel
	On/Off Ramp		Footbridge

REGIONAL ROUTES

	Tollway, Freeway.
	Primary Road
	Secondary Road
	Minor Road

BOUNDARIES

	International
	State
	Disputed
	Fortified Wall

HYDROGRAPHY

	River, Creek
	Canal
	Lake
	Dry Lake; Salt Lake
	Spring; Rapids
	Waterfalls

TRANSPORT ROUTES & STATIONS

	Train		Ferry
	Underground Train		Walking Trail
	Metro		Walking Tour
	Tramway		Path
	Cable Car, Chairlift		Pier or Jetty

AREA FEATURES

	Building		Market		Beach		Campus
	Park, Gardens		Sports Ground		Cemetery		Plaza

POPULATION SYMBOLS

◌ CAPITAL	National Capital	● CITY	City	● Village	Village
◉ CAPITAL	State Capital	● Town	Town		Urban Area

MAP SYMBOLS

●	Place to Stay	▼	Place to Eat	●	Point of Interest

✈	Airport	⚓	Fountain	🏛	Museum		Swimming Pool
	Archaeological Site		Golf Course		Parking		Synagogue
	Bank		Hospital		Police Station		Theatre
	Bus Terminal		Internet Cafe		Post Office		Tomb
	Cave		Lookout		Pub or Bar		Tourist Information
	Church		Monument		Shopping Centre		Winery
	Cinema		Mosque		Stately Home		Zoo

Note: not all symbols displayed above appear in this book

LONELY PLANET OFFICES

Australia
Locked Bag 1, Footscray, Victoria 3011
☎ 03 9689 4666 fax 03 9689 6833
email: talk2us@lonelyplanet.com.au

UK
10a Spring Place, London NW5 3BH
☎ 020 7428 4800 fax 020 7428 4828
email: go@lonelyplanet.co.uk

USA
150 Linden St, Oakland, CA 94607
☎ 510 893 8555 TOLL FREE: 800 275 8555
fax 510 893 8572
email: info@lonelyplanet.com

France
1 rue du Dahomey, 75011 Paris
☎ 01 55 25 33 00 fax 01 55 25 33 01
email: bip@lonelyplanet.fr
www.lonelyplanet.fr

World Wide Web: www.lonelyplanet.com *or* AOL keyword: lp
Lonely Planet Images: lpi@lonelyplanet.com.au